Praise fo

D0861149

"*Madness of the Q* is a                                               ith Sam
Teagarden on the run, desperate to connect with the right people
and evade the wrong ones from New York to Israel to Italy to
Germany in a non-stop plot that reminds us of Dan Brown, Lud-
lum, Fleming, and maybe even a bit of Umberto Eco."
—Thomas Perry, author of *The Butcher's Boy*,
The Burglar, and A Small Town

"This would make for an exciting movie in the Dan Brown genre.
It's a thrilling story that you'll be glued to from start to finish!"
—Brenda Repland, Eyes on World Cultures

## Praise for *Flight of the Fox*

"Intriguing...Jason Bourne fans will have some fun."
—*Publishers Weekly*

"*Flight of the Fox* is an explosively paranoid thriller that pays
homage to classics of the genre. Basnight delivers nonstop action
and an everyman hero to root for."
—Joseph Finder, *New York Times*
bestselling author of *The Switch*

"Basnight's novel does double duty. It's both a fast-paced and
furious thriller, and a thought-provoking commentary on a
government gone wild. Read it."
—Reed Farrel Coleman, *New York Times*
bestselling author of *What You Break*

# MADNESS
# OF THE Q
*A Sam Teagarden Thriller*

## ALSO BY GRAY BASNIGHT

*The Cop with the Pink Pistol*

*Shadows in the Fire*

*The Sam Teagarden Thriller Series*
*Flight of the Fox*

# GRAY BASNIGHT

# MADNESS OF THE Q

*A Sam Teagarden Thriller*

Down & Out Books
3959 Van Dyke Road, Suite 265
Lutz, FL 33558
DownAndOutBooks.com

The characters and events in this book are fictitious. Any similarity to real persons, living or dead, is coincidental and not intended by the author.

Cover design by Zach McCain

ISBN: 1-64396-088-1
ISBN-13: 978-1-64396-088-3

With appreciation for those readers of *Flight of the Fox* who requested a second novel featuring Sam Teagarden.

"Men, it has been well said, think in herds;
it will be seen that they go mad in herds,
while they recover their senses slowly,
and one by one."

—Charles Mackay, *Extraordinary Popular Delusions
and the Madness of Crowds* (1841)

# PREFACE TO MASS MADNESS IN 2025

In the nineteenth century, after meticulous comparative examination of the New Testament, both secular and devout scholars concluded that a lost voice existed. Named Quelle, German for the word "source," it became known as the Q Document.

Over the decades, conflicting theories of its purpose evolved: apostolic message heralding the Messiah's return, prologue undergirding existing scripture, or intentionally suppressed evidence of historic deceit.

Thus, in the twenty-first century, word of a newly discovered text ignited a global contagion of savagery.

# THE MADNESS BEGINS
## CHAPTER ONE

*Friday, February 21, 2025*

A hard rap at the ancient door was the last thing he wanted to hear.

Dr. Pablo Zurbarán was intently fixed on a scrap of two-thousand-year-old parchment secured beneath the aperture of his microscope when the unwelcome knock intruded. Because of the relentless parade of calls, he escaped to his cramped laboratory below the cathedral at Santiago de Compostela. The deluge began after the annual meeting of The Ecumenical Apostles a fortnight earlier in America where he presented his latest archeological finding. Since then, he'd been the target of a full-blown media barrage. Requests for interviews arrived by old-fashioned door knocks and phone calls, as well as the ambush approach on the street and every possible e-based means. The pressure compelled him to seek sanctuary where piles of maps, books, bones, and antiquities were stacked against the stone walls. Because there was no telephone or cell signal, it was the only place where he could work in peace.

When the knock came, he looked away from the ocular and rubbed his eyes. He'd been staring at the lettering of Fragmento Diecisiete for nearly an hour. All pages in the newly recovered codex were wonderful to view with the clarity of magnification.

But that one passage was breathtaking. Two days earlier, after fully decoding the seventeenth document, he found its contents so astonishing that he pronounced it "El Fragmento de la Santa Mierda" to an administrative priest from the diocese of Galicia. In English, it meant "The Holy Shit Fragment."

He almost called out, "Who's there?" Instead, he decided to ignore the knock, hoping the unwanted visitor would give up and go away.

The media onslaught made him a celebrity within religious circles. The callers wanted interviews and photographs of him and the documents. In exchange, some extended invitations to prestigious events. The more aggressive appeals were not from reporters, but from priests, ministers, rabbis, churches, synagogues, diplomats, lawyers, and publishers. Some were complimentary, some were angry, and some were from people without knowledge of his work, yet ready to challenge the integrity of his research.

That morning, his wife, who'd been with him at the excavation in Israel, fielded two calls offering money, and one anonymous voice threatening academic condemnation. Afterward, she described the volume of inquisitors to be endless in both variety and motivation. Yet there was one consistent fact. Not one entreaty made it to his underground hideaway lab.

The cathedral had only one entrance to the cellar's meandering corridors. It was *inside* the basilica, through the carefully guarded Door of Fidelity near the small Quintana Chapel. Once admitted, the visitor descended a spiral staircase to the underground labyrinth where there was no directional signage. Because of these safeguards, all public appeals had arrived only at his home or university office.

Ignoring the knock did not work. The rap came again, harder and louder.

"¿Quién es?"

"I am sorry, professor. No hablo Español. My name is Archbishop Tasso Tadros. I am with the Vatican Antiquities Lab. Many messages have been left for you pertaining to my visit this evening."

"What do you want?"

"Sir, I am an emissary of Our Most Holy Father on a matter of great urgency. I must speak with you."

That explained his being admitted to the underground through the Door of Fidelity. The cathedral guards would not challenge an archbishop. And with papers authorizing him as an envoy of the Pope, they'd happily escort him through the maze to his subterranean office.

"Un momento, Your Grace."

Zurbarán stood and shuffled to the door, which was among the oldest in the cathedral and made of black mulberry brought from the Holy Land after the Third Crusade. He glanced at his image in the small mirror by the coat rack. His eyes were tired. He needed a shave and his gray hair, always disorderly, was overdue for a trim. He tucked the rumpled edges of his shirt into his trousers, unlatched the bolt, and tugged steadily on the handle.

The man standing in the semi-darkened corridor was smiling, hands clasped at the front. He was attired in full collar shirt and cassock adorned with magenta piping, overlaid with a matching amice vestment that draped his shoulders. Atop his amice hung an ornate Latinate cross with a noticeably short crossbar and uniquely long vertical shaft.

Only after scanning the traditional vestments of the faith did Zurbarán turn to his visitor's countenance. The face was stout and hardy, with features denoting a long-lineage Mediterranean native of Greek or other Middle Eastern heritage. He had fully rounded lips of a healthy pink, like those seen on robust courtesans in Baroque paintings by Caravaggio. His deep-set eyes were moist with kindness and his cheeks glowed with ruddy ardor. The overall appearance led to only one possible conclusion: this man was important.

"Your Grace, this is an honor." He peered into the corridor to see if the visitor was accompanied by cathedral guards, but he was alone.

The archbishop smiled. "It is only me. At my request the

kindly basilica attendants provided directions. I got lost once, but not very badly."

"I see. Please come in."

"Thank you. I apologize for not speaking Spanish."

"It is all right."

"In fact, I do speak the language, though not well. It is such a beautiful tongue that I do not wish to offend with improper grammar."

"Are you permanently posted to the Vatican?"

"Oh yes, yes," the archbishop said with enthusiasm. From a pocket in his cassock he withdrew papers. "I am here at the direct request of the Holy See. I will return directly to His Holiness at St. Peter's to brief him on our conference."

"Oh, my," Zurbarán said, betraying a sense of flattery. He pushed the ancient door closed and reset the latch. He wasn't a religious man, though he was a lifelong Catholic and could hardly deny admission to this esteemed visitor. After moving stacks of writing pads, boxes filled with bones, and other office clutter, he gestured for the archbishop to sit on a rusty metal fold-up chair. It was not appropriate to his guest's high office, but he had no other. "Your Grace, please tell me, how I may assist?"

"I, too, am an archeologist," Archbishop Tadros began after sitting. "As I said, I am with the Vatican Antiquities Lab." He glanced around with friendly acknowledgement at the professor's restricted quarters. "My office is also in a crypt." His eyes glinted with humor. "Mine, however, is below the Vatican, which is considerably more spacious than your...laboratorio pequeño."

Zurbarán nodded at his office clutter. He patted the nearest human skull within easy reach. "It is true, Your Grace. I must make do with what can be spared by the archdiocese here in the Galician province. I have a university office, but it's little more than a cubicle. Therefore, I do my research here. Beyond that back wall lies the body of none other than St. James himself. I occasionally think my proximity to him is preferable to having greater space."

The archbishop chuckled politely at Zurbarán's repartee. "Getting down to business, if I may, I am here, of course, because of your presentation to the recent gathering of The Ecumenical Apostles in the American city of Dallas."

"Yes?"

"Professor, it was there that you announced discovery of the Quelle Document, the long missing source for much of Matthew and Luke."

"Yes. None other."

"Are you certain?"

"Oh, yes. It is indisputably the Quelle Document. It is in fragments of course. As I explained earlier this month in Texas, there are seventeen remnants of the full Q Codex available to us."

"Yes. And only the final four were encoded?"

"Correct. Only the final four. As I announced, the first thirteen are straight affirmations of the two gospels. They did not fully survive the passing of two millennia because the amphora suffered damage. It was secreted in a tunnel below Megiddo Church in Israel. Thankfully, the remnants that did survive are quite legible."

"Professor, I regret the unpleasant nature of this next question, but His Holiness very much wishes to know. Did you present a translation of any fragment, or photos of the document, at any time during your visit to America?"

"Oh, no. The only photos I presented were of the tunnel, the amphora, and the papyri bundle before separation."

"Ah, very good. But you did announce to the audience that the final four fragments were written in code and that you were, at that time, laboring on decryption?"

The professor responded slowly.

"Yes," he said, wondering if the archbishop's tone was becoming aggressive.

"And you also announced that you would continue a study of all seventeen fragments with the eventual goal of publication? You told the gathering to be patient, that a great announcement would be forthcoming. I believe you used the word 'soon.'"

"Well, yes-s-s. That is what I do," Zurbarán said. "I am a scholar of papyrology and an archeologist of ancient Judaism and Christianity. I am working on an article and have plans for a wider, more thorough presentation of my discovery."

"Hmm," the archbishop said, his eyes growing less friendly.

"Your Grace, I am confused. My presentation in Dallas was a matter of public record. Additionally, I work only with photos. The original fragments were immediately dispatched to St. Peter's. As an archeologist and supervisor with the Vatican's antiquities lab, have you not seen and worked with them yourself?"

Tadros was ready for the question.

"Yes, yes, of course I have." He gave a small eyeroll, as if to say it should be obvious. "But you see, the team I oversee is also working only with photos. The original papyri are now subjected to preservation under UV light, and will remain isolated for some time. Professor, this visit isn't about photos versus originals, or about what I have or have not seen. As I explained, His Holiness wishes me to make direct inquiry as to your announcement in Texas so that we may incorporate *your* findings with our own."

"Ah, yes. I understand now."

"So then, *are* you still trying to decrypt the final four fragments?"

"Oh, more than merely trying. That job is done. They are now fully decrypted."

The archbishop's lips thinned and turned inward, which Zurbarán took to be an expression of disapproval. Seeing that, Tadros quickly recovered with a deceptive question.

"It is very curious, isn't it, Professor? Tell me, why do you suppose our Lord chose to conceal his voice with a first-century cipher?"

"Oh, I do not ponder such things." Zurbarán pushed his gray hair from his forehead with one hand, while giving a small dismissive wave with the other. "Yes, of course I was raised in the faith. I am also a scientist. It is my job to find, uncover, discover, and preserve. But explain the mysteries of Our Father? Truly,

Your Grace, that I cannot attempt."

"No, of course not. But tell me, when it came to analyzing remnants fourteen through seventeen, was it a difficult matter to, as they say in American movies, 'crack the code'?"

"Yes, at first. Not only are the final four fragments encoded, they are also in ancient Greek, as is the entire codex. I struggled with that and sought help from a professor of Greek at the university and also from a visiting Greek Orthodox priest. The language is no longer spoken, but the vocabulary basics can be determined by most speakers of modern Greek."

"Did the two characters who assisted actually view your decoded remnants?"

"No, Your Grace." Zurbarán found it odd that he would describe a man of the cloth as a "character." "They assisted me only via email, and even then, only on a few lines at a time."

The archbishop nodded. "Good, good, good. That is very good," he said. "In that case, I may leave those two in peace for now." Zurbarán was set to respond when Tadros interrupted in a voice louder than before. "But what's important is that you *have* decoded the final four?"

"Yes, Your Grace." He tapped the nearest paper pile at his elbow. The top of the foot-high stack held a file folder labeled Q Doc, which contained photographs of all the remnants. "I am no linguist. And I confess, I am not a trained cryptologist by profession, but once I discovered the cipher, piecing together the bones went quickly."

"And what marrow have you extracted from those bones?"

"Ah yes, the marrow," Zurbarán said. He took a satisfying breath. "As I've explained, most of the document is a reaffirmation of the Gospel as we already know it. The great wonder, of course, is to lay contemporary eyes upon the original. It is glorious indeed!"

"You said, 'most of the document.' Tell me, which portions are *not* a reaffirmation of the faith?"

Zurbarán grew increasingly uncomfortable with the line of

inquiry, yet still could not bring himself to pose an objection. He held only a bearing of respectful deference.

"The decoded final four do indeed cast new light upon the earliest days when our faith was being structured by Saul of Tarsus, whom we know as Saint Paul."

"Yes, my team has also managed to cast some light upon those final four pieces of papyri."

This delighted Professor Zurbarán. Not only was the archbishop sharing news of his own work but appeared to open the door to collaboration.

"Ah! Very good. Perhaps we may compare our discoveries to confirm accuracy for analysis and eventual release to the public."

The archbishop ignored him. He sighed and glanced at the file folder between them.

"Yes, yes," he said. "Vatican scholars have decoded them. That is why I am here. Tell me, Professor, what exactly have you learned from your decryption work about those early days when our young faith was in the sainted hands of Saul of Tarsus?"

Now feeling a sense of collegiality, he was pleased to address the archbishop's request. He unpinned the clip he'd been studying when the unwanted knock came to his door. After removing the photo from the microscope, he held it high against the ceiling fixture to admire it.

"Your Grace, my effort to shed light on the final four fragments tells me that, like Judaism, Islam, Hinduism, and all the great faiths of our species—God's message was accompanied by the collaboration of men, ordinary and extraordinary, doing the work of their Lord and Savior."

Tadros did not care for the answer. He snatched the photo from Zurbarán, opened the Q Doc file folder, placed it atop the many other photos stacked inside, and closed the manila binder with an imperious flair.

"So, you are neither a linguist nor a cryptologist," he began. "Well, well, well. What exactly *are* you then, Professor Pablo Zurbarán...P-h-D...University of Chicago and the University of

Oxford...professor of Israeli Antiquities for the University of Galicia and the Cathedral of Santiago de Compostela here in the northwest corner of the very *Catholic* nation of Spain?"

Zurbarán was dumbstruck. His jaw slackened. He wanted to please this emissary of the Pope inquiring about his presentation in America. Yet whatever he'd done to displease him was a mystery.

"If I may say, Your Grace, I hope you do not feel I am questioning our faith. The mystery of faith is inviolable. As to the Q Document itself, what Your Grace may find quite interesting is—"

Tadros grunted noisily. He put up a hand, palm out.

"What His Grace finds quite interesting," said the holy man, "is that *you*, a layman, a digger of ditches, a sifter of dirt and rock, presume the unholy right to transpose and construe and interpret and paraphrase the voice of God the Father Almighty. You may think you are merely discovering and reporting facts. I assure you, you are not. Only His Holiness decides facts. And as his emissary—*I*—am the decider where—*you*—are concerned."

"Your Grace, it is my work and I—"

Before he could find the words, Archbishop Tadros gripped his cross by the short crossbar and yanked a thin blade from the unusually long shaft.

"Oh, 'my *wor-r-k*,'" the archbishop whined in mocking sarcasm, grasping the dagger's hilt with interlocking fingers. "We can't have you fumbling about with the voice of God the Father, now can we?"

"But, Your Grace—"

The archbishop calmly inserted the blade into Zurbarán's throat. As his victim's eyes flared with shock, the assassin reached with his free hand to grip the back of the helpless professor's neck. In that position, the pressure on the larynx and trachea doubled, tripled, and quadrupled with every hardened thrust coordinated by two powerful hands working together like a crankshaft on a piston. Zurbarán's struggles to breathe sounded like leather boots scraping mud on a doormat.

When Zurbarán was dead, the man posing as an archbishop

withdrew the wet dagger. He twice wiped it on his victim's shirt and replaced it in the ornate sheath dangling from his neck chain. Turning to the professor's nearby laptop, which remained logged on, he clicked the email icon, then the Sent file to examine recent outgoing communications. What he found surprised him. His employer wanted him to kill Dr. Zurbarán *before* the decoded findings were dispatched to anyone. The assassin assumed he'd done precisely that, but now realized otherwise. He'd arrived too late. Earlier that evening, the professor had emailed a full decryption of the final four Q Document fragments to each officer of The Ecumenical Apostles located around the globe, all of whom had attended the Dallas convention.

The killer's reaction was a mixture of surprise and ambivalence. "לעזאזל" he said in Hebrew, which meant, "Shit!" He picked up the thick Q Doc file, tucked it under one arm, and sighed. "Well it's not my fault," he mused in English. "If they had hired me one day sooner, he would have been killed one day sooner."

Careful not to tread on the oozing blood below Zurbarán's chair, he stood and moved toward the ancient door. In Hebrew, he muttered, "וב, עבודה אחרת פירושה עוד יום משכורת", which meant, "For me, it means another job and another day's pay." In English he said, "For now, I am hungry." And finally, in perfect Spanish, he said, "Bueno, es la hora de cenar. Cuando esté in Galicia, siempre debe comer pulpo."

Back in the main basilica, he strode to a vestibule leading to a private restroom where he removed all sectarian vestments and discarded them in the waste bin. He leaned into the mirror to cleanse ruby blush from his face and wipe pink gloss from his lips. Dressed now as a tourist, he tucked the crucifix below his undershirt and returned to the narrow streets of Santiago de Compostela. With a sightseeing map of the old city, he set off upon the cobblestones to find a traditional Galician restaurant offering his desired repast of boiled octopus over sliced potatoes with garlic and anointed by generous splashes of olive oil.

# THE HERD MENTALITY
## CHAPTER TWO

*Saturday, March 1, 2025*

The first incident of mass madness among ecclesiastics occurred near the town of Baiona, Spain.

Eleven Benedictine monks of the Monasterio del Nuevo Mundo shunned a gathering of novices and postulants waiting in the abbey for First Hour prayers. Instead of joining them as expected, the monks walked to the cloister where ten of them kneeled in the warmth of the early sun. Any casual observer would assume they intended to pray ahead of the day's routine. Once positioned, the final monk, who was the abbot, walked behind and cut each of their throats with a straight razor.

When finished, he kneeled in the flowing redness and turned the blade on himself, managing only to sever his left external jugular before surrendering to the pain. Compared with the others, this caused a lesser surge of blood. It was slower and more painful. Still, it was sufficient to accomplish his goal.

# CHAPTER THREE

*Sunday, March 2, 2025*

The next episode occurred near Matamoros, Mexico.

Campamento de la Verdad was a Christian-based cult composed of men and women from around the world, though primarily from the United States. On that morning, the man known as Shepherd One led all four hundred thirty-one of his followers from makeshift dormitories to a fallow sorghum field. There had been an unusual chill in the air, yet the temperature grew warm as they paraded under his direction into a spiral formation. Just behind the leader, a boy of eleven pulled a child's wagon laden with jars and bottles. From the center of the helix, Shepherd One methodically worked outward along the concentric pattern. Pausing at each member of his flock, he administered a generous spoonful of ricin mixed with sweet applesauce, followed by a long swig of vodka.

When nearly finished two hours later, he paused to look upon his work where four hundred thirty bodies lay in the same design as God's home base, the spiraling Milky Way Galaxy.

"The flock remained loyal," he said to the boy. "Not one of them ran."

"Yes," agreed the boy, "no one ran away."

The next spoonful was for the child whose wagon, by then, held only a single smeared jar of applesauce and one nearly depleted magnum of vodka. All other containers had been cast off when emptied near fallen receivers of the final sacrament.

Lastly, Shepherd One consumed his own homemade mixture of quick death.

# CHAPTER FOUR

*Sunday, March 9, 2025*

The third event took place one week later in Falkland, a rural crossroads in West Virginia's Appalachian region. Besides the Falkland Sawmill, which had been operational since 1929, there were two trailer homes and one recently constructed, modest ranch-style house of red brick. The only other structure was the Pentecostal Church of the Revivalist Rock, a concrete box the size of a two-car garage with the date "June 1971" carved into a cornerstone.

After the call to worship and opening prayer, the preacher departed his liturgical norm. He summoned all twenty-four parishioners to stand shoulder-to-shoulder in pairs. Once in place at the altar, he withdrew a plastic U.S. mail crate from behind the plywood pulpit. It was covered with a double-folded red beach towel secured at the rim with bungee cords and heavily laden on the inside with rattlesnakes, water moccasins, and copperheads. There was also one coral snake. Proclaiming the time had come for a communal test of faith, he worked the line of believers from one end to the other.

The first pair was a retired coal miner who lived in the modest brick house and a ten-year-old girl from a town one valley to the east who wore an outmoded pleated dress over a crinoline half-slip and a long white hair ribbon. They were told to interlock fingers and insert their affixed forearms through a tight rent in the top of the towel. Only the girl winced as the vipers struck each hand and wrist numerous times. Afterward, the preacher lowered the crate, absolved them, and moved to the next couple. He made a total of twelve stops.

Later, when the bodies were discovered, all but two were seated in pews. The preacher was slumped on a brown-metal folding chair near the altar, arms draping at his hips, chin resting on his chest. The girl with the white hair ribbon was sprawled on the front mud mat, her upper body twisted awkwardly against twin doors. She was held there by her right arm, still straining where it looped in desperate struggle with a heavy chain that secured both doorknobs by a thick padlock.

# CHAPTER FIVE

*Monday, March 10, 2025*

Wycoff Cranston had been on the job as White House advisor for domestic affairs only two weeks. When he made the call to assistant FBI Director William Drakken, the exchange was brief.

"Yeah, hello. Drakken here."

"How're you doing? This is Cranston, the new guy for domestic counsel over here at sixteen hundred."

"Right. Saw you got tapped from Interior. Give it two more weeks. With this administration, you'll be the veteran and everyone else will be the FNG."

"Yeah," Cranston said. "People come and go around here. Sometimes they just disappear like Stalinist Russia."

"Uh-huh," Drakken grunted. "And I'm the prick that made some of those fuckers go bye-bye."

"Good, good. Then you're just the man I need to speak with. Listen, about this suicide thing making headlines all over the world."

"I figured this call was about that clusterfuck of cuckoos."

"You got any ideas?"

"I think the boys here at J. Edgar HQ can come up with something you'll like. It'll probably mean coordinating with Langley for international recon. That'll mean a platoon of goddamn lawyers from half a dozen agencies climbing up my ass, but I'll beat 'em back after justifying it with the House Intelligence Committee where I've got a couple of golf buddies."

"Good, good. Interagency co-op between the FBI and CIA gets good press, so long as everyone stays in their lane. Whatever it is, send it to the press office at sixteen hundred so we can announce it. I need to make POTUS look like he's doing something on this. Kinda important. He's taking a beating from the lightweights on the Hill for being a no-show on this hara-kiri fad."

"I can do that for you. Listen, last month's terror thing in Manhattan drained my contingency funds for the year. Since the perp was just another domestic asshole, the military is getting a pass and the FBI is handling a nationwide search for accomplices."

"Yeah, so? That's what you're supposed to do."

"Right." He cleared his throat. "What I'm getting at is—we're picking up the whole check. My terror budget is already fully tapped for the whole year. So how about I plug into the Justice Reserve Budget slotted for unforeseen domestic shit? If that works for you, the fucked-up rules approved by those same lightweights require POTUS to okay it."

Cranston gave a hard exhale. This G-Man was looking for a quid pro quo. He wanted a budget boost in exchange for generating clap-clap that'll ramp-up approval ratings for POTUS.

"Yeah...go...ahead," he said, unhappily hammering each word. "Send the forms over and I'll push it through during this afternoon's facetime in the Oval. But listen to me, POTUS is going to have a press conference middle of next week. We've got our position on the Manhattan terror thing covered. But I need something real sexy on the suicide thing. Even though it's a global crisis, I want you to make it as red, white, and blue as you can. Put Lassie and Seal Team Six in the photo op if that's what it takes. This will be my first day for show-and-tell on the job, so do *not* leave my limp you-know-what flapping in the wind."

"Yep, I get that part," Drakken assured. "I'll send over something goddamned good for you, POTUS, the press, and all mankind."

"Excellent."

They both clicked off at the same time.

# Extraordinary Delusions
## Chapter Six

*Friday, March 14, 2025*

Sam Teagarden mistook the tiny drones for a swarm of ravenous bugs drawn to the apple core on the corner of his desk, the remains of a late lunch. He swatted absently while grading the last of the day's midterm exams.

That afternoon marked the traditional Friday kickoff of spring break. The annual craving for south Florida was getting underway later than usual because of February's terror attack in Manhattan, which set the academic calendar back by one week. Fourteen people were killed, and dozens injured by a series of remote-controlled bombs spaced around the city. After paralyzing Manhattan for several days, the NYPD said it was the work of a single suspect—a thirty-three-year-old carpenter from Enfield, North Carolina named Jeffery Nash. Angry about a new prohibition on the sale of assault rifles, Nash blamed New York City as the incubating capital of un-American liberality. Fearing they'd be next, community groups in Chicago, L.A., and other equally big and liberal cities demanded that the FBI verify that Nash wasn't part of a wider network.

As individual stories of the New York victims emerged, national mass media found one to be particularly poignant. A father was walking his seven-year-old daughter to her public school when it happened. He was killed; she survived, though just barely. Unidentified at first, the hospital listed her as Little Girl Blue because of her blue dress. Finding it endearing, the press and public became fixated with sympathy which made her a cause célèbre. The collection of flowers, balloons, and stuffed animals grew so large it had to be moved from the hospital room, to the hospital lobby, and finally to a makeshift shrine in a military tent erected in a nearby park. Additionally, the hospital began releasing daily updates on Little Girl Blue's condition.

It was small compensation that the delay of spring break was accompanied by early arrival of spring weather, allowing Teagarden to open his office windows in the Columbia University math building. Outside, the air smelled of photosynthesis, and the few students still on campus were already wearing tees and flip-flops. Some cited the season's prematurely warm temps as the latest evidence of ongoing climate change, yet no one complained.

For a second time he waved with distraction at the buzzing. Reaching with one hand, he folded the wrapper to seal the apple core and scraps of bread crust from his turkey sandwich.

The final paper belonged to his star pupil, a brilliant young man named Aken Okeke from Namibia, who breezed through a previous course on Fluid Dynamics. This class was a graduate-level calculus requirement called Advanced Probability, though the midterm subject had been a curve ball about Random Patterns. A surprise that ruffled feathers for everyone, including Okeke, it was an experiment to see if anyone retained creative thinking after weeks of hard number-crunching. The test challenged them to find, analyze, and interpret useful patterns in things like stock market trading, traffic accidents, public health crises, even terror attacks. Once discovered, the theory goes, a hidden pattern might be put to good use by making money on the stock market, preventing traffic accidents, avoiding public health crises, and even intercepting terror attacks. After all, what's the use in being a math whiz if all you become is a tax accountant?

Most students did poorly on the exam. A few did moderately

well, particularly the two women in the class. At a quick glance, it appeared that Okeke would be among those who scored average at best.

After a third swipe at the irritating bugs, Teagarden snatched the wadded wrapper to heave into the wastebasket in the corner, hoping it would send them in pursuit. When they didn't budge, he looked closer and saw that they were not flies, gnats, or insects of any kind. In that moment, his spinal fluid stopped flowing.

They're drones. Ultra-mini drones!

Teagarden froze. About the size of a housefly, each had pore-like openings resembling the eyes of a spider. Below their egg-shaped bodies was a set of tiny rotor blades that tilted to adjust for altitude and flight path. When close, they made a vague buzzing noise. When not hovering, they flew around so fast he couldn't count their number, but estimated at least ten, maybe fourteen.

No. Not again.

Teagarden had been in this position before. Six years earlier, the drones were about the size of a baseball, sent to kill him and retrieve what became known as The Dear John File. It was no surprise that these were smaller. Recent advances had turned the U.S. Air Force into a military branch consisting almost entirely of UAVs, unmanned aerial vehicles. They ranged in size from regular planes, to dragonfly-sized machines that spit fire, poison, and micro-bombs by the hundreds of thousands, all with great precision.

He had no idea why these were in his office, but he had no intention of waiting to find out. The nastiness of that previous odyssey in 2019 made the idea of a sequel a big "no thank you."

Been there, done that.

He made a snap decision *not* to bolt. If these bugs were armed, it would be unwise to run like a fox. Instead, he casually eased back from his desk, slowly stood, and shifted toward the open door as calmly as he could manage. He watched to see if they were more interested in him, or the test papers examining consistencies in the law of large numbers.

Uh-oh!

They split the difference. About half stayed with Aken Okeke's open test booklet, the other half followed him. He took two side-steps closer to the corridor. The pattern was the same. He turned and made two strides. Still, they were evenly divided. He glanced to the hallway, hoping someone walking past may scare them off.

Yeah, right. On the first afternoon of spring break? Not a chance.

Okay, enough is enough. If he was going to get zapped, it would have to be in the back. He made a break for the door and into the empty hallway as fast as his creaky knees would carry him. At the stairwell, he leaned on the bannister and partially slid to the first landing.

From there, he did another half-slide to the ground floor, high-stepping like a daddy longlegs. On the way down, a janitorial pushcart parked in the main corridor caught his attention. It was loaded with hooks, brackets, and compartments that held implements for sweeping, scraping, and swabbing. The push broom, dust mop, and spritz bottles had no value to him. The yellow dustpan, however, might be useful.

Skipping the final two steps, he hurried to the cart, grabbed the yellow handle, spun to regain his footing, and readied the dustpan for use as a gladiatorial flyswatter. Mysteriously, only two drones separated from the pack to follow him. The others were nowhere to be seen. It didn't matter. One was more than enough to kill him in an instant with epipoxilene, or any of the latest weapons that could dispense instant death.

At the bottom of the stairwell, they paused to hover and observe their target. Whoever was monitoring the remote video screen must have laughed to see Sam Teagarden ready to defend his life with a dustpan.

Don't just hover. Do something.

When one of the bugs revved its engine, the sound was audible from several paces away.

Great. I've seen this before, like maybe in a Bugs Bunny cartoon.

The assault wasn't what he expected. He imagined it would

dive, retreat, gain altitude, and dive again from a different angle like a mad hornet. Instead, it whizzed past him as if it had somewhere else to go. Teagarden easily blocked its path with the back of the dustpan which made it suddenly halt midair. Seeing opportunity, he reared his backhand and sliced forward, bashing the drone with a powerful crack. It ricocheted off the wall, made a *zuh-h-h* sound of electronic death, and plopped to the floor.

He thought of picking it up to examine it, but the second drone was still hovering and watching. With one down and one to go, Teagarden took what seemed his best option. He bolted. He hurried down the corridor, through the lobby, and out the main door. Once outside, he saw why the other drones had not followed. They'd returned to his office and flown out the open window where they hovered about ten feet overhead. From that distance, they appeared to be nothing unusual, a vague grouping of flies or black wasps just emerged from their nest in the early bloom of spring.

He strained to keep an eye on them as he hurried across the campus green, unaware that his cell phone was buzzing in his pocket, or of the two men watching him from the sidewalk. One was the UPS man, the other was Josh, the building custodian who called out, "What's wrong, Professor?...Professor is there something wrong?" But the only thing Sam Teagarden heard was the voice inside his head screaming one word.

Run!

# CHAPTER SEVEN

The subway station was a logical choice. Not that the drones couldn't follow him there. And once they did, it would be easy to chase him to the edge of the platform where he'd plunge to the tracks and be sliced under heavy steel wheels or electrocuted by the third rail.

An uptown Number One train pulled into the station as he pushed through the transponder turnstile that read the credit card inside his wallet. He didn't need to take the train to get home because his apartment was one block from the university's math building. In his panic, he hoped the underground station would be a good refuge and a moving train even better.

Only after the twin doors slid open and shut behind him did he look back through the windows. Nothing seemed out of the ordinary. There were no drones on the platform, and no buzzing clouds of bugs zooming through the turnstile. He guessed it was because they didn't want their attack captured on transit security cameras.

Standing against the door window, trying to catch his breath, he withdrew his cell phone and saw a missed call from his wife. He started to dial her back when the signal was lost. Every station was equipped with cell signals, but not the trains themselves.

You'd think in the year 2025, they'd have solved that glitch. They can suck money from your wallet as you walk through turnstiles. And they can use algorithms to mark you as a suspicious character for video surveillance. Yet they still can't equip trains with Wi-Fi.

Teagarden inhaled the stale air of the subway car. The last time this happened, he was forced to run from his home in the Catskill Mountains down the East Coast to Key West, leaving a trail of death along the way. Now, six years later, the trauma still lived with him every day and haunted him every night. Yet he stayed silent about his PTSD. Because of him, history books had been rewritten. His survival in 2019 led to published proof that JFK, MLK, and RFK were targeted by a black ops program managed by one of the sickest minds of the twentieth century. Consequently, many around the world celebrated him as the American Prometheus, which compelled him to keep the emotional damage to himself.

Not all agreed. Plenty of people hated him. On balance, the death threats versus adulation were just about even. Thankfully, by 2025, the media had moved on. He remained a lengthy entry on Wikipedia, but demands for interviews and television appearances had nearly stopped. Hate-mongers either accepted the reality that rogue elements within the government committed unspeakable crimes in the 1960s, or they didn't. If they didn't, they said so, and moved on to the next crisis. In America, there's always a new crisis lurking in the next day's headlines.

Cynthia Blair knew he suffered PTSD. She was his second wife and did more than anyone to help him adjust. It was her idea to search for comfort in a local church. Neither had been big believers, and neither felt destined for intense religious conviction. Yet she wanted to explore the possibility that human kindness grounded in faith would advance the healing process. She was right. In the last few years, he noticed a gradual increase in personal happiness and peace.

And now—this.

Teagarden edged away from the door windows in case the drones buzzed north to an uptown station.

Okay, so who's trying to kill me this time?

He had no answer. Six years ago, it was the FBI. Six years

later, the FBI was his best guess. Or maybe, just maybe, it was a group that harbored hate for him because of the changes he wrought. That seemed unlikely. Americans who wanted history books to remain unchanged weren't the sort of people to come into possession of a dozen micro-drones.

He watched the uptown stations arrive and depart like quick dreams in a night of fitful sleep. First was 125th Street in Harlem, where the train lumbered from the earth to make an above-ground stop before reentering the tunnel. Then came stops at 137th, 145th, and 157th. It reminded him of the first day in Advanced Probability class back in January. He'd drawn a list of numbers on the board and gave the students five minutes to discover a meaningful, random pattern. The numbers were: 14, 18, 23, 28, 34, 42, 50, 59, 66, 72, 79, 86, 96, 103, 110, 116, 125, 137, 145, 157, 168, 181, 191, 207, and 215.

At the four-minute mark, he said, "No one? Really? Oh come, come class. It's so obvious that it should take only a few seconds of creative thought."

After five minutes, no one had an answer.

"They denote all numbered street stops of the Number One subway train from Greenwich Village to northern Manhattan."

There were groans all around. Several called it unfair. One student, thankfully not the brilliant Aken Okeke, claimed it wasn't a math question but a "parlor trick."

"Really?" Teagarden said. "Do you believe numbers will always behave in ways that comport with your view of what is, and what is not, true mathematics?"

That student surrendered with a blush of regret.

He checked his cell phone at each passing station, though the signal didn't last long enough to make a call. At 145th Street he saw a text from his wife: *call me...important.*

He exited at the next stop and ascended to 157th and Broadway, dialing as he walked. There was no casual "hello" when she picked up.

"Oh, God, are you all right? You didn't get hurt running from them, did you?"

"What? No, I'm okay. How did you—"

"Thank God. I was afraid you'd get hurt in the panic. Listen, he's here at the apartment. Where are you?"

"I'm uptown. I escaped on a Number One subway to Washington Heights. What do you mean? Who's at the apartment? And how do you know about this?"

"Sam, please come home immediately. We'll explain when you get here. His name is Klassen. He's an FBI agent. But it's okay. He's okay. Just come home. I've been worried to death since you fled your office."

# Chapter Eight

The downtown cab was one of the new driverless models owned by QuickCo, whose advertising slogan was "Hey...wanna catch a Quickie?" When the trademark phrase first went public, some were offended and tried to shame the company into changing it, but QuickCo was too big. As the mightiest online advertising outfit, it was responsible for more pop-up ads than any other. Every human on Earth hated pop-up ads, yet the company most responsible for them had become the third wealthiest in the S&P 500. For Teagarden, it was one of the greatest mysteries of commerce—all consumers despised pop-up ads, yet no one abandoned their apps because of the relentless intrusions, including him.

He climbed into the back seat of the Quickie Cab and interrupted the prerecorded greeting by calling out his destination. Unfortunately, there was nothing quick about a Quickie. In violation of every New Yorker's demand for haste, it never broke thirty miles per hour and obediently stopped for every yellow light along heavily trafficked Broadway. Because it was driverless, there was no way to put in a request to drop the pedal.

It didn't help that Teagarden was personally targeted by a massive *public* pop-up during the trek, probably caused by the GPS tracer on his cell phone. Public pop-ups were the worst. They were far more annoying than web-based interruptions. It had already happened twice on the screen in the back of the Quickie car. Now it was a huge electronic billboard atop an apartment building. Each time the commercial was for Caribe Caramba!, an online travel service:

> Hello, Professor Teagarden,
> Escape the snow this winter!
> Check out these low rates for Bimini, Freeport
> and Nassau.
> All luxury deals include airfare, four-star hotel
> and car!

He easily clicked past the ads on the Quickie's back seat screen but had no such option with the rooftop jumbotron flashing his name all over upper Broadway. The ads stemmed from his wife's search the previous evening. They'd considered a last-minute trip to the Bahamas. That morning, she rejected the idea because of the expense, suggesting instead that they choose a week of stay-cation R&R. The itinerary would include dinner and a show, long dog walks, ordering-in Chinese food, enjoying bike rides along the Hudson, and leisurely sex when neither was too exhausted. He happily agreed.

"Ugh," Teagarden grunted, looking at the garish rooftop billboard. His name was in giant lettering accompanied by a selfie of him and Blair walking in the deep snow of Central Park during last winter's big blizzard. Seeing it now made him regret sharing it on social media where it would live forever like Styrofoam in a landfill.

Individually targeted public pop-ups were the subject of major controversy. Anyone was a potential target. Turning off your cell phone usually stopped them. The more sophisticated billboards, however, could default to credit card chips and even key fobs. Some people loved them and took selfies for posting. Generally, anyone with a modicum of self-respect considered them a crude invasion.

At his building on 116th Street, Teagarden tapped the Quickie Cab's transponder with his wallet to pay the metered fare and ignored the option to input an additional fifteen percent tip for the driver who did not exist.

He rushed through the lobby without the usual wave to Luis, the afternoon doorman. Blair and Coconut Too, their blond lab, were waiting in the corridor on the twenty-third floor when the elevator doors swooshed open.

"How did you know it was me?"

"We watched you on the aerial monitor." She took one arm to pull him closer for a quick heads-up whisper. "Sam, it's okay. He's on our side."

"Monitor? What monitor?"

"Sam, listen to me. He's here to help. He—"

But Teagarden was too frantic. She squeezed his hand as he moved past her. Aware of his agitated state, the big dog followed like a protective escort. Inside, a skinny man in a rumpled white dress shirt stood with his back to the entranceway. His suit jacket was draped over the back of a stool at the breakfast bar, where two tea mugs rested. From the rear, Teagarden saw that he was busy with a handheld device as though playing a video game. He was gazing through the sliding doors, steadily fixed on the eastern skyline. Outside on the balcony, a valise sat on the wrought iron table, a flat-screen monitor visible in the opened, upright lid. The video image on the monitor bounced between a single aerial shot of the Columbia campus and a patchwork grid of a dozen images too small for him to make out. The bottom of the case was a thick slab of foam rubber, precisely cut into little compartments.

"C'mon now," the skinny man said, working the device with both hands. "C'mon, lil' guys, don't be stubborn."

Before Teagarden could ask what he was doing in his living room, they appeared en masse. First, there was nothing, then suddenly—they were there. All of them. They paused just beyond the balcony railing, looking like a swarm of flies. The same drones he'd fled, thinking they'd come to kill him. Holding at the railing, they appeared to be waiting for their next instruction. The skinny man keyed in directives with both index fingers and maneuvered levers with both thumbs.

"Okay, in you go," he said in a kindly voice.

Coco Too's ears perked up as he watched. The drones revved, adjusted their pitch, and dove two-by-two straight into their snug foam compartments.

"Okay," the man said. "One more to go."

This time only one drone appeared at the balcony rail. It was larger than the others, about the size of a bumble bee. After more adjustments, it buzzed toward the open chambered nest, where it hovered overhead. In that position, Teagarden could see that, unlike the others, it had claw-like talons that clutched one of the smaller drones. Coco Too growled in his lowest possible canine octave. With another input on the remote, the talons opened, the mini-bot dropped into the box, and the lid closed.

"Was that the one I swatted with the dustpan?" Teagarden asked.

"Oh shit!" the skinny man shouted. He put a hand on his sternum. "Sorry," he said, "I didn't see you there. Yes sir, that's the K-48 you wacked. They're known as Baby Bug Bots." He nodded enthusiastically. "It had to be retrieved. You know, the technology is proprietary. It would be my butt if all its little internal secrets fell into the wrong hands."

"Proprietary to whom?"

"Technically to the U.S. Air Force, in this case to the Federal Bureau of Investigation." He extended his right hand. It was an honest, if awkward, gesture. "I'm Special Agent Aaron Wechter. I apologize for startling you at your office."

Teagarden ignored him. His dog plopped at his feet, worried about the room's rising tension. Outside, the slightly larger drone with talons still hovered at the balcony rail where the skinny man left it. Blair edged closer to her husband. Teagarden glanced from mini-drone to wife to Special Agent Wechter, back to mini-drone, and back to Special Agent Wechter. He saw that the agent was no older than mid-twenties and his face still held a boyish soft-ness. With messy hair and a general unkempt appearance, he looked more like a classic computer nerd than a federal agent.

"You *apologize* for startling me? You apologize for *startling* me."

"Sam, please," his wife said. "He's here to—" Teagarden cut her off.

"That's what you call fear of being murdered by a swarm of killer bugs? You call that being '*startled.*' Do you have any idea how many people were killed six years ago during my run from Bethel, New York to Key West?"

"Uh, sir..."

"I lost count at nine. Murdered."

"Well..."

"Is *that* startling to you? Would you care to apologize to all of them for being startled?"

"Sir, I am aware that..."

"Oh, you are *aware!* That's sweet. Are you aware that I was so frightened of those robotic vermin that I was ready to bolt straight out of my office window and break my neck in the fall? Were you aware that I'd rather go splat on the sidewalk than endure their untraceable poison? Were you aware that I'd risk electrocution on the third rail to avoid getting zapped with epipoxilene?"

Nearly nose to nose, and staring into his befuddled eyes, Teagarden finally stopped. The young agent tried to find words but was so flummoxed he stood silent. Instead, he turned back to the remaining mini-drone and made one final input on the remote control. A second lid on the valise popped up. The bumble-bee-sized drone adjusted its pitch, revved, and dove straight into the open reservoir. A moment later, that cover also closed.

"Now that you're home safe, my job is done." He walked to the balcony, snapped the locks on the valise, picked it up, and walked back into the main room. "I apologize again." At the breakfast bar, he leaned beyond the counter. "I'll be going now, sir," he said.

"Right," a voice responded from inside the kitchen. "Set up shop in the van. Send the bugs up to an altitude of about fifty feet and spread them over a two-block radius. Tell Agent Utrillo to keep eyes on the service entrance."

"Yes sir."

Teagarden's jaw went slack. He had no idea there was a second man in his apartment. He watched his wife open the door for Agent Wechter and give an apologetic nod as he departed. Breaking from his stupor, Teagarden stepped toward the breakfast bar to peer into the kitchen.

The man standing by the refrigerator was older, about fifty-five, approximately five-feet-five, with remarkably broad shoulders. He was heavier, at least two hundred pounds, and had a rounded, weather-beaten face. His right hand held a mug.

"What are you doing in my kitchen?"

"Refilling my tea mug with hot water from the kettle," the man said. "But if you mean to ask, what am I doing in your apartment, the answer is—saving your life."

Stunned, Teagarden dropped to the sofa. Coco Too jumped to sit next to him.

# CHAPTER NINE

"Sam, I'm sorry," Blair said. She too sat on the sofa next to Coco and leaned into her husband. "I tried to tell you. Of course, your reaction was understandable. They had to come on strong. They were afraid for your life."

The short man with broad shoulders and sun-burned complexion slowly walked from the kitchen, steaming tea mug in hand. He was wearing a conservative pinstripe suit with a vest, blue dress shirt, and red necktie, minus the jacket. It was *his* jacket draped over the back of the stool, not Wechter's.

"She's right Professor Teagarden. The fact is, we did save your life. I realize we violated your breakpoint. I apologize for that. It had to be done because your life was in immediate danger. And it still is. Extreme danger."

Teagarden cleared his throat. "And who might you be?"

"Supervisory Special Agent Bernard Klassen. Along with agents Aaron Wechter and Mariana Utrillo, who's outside in our van, plus others at the downtown office. We constitute Operation Five O'clock."

Teagarden reflexively looked at his watch.

"It's not a reference to the time, Professor Teagarden. You are Operation Five O'clock."

"Excuse me?"

"Your name—Teagarden. It was Agent Wechter who came up with it. He attended primary school near London, where teatime begins at five p.m." He raised his tea mug as if offering a toast.

"Clever, don't you think?"

Teagarden found his voice. "When do I get to know what this is all about, and why am I the object of another operation managed by the Federal Bureau of Incompetence?"

"Sam, please," his wife objected. She gripped his arm. "Try to listen to him; he's on our side."

Klassen smiled slightly. "It's all right. I understand your frustration. May I sit?"

"Yes, of course," Blair said. She gestured to the armchair closest to the sofa.

"Professor Teagarden, did you notice the man near the front of the mathematics building as you fled?" He paused to sip his tea. Receiving no answer, he continued. "It's even less likely that you noticed him following you to the subway entrance."

"I do recall that there were two men."

"Right. One was the building custodian. The other man was the reason the K-48s entered your office window. I'm talking about the one in the brown UPS uniform. He was not a real UPS man. He knew you were alone. He was about to enter the building to kill you. He'd have killed the custodian as well. Fortunately, the drones confused him, and you bolted so fast he didn't have a clear opportunity. By the way, only two K-48s followed you down the stairs because the others returned outside to monitor your assassin."

"Do they shoot epipoxilene?"

"No. Shooting the mother's milk of the dark ops is an obsolete delivery method. These new mini-drones inject it, mosquito style. Plus, they're far more maneuverable. No radar in the world can spot them. They approach a human target, land on the skin, inject the poison, and fly back to Agent Wechter's 'air-*base* in a suit-*case*,' as it's called."

Teagarden considered the information.

So this guy really is with the FBI, and he really means me no harm.

Allowing that reality to sink in was a challenge. Once it finally penetrated, he realized that the most important question remained unanswered. Perhaps intentionally unanswered. He guessed that Klassen was deliberately holding back, letting the explanation unfold at its own pace.

"All right, then," Teagarden said, "time for Agent Klassen to fill in the X's and Y's."

"Beg pardon?"

"Algebraic equations, Mr. Klassen. If X is trying to kill Y, who is X and what is the value of Y's death?"

"Oh, yes."

"While you're at it, kindly enlighten me as to why you didn't knock at my door, call, email, text, MotherBoard, Snapchat, Facebook, or tweet?"

Klassen nodded, sipped his tea, and leaned forward. He withdrew a handkerchief from his hip pocket to dab the growing moisture at his temples. Blair gave a small sigh of relief that her husband's anger was easing.

"It's like this," Klassen began. "The FBI received a tip from certain confidential Israeli sources that three persons of interest were bound for the U.S. Once it was determined that they were not Islamic terrorists, the tip got passed to my team."

"When did that happen?"

"This morning."

"Wait a second. Operation Five O'clock has existed only since the morning?"

"Oh, no. Operation Five O'clock has existed only since about four o'clock this afternoon." He looked at his watch. "It's less than ninety minutes old."

"Explain."

"That's when we learned you were the target. We've been tailing them since the wee hours this morning. Unfortunately, they split up and we lost the third one. The two we were still tailing came here and asked the doorman, Mr. Luis Comacho, for you."

"It's my fault," Blair said. "They told Luis they had an appointment with you. When he buzzed me on the intercom, I said you were at the office. Luis told them to try the campus math building." She gestured at Klassen. "Five minutes later, the FBI was at the door."

"And *that* is when Operation Five O'clock was officially formed. When we realized you were the target."

"Why didn't you just arrest them?"

"Now we will. At the time, we had to move quickly to save you because we feared the missing third man was already on your campus, which of course, he was. And saving you meant dispatching K-48s. There are more K-48s than there are of us, and they don't get stuck in traffic."

Teagarden rubbed the head and neck of his dog and looked from his spouse to Klassen. "Is it possible they'll show up here and shoot me?"

"Yes," his wife said.

"That's why we're in your home now, Professor Teagarden, though they will not try to shoot you because they do not have firearms."

Teagarden wanted answers to the big questions but couldn't help being distracted by puzzles that popped up. "How do you know they don't have guns?"

Klassen hesitated. "It's not public knowledge, but I'll show you anyway. It's called the OMD. Stands for ocular metal detector." He withdrew what looked like an old-fashioned monocle from his vest pocket and fit it over his right eye. "This mini-version is standard-issue to all federal law enforcement including Homeland Security. Not totally reliable but works fairly well. More advanced versions are known as God Glasses." He squinted one eye and scanned Teagarden from ankle to scalp with the thick lens snugly covering the other eye. "You have six flathead screws in each of your knees and a small pocketknife attached to your keychain." He removed the monocle and replaced it in his vest.

"So why didn't the killers just buy guns once they entered gun-liberal America?" he asked.

"Probably because they entered America through gun-conservative New York City. Also, since two of them are prelates with one of the oldest churches in the world, I doubt they'd know how to approach street gangsters to make illegal firearm purchases.

"Prelates?"

"Yes sir."

"As in, priests?"

"One is a priest from Santiago de Compostela, Spain. The woman is a nun with a cloister called Sisters of the Order of St. Genesius. That's near the town of Muxia, also in northwest Spain. The third was the man in the UPS uniform that you bolted past on the Columbia campus. Very dangerous. He was your primary assassin, who happens to be ex-Mossad."

# CHAPTER TEN

Blair's gasp was nearly inaudible. Teagarden went slack-jawed. They were all quiet for a while. Klassen too became contemplative, as though working on the end game of Operation Five O'clock. Teagarden was now certain that Klassen was intentionally releasing details slowly. It was smart, and made him guess that Klassen was more than a cop. When cops want you to know something, they just tell you. If you don't get it on first pass, that's your problem. Coddling sensibilities is not in their repertoire, nor is it supposed to be.

"What else have you done with your life?" Teagarden asked. "I'm thinking you haven't been a fed your entire career."

Klassen's eyes glinted slightly. "You'd never guess."

Blair welcomed the friendly change of subject.

"Army officer," she said. "Military intelligence. I'll bet you helped capture Osama."

"Afraid not."

"Lawyer and then a judge?" guessed Teagarden.

"No."

"Not a preacher?" asked Blair.

"Correct. Not a preacher. And neither a priest nor a rabbi."

"Grade school teacher," she said.

"Getting closer. All right, I'll tell you. I was a psychology professor not far from here at City University. I had a private therapy practice two nights week. Tuesdays and Wednesdays were totally booked. You know, troubled marriages, getting fired, hating your

40

mother. General modern anxiety stuff."

"After today I'm going to need therapy," Teagarden said.

"Me too," said Blair.

"Why'd you change careers?" Teagarden pressed.

For the first time a flash of regret came over Klassen's face. "My partner was a numbers-crunch guy. He worked for one of the big brokerage houses. I lost him at 8:46 a.m., Tuesday, September 11, 2001." He took another sip of tea and replaced the mug on the coffee table. He wiped his mouth with his handkerchief. "He was on a high floor, so, it was quick."

It made Teagarden appreciate him. Their stories were not unrelated. His first wife was killed in an accident on the New York State Thruway almost seven years ago. He suffered two broken knees and endured months of recovery and physical therapy before he could walk. That was followed by his now well-documented run for his life down the East Coast that led to the American Prometheus moniker.

Another moment of silence passed between them, this time without discomfort. During the pause, sounds of motorized traffic floated up from below. The loudest was caused by a rushing fire truck with a klaxon that even the deaf could hear. They were on the verge of renewing conversation when all three snapped alert, drawn by an extraordinary shriek that seemed to come from outside on the balcony. Yet nothing on the small terrace seemed unusual. When the shriek sounded again, and its source dropped from the sky like a wounded bird, they all hurried to the glass doors. It was Special Agent Aaron Wechter, who managed to break his fall from the roof with a desperate grasp on the handrail.

Klassen was the first outside where his partner struggled to hold on to the far side of the banister with one tangled arm, his face grimacing with the pain of smashed bones and torn tendons. Before Klassen could extend a hand, Wechter lost his grip. When Teagarden and Blair caught up, they all peered over the edge to watch in shock as the young agent tumbled twenty-three floors. It seemed to happen in slow-motion. Halfway down, one leg snagged a plant holder, sending him spiraling outward to a concrete sidewalk ten feet from the base wall. He hit bottom on the back of his left shoulder and crumpled like a jacket tossed into a laundry hamper.

"Oh, God!" Klassen shouted. He pounded the balcony railing with a fist. When he turned to look up, Teagarden and Blair did the same. Two floors above, a man wearing a brown UPS uniform peered over the rooftop parapet. Having confirmed Wechter's death, he withdrew from the parapet, which sent Klassen racing back through the apartment, into the hallway, and toward the stairwell. Seeing it all, Coco Too's hunting instincts kicked in, making him follow.

"Is that the man you saw on campus?" Blair asked.

"I think so. Wechter must have seen something suspicious and gone up to the roof instead of down to the van as Klassen instructed."

"Sam, look!" Blair shouted, pointing below.

In the distance, a woman wearing a blue FBI windbreaker ran toward Wechter's body, unaware that she was being followed by a man and a woman. The pursuing man carried a chunk of what appeared to be broken curbstone, the woman carried a red plastic jug.

"Sam, that must be Agent Utrillo."

"And those two behind her must be the nun and one of the priests."

"They came from that double-parked van. Sam, this is bad. I think they're going to attack her."

When Agent Utrillo arrived at the ruined body of Agent Wechter, she turned and doubled over to vomit. Retching on the adjacent grass, with traffic booming in the background, she could not hear the desperate warnings screamed by Teagarden and Blair from twenty-three floors up.

A moment later, she gazed upward. Perhaps it was a shift in wind direction, or a lull in traffic noise caused by synchronized red lights. Whatever the cause, Agent Utrillo finally heard the shouted alarms. She looked first to the balcony, then turned to see the danger and managed to scramble away, pivot, draw down, and shoot the priest as he raced toward her with the curbstone held over his head.

After he fell dead, his female companion with the red plastic jug backed away. Ignoring orders to halt, she uncapped the container and showered her body with reflective liquid. One flick with a disposable lighter, and her body flashed over. At first, she stumbled in shock. Then, before falling and fully succumbing to the fire, she rallied. In a final act of passion, she rushed toward the woman in the FBI windbreaker and tried to embrace her so they'd both pass from this world in a grip of blazing death.

Seeing her intention, Special Agent Mariana Utrillo stood her ground, aimed, and killed the woman on fire with a single shot.

# CHAPTER ELEVEN

*Saturday, March 15, 2025*

"We don't really know much."

It was the third time Supervisory Special Agent Bernard Klassen spoke those words. It was careful, language. The type of language that made Blair's lawyerly instincts kick in, making her antennae vibrate on behalf of her husband.

"Please share what you *do* know," she said.

He had insisted that Blair and Teagarden be admitted to his hospital room after he came out of surgery the second time. They figured he wanted to thank them for saving his life on the roof of their apartment building by stanching the blood flow from a knife wound to the femoral artery in his right leg. Many others continuously entered and exited the cramped room: doctors, nurses, uniformed NYPD, men and women in blue FBI windbreakers, and men in suits. Klassen made certain that all feds gave Blair and Teagarden "hands off" recognition as civilian "friendlies." Still, they had to stand flat against the wall to avoid impeding foot traffic.

Klassen looked bad. The assassin had nearly killed him on the roof after beating and tossing Agent Wechter over. In addition to a knife wound, Klassen had a concussion, broken ribs, and a broken right hand. Both eyes were swollen shut with concentric auras colored black, blue, and maroon. According to him, if Coco Too hadn't interceded, the assassin would not have retreated when he did.

"Only a few more minutes," a nurse announced. "The patient has been given a strong sedative and needs rest." She turned to review a machine over his bed that flashed digital readings on a dozen body functions.

Two uniformed cops mumbled acknowledgment to the nurse and departed. Klassen felt for the morphine pump pinned to his blue gown and gave the button a single push. He jammed up two pillows with his uninjured left hand.

"Ms. Blair," Klassen began. "We need to talk."

"My name is Cynthia. You saved my husband's life. Then we saved yours. I think we can move to a friendlier footing."

That did not sit well with the other feds. They halted as though someone pushed a universal pause button. Klassen sensed it, though his swollen eyes made him essentially blind. He knew resentment against Teagarden ran deep in the Bureau's upper echelons. Younger agents had accepted changes wrought by the scandal known as The Dear John File, which was decoded and published by Teagarden. Older agents, however, projected only a veneer of tolerance. Their anger still simmered. They had endured internal investigations, purges, and management overhaul but had not resolved the fury they held for the mathematics professor.

"Right," Klassen said to Blair's insistence on first names. "It's not that I'm not appreciative of your actions and your fast call to nine-one-one. I am. Under the circumstances, however, perhaps it's best that we stick with old-fashioned formalities for now."

That pushed the universal play button. The suits and windbreakers resumed cell phoning, texting, and pacing in and out of the room.

Blair acquiesced. "Yes, of course," she said.

"Agent Klassen," Blair continued, "my sense is that the ones who targeted my husband and assassinated that young FBI agent are still out there and still seeking to harm my husband. I must ask you again—"

Klassen interrupted her. "Sir?" he said, as loudly as his vocal cords allowed.

At first, Blair didn't understand. Then she noticed that one of the suits lowered his cell phone and looked straight into her eyes. It was clear to her that this was the man Klassen was addressing for permission to explain. He was a big-boned man. His large head sat atop a thick football neck that sprouted from massively broad shoulders. She pegged his blue suit as an off-the-rack poly/wool from one of the chains that cater to oversized men. His deep-set eyes were quick and observant, letting her know that he outranked everyone in the room in both intelligence and authority.

"Yeah, yeah," the big man said with an irritable voice. "Looks like you're going to live, Klassen, so we'll go with your no-good idea for now. Understand this—if he gets over there and creates another clusterfuck, this time with *international* consequences, it *will* be on you."

"Yes sir," Klassen said, his puffy face nodded in the affirmative.

"I've got to send something to sixteen hundred anyway," the large man continued. "That means you better not leave me digging for a gold nugget buried inside a pile of shit. You got that?"

"Yes sir."

"And be advised, I'm ordering accounting to allot the lowest budget possible. Coach class. No booze. And no room service. If it's my tit that gets caught in the wringer, at least there won't be any fucking limos or shit-silver-dollar five-star hotels on the taxpayer tab for the Washington Bozo Post to run on the front page." He turned to Teagarden. "We'd better have some goddamned positive results by the middle of the week when POTUS has that presser. And I want the whole thing wrapped with a pretty ribbon at that Jesus clambake happening in Berlin next week. That's the timetable. You got that?"

He was looking at Teagarden; it was Klassen who answered.

"Yes sir, I understand."

"Good." His irritable tone settled as he turned back to Klassen in the hospital bed. "Now here're some more facts for you. Agent Utrillo gets a career citation. Wechter gets a posthumous Star Medal presented to his momma. As for you, I'll put a nice attaboy

46

in your file—but not until *after* Op Five O'clock is put to bed with my satisfaction."

"Understood, sir."

The triple-X sized man turned and made an announcement for all gathered feds. "New York response team and all D.C. personnel, we're out of here. Return to base."

He gave Blair and Teagarden a quick scowl before departing. The blue windbreakers and remaining suits lined up like ducklings to follow him, leaving only Blair, Teagarden, the senior nurse, and the patient. The nurse tenderly patted Klassen's uninjured left hand.

"You have interesting colleagues," she said.

"Don't I?" He tried to roll his eyes but couldn't. "Such charming gentlemen they are."

"Just two minutes more," she said with a glance to Blair and Teagarden, though without attitude. "That sedative is about to take effect and it will have an impact on his cognitive ability. Don't worry, it's good medicine. The deeper the sleep the faster he'll recover." She glanced once more at the machine monitoring pulse, blood pressure and respiration, gave them all a small nod, and left the room.

"Wow," Klassen said, "I'm going to lose 'cognitive ability.' Guess I better talk fast before I babble. Here are the answers to questions I'm sure you're wondering. The name of the big man who just departed as though he were General Patton is Assistant FBI Director William Drakken. You can imagine the nicknames. Dracula is the favorite, followed by Count Drakken and Drakkenstein. Of course, he is the boss. As someone once said, 'Whatever else you can say about the boss, one thing is certain—he is still the boss.' I think I heard that in a spy movie. Was it with Tom Hanks? Did either of you see that one?"

Thinking the question silly and an indication of his loss of cognitive reliability, Blair and Teagarden ignored it.

"I just hope Dracula appreciates what you did," said Teagarden. He gestured to Klassen's elevated right leg and swollen eyes.

"You risked your life pursuing the man who killed Agent Wechter, the same man who tried to kill me."

"Nah. I emptied a full clip but he still got away. That's not something Dracula would appreciate. The FBI has an unwritten rule. When we shoot *at* a man, the bullets are supposed to *drop* the man. I failed. Agent Utrillo, however, did good. Real good. She dropped both those crazies."

"At least you shot your assailant."

"Correction. I *think* I shot him. I was slipping into cadaver stage at the time, so I'm uncertain. I'm told there were two blood types at the scene, and mine was one of them. Either I shot him, Wechter shot him, or your dog drew some of his hemoglobin. Frankly, I put my money on the dog because by then, my leg was bleeding like a spaghetti strainer. He had some sort of dagger that he wielded like a platoon of men with fixed bayonets. If you hadn't arrived when you did...well, you know that part of the story."

"Right," Blair said. "Before you go to sleep, please tell us the other part of the story. The part that explains Mr. Drakken's, shall we call them, *comments,* to you and to my husband?"

The patient took a breath and struggled to collect his thoughts before he lost them to the influence of medication.

"It's like this," he said. "Some people who know what you did six years ago think you're just the right man, or even the *only* man, for this particular job." His speech slowed as he searched for the words. "They want to send you...abroad...they think... um...a document may be...uh...linked to the mass suicide madness...and the attempt on your life...they want you to see...a church deacon at the excavation site...a man who secretly photocopied...uh...the document."

"A church deacon where?" Teagarden asked.

"U-h-h...little county...over...in the de-desert."

"What little country?"

"Izz...uh-h-h...Izz-ray-el-l-l."

"Israel? Why Israel?" Teagarden asked.

"Q. The Q...they...call it...the Q Doc...u...ment."

# CHAPTER TWELVE

*Monday, March 17, 2025*

Two days later he stood at a JFK departure gate. The morning flight from New York to Tel Aviv was a grueling sixteen-hour haul in an airborne Greyhound bus with a layover at Charles de Gaulle Airport in Paris. It would have been far worse had Teagarden not used his MasterCard for an upgrade from coach to business class.

Before takeoff, he did a final e-check with all parties on his Flexi-Flat laptop that had been rolled up in his carry-on:

> **From:** cynthiablair@solarvector.com
> **To:** samteagarden@solarvector.com
>
> just heard from klassen…he's feeling better and says dracula ok'd him to manage you and 'operation 5 o'clock' from his hospital bed…says u.s. security diplomat named eveillard will meet u in jeru. agent utrillo is staying here with me at the house in bethel…so i am safe…you be safe too and come back quick…in two or three days!!! ps: i packed socks for u.

It was her only complaint about his personal habits. He preferred wearing loafers without socks. Even at work.

**From:** samteagarden@solarvector.com
**To:** cynthiablair@solarvector.com

i will be safe and will come back quick… so what sort of gift would u like from the mideast? also, it will still be cold in the catskills, so make sure there's plenty of oil in the tank. ps: i will consider the socks, i promise (hee-hee).

**From:** bklassen@fbi.gov
**To:** samteagarden@solarvector.com

Professor Teagarden, Thank you once again. I am definitely better after a brief drug coma. Your mission will be a quick two or three day turn-a-round to get a look at the document in question, which we understand is encoded, and which is precisely why you're our man for the job. We believe the Q document is the reason you were pre-emptively targeted in New York. Naturally, it's hoped you will decode it and inform us if it factors into this contagion of global flash-mob suicide, which the U.S. aims to halt. I regret not being able to accompany you. Your security contact at Station Jeru is Emmanuel Eveillard, a darn good man. And take care in that relentless sun. I got a mild case of heat stroke last week in Megiddo. Drink plenty of water.

With appreciation, Special Agent Bernard Klassen

Agent Klassen's formal style of writing email was rare and made Teagarden like him even more. Even so, he responded informally.

**From:** samteagarden@solarvector.com
**To:** bklassen@fbi.gov

understood...will brief u asap...meantime i apologize for my discourtesy to you and agent Wechter in my apt....I regret that—sam

**From:** elandrew@usnavy.mil
**To:** samteagarden@solarvector.com

dad...so proud u'r wking w/newly reformed fbi... all good here...come to the keys to visit me, marnie and casey if you have time left in spring break. your granddaughter misses you! ...eva

**From:** samteagarden@solarvector.com
**To:** elandrew@usnavy.mil

it's a deal...see you all in a few days... in key west... love to all, especially my sweet granddaughter.

**From:** cynthiablair@solarvector.com
**To:** samteagarden@solarvector.com

no worries on furnace oil...it's unseasonably warm up here. need no gift from mideast...except your safe return...because i love you. dig?

Everything was good.

All the people he loved were safe. His wife, Coco Too, and Agent Utrillo were ensconced in their getaway home within sight of the hillside where the Woodstock rock festival took place and where he happened to be born. It was the same place where drones first attacked him in 2019. His daughter, granddaughter, and son-in-law were safe at their Key West home. Now he could indulge in a bit of ego. He was serving his nation as an investigator of an ancient document with potential religious significance that was causing people to punch their own ticket.

International investigator—hey, that's kind of cool.

But it also meant he was an employee of the FBI.

And that's weird.

If the job ended well, maybe it would neutralize him in the FBI's memory bank. Not that he did anything wrong. Even so, it was clear that the older guys still hated him. His tax returns had been audited every year since 2019 and being tailed while walking Coco Too was a periodic reality. At least he wasn't getting pulled over by the NYPD, so the FBI had some limitations. If this trip paid off in fence mending, it could end all punitive federal surveillance.

*That would be a relief.*

During the first leg of the flight, Teagarden read the FBI report previously downloaded to his Flexi-Flat. One great benefit of that particular laptop, aside from portability, was being able to bend the edges to prevent gawkers reading over-the-shoulder.

Aside from revealing woeful writing skills among government bureaucrats, the official report did little to shed insight into Klassen's drug-induced blabbering, or Drakken's hemorrhaging profanity.

*I too indulge in four-letter words here and there, but that macho Drakken is scary.*

The opening of the briefing was perfectly ludicrous:

Page One

This electronic document will be available to the recipient for two hours, after which the allowed read-time will expire and the document(s) will be automatically deleted. Once opened, the document(s) may be read/perused once (and only once), after which, the document(s) will automatically delete. If the recipient attempts to save, print, photograph, alter in any manner, or forward any of the document(s) to any other party, the document(s) will automatically delete and the responsible party may face charges in accordance with violation of title 69.2 that could result in a fine of $50,000 and imprisonment of not more than 15 years.

NOTE: The font of this e-document is backlighted with ApacheCom flash pulses that detect and prevent photography. Should any reader attempt a photographic screenshot, the e-doc will immediately delete, and all possible criminal charges enumerated above will initiate electronically without regard for circumstance, motive, or rank.

Oh brother. The Mission Impossible team never faced legalese crap like this. Once Jim Phelps and Ethan Hunt heard the audio tape, it simply self-destructed.

Page Two

Office Memorandum
UNITED STATES GOVERNMENT
**To:** Director, FBI
**Date:** 3/16/2025
cc: Asst. Dir. William Drakken,
White House Advisor on Domestic Affairs,
Wycoff Cranston

**From:** Supervisory Agent Bernard Klassen
**Subject:** Operation Five O'Clock
Mass Suicides
Purported "Q Document"

**Status:** Confidential/Eyes Only

**Internal Report:** As per your approval, am moving immediately to accommodate inter-diplomatic request from Station Jerusalem, via diplo-channels—ambassador, ranking allied sources (Prime Minister, Knesset Speaker), U.S. intel-research, et al—to dispatch requested American Sam Teagarden (private citizen, U.S.). Said dispatch will be for 48 hour (maximum) assist with local religious orgs for analysis and/or decrypting of newly surfaced documents theorized to hold value pertaining to history/ancient religion/regional interest.

Intel report issued via standard CIA channels/Station Jeru, suggests said document may bear relation to ongoing mass suicides. To date, 1,042 are dead in eleven known incidents in seven nations.

Said U.S. citizen (SUSC) will travel via commercial aviation, with escort by FBI security to aircraft at JFK, and be met by U.S. security/military/intel at Station Jeru. Upon arrival, at no time while on international soil, will SUSC be without U.S. authorized escort.

As previously noted, this request follows attempt on Teagarden's life in NYC, deaths of two foreign (previously unknown) agents, and the murder of Special Agent Aaron Wechter, of the FBI Mobile Aerial Surveillance Div. It was media coverage of that NY attack that resulted in a request for Teagarden's assistance issued by concerned religious leaders via the World Judeo-Christian History Council headquartered in NYC, scheduled to gather next week in Berlin at the Charlottenburg Grüner Park Hotel. Said request was brought to the attention of intel at Station Jeru as passed on from verified/cleared allied authorities that Teagarden may be appropriate interim ISR means to address matters of int'l concern while maintaining minimum expense and media exposure. First and only stop in Israel will be at the Church of Megiddo, allegedly the world's oldest, where a deacon is believed safeguarding original or copy of newly discovered Q Document.

**Goal:** Presence of SUSC will encourage local church official to cooperate/reveal/share said document with said accompanying U.S. intel personnel.

Note: said dispatch of private citizen will retain original codename: Op Five O'clock.

Teagarden stumbled over the reference to "ISR." He figured it was an abbreviation for Israel, though it made no sense in context. He departed the CIA file to click onto his Flexi-Flat's downloaded dictionary and encyclopedia. Possibilities for ISR definition were:

Institute for Systems Research
Inside Sales Representative
Interrupt Service Routine
Illegal Street Racing

None of them made any sense. Then there was the military reference: Intelligence, Surveillance, and Reconnaissance.

Yep, that's the one. Assistant Director William Drakkenstein not only saw to it that I'm a "minimum expense," which basically means I'm a bargain-basement secret agent. Worse, he also classified me as an "interim ISR." That means he considers me little more than a freelance office spyboy, an expendable recon scout. Hell—he might as well call me a disposable human drone!

It was language that smacked of a bureaucratic poke in the eye. Teagarden wondered if he was being paranoid to suspect that Drakken instructed that the phrases "interim ISR" and "minimum expense" be left in the redacted files just to make certain he saw them. His own answer to his question was—no, he was not being paranoid. And, yes, he was intended to see them. It left no question that Drakken remained bitterly resentful that Teagarden had exposed dreadful crimes committed by the FBI that caused American history to be rewritten.

He clicked forward in the files.

Page Three

Q Document
Precis:

The Q Document is a theoretical source for two of the four Gospel accounts in the New Testament. Believed by some to be both a missing Gospel and/or a principal source of Matthew and Luke. The name is drawn from the German word "quelle," meaning "source." Should it be found, said document would hold interest for religious scholars and institutions. Could have repercussions for nations where multiple faiths vie for influence in social and governmental affairs.

See: Wikipedia.

Really? "See: Wikipedia"? Great. Our American tax dollars at work. Some analyst gives the FBI director one paragraph of info and directs him to Wikipedia if he wants more data. Very sophisticated. No wonder a cabal of morons are running the U.S. government.

Page Four

Mass Incident Details

One:
3/1/25
Location: Monasterio del Nuevo Mundo, Baiona, Spain
Toll: 11
Means: submission to severed jugular (suicide)

Two:
3/2/25
Location: Campamento de la Verdad (Cult), Matamoros, Mexico
Toll: 432
Means: voluntary ricin consumption (suicide)

Three:
3/9/25
Location: Pentecostal Church of the Revivalist Rock, Falkland, West Virginia
Toll: 25
Means: voluntary exposure to venomous snake bites (suicide/one murder)

Four:
3/10/25
Location: Sunrise prayers for (ad hoc) Church of Wounded Vets, Ford Island, Oahu, Hawaii
Toll: 9
Means: Glock 19 (passed down the line for voluntary murder/suicide)

Five:
3/10/25
Location: Cathédrale Notre Dame de Vénissieux, Lyon, France
Toll: 227

Means: cyanide-filled communion wafers (considered murder/suicide)

Six:
3/11/25
Location: Orthodox Church of the Holy Spirit, Vitovka, Belarus
Toll: 52
Means: cyanide-filled communion wafers (considered murder/suicide)

Seven:
3/11/25
Location: Santuário Evangélico de Ipanema, Rio de Janeiro, Brazil
Toll: 18
Means: carbon monoxide (suicide)

Eight:
3/11/25
Location: Gate of the Anointed One (Cult), Wooded Mt., Vancouver, Canada
Toll: 37
Means: voluntary hanging (suicide)

That's enough!

Teagarden only scanned details of the remaining suicide events. One of which was somewhere in the jungle of Colombia where everyone stood at the edge of a fiery pit, held hands, and jumped in. And how did investigators figure that out? Simple. Victims of their own zealotry propped up cell phones in nearby trees and set them to record.

Regardless of technique, the question was, why?

Why were they doing this to themselves?

Other questions were easily answered: the what, when, where, and how. Knowing why is always the most difficult. Cops, reporters, lawyers, and judges all say that most of the time the *why* goes unanswered, and therefore it's best left to poets and novelists.

Teagarden was sickened, particularly with the suicide by fire. All the death displays were horrific. But fire? Of all ways to die, he thought, incineration must be the worst. And the other big question, besides why, was—why didn't some of them bolt? Bunches tried to flee the Jonestown mass suicide back in 1978. In all these cases, only one person was described in media reports as having made an effort to save herself. That was a ten-year-old girl in Falkland, West Virginia who succumbed to snake venom while straining against a heavy chain that locked the church door from the inside.

The only common thread was cult-driven religion. Beyond that—there was nothing, at least, nothing substantial. There was no definite connection to the discovery of an ancient document in Israel. That part was only a theory.

As to whoever requested Teagarden by name, that was another puzzle. Judging from the file he was reading, not even the FBI or CIA knew for certain who asked for his involvement. All they were saying up and down the food chain was that the request had been made through "approved channels."

Let's hope that's not a problem for the man they're referring to as "said U.S. citizen" (SUSC). Imagine that Orwellian phraseology in a newspaper obit: "An SUSC was killed in Jerusalem when...blah-blah-blah...but his presence there was totally authorized through approved channels."

The giant Airbus A380 surfed into waves of turbulence, causing the *ding-dong* to sound and the fasten seatbelt sign to illuminate. It wasn't a problem for Teagarden because he'd never unbuckled. He pushed farther back in the business-class seat and pulled the laptop closer to continue reading.

Page Five
Addendum:

Subject
Intelligence Analysis of Mass Suicides (Various)

Domestic (CIA, NSA)

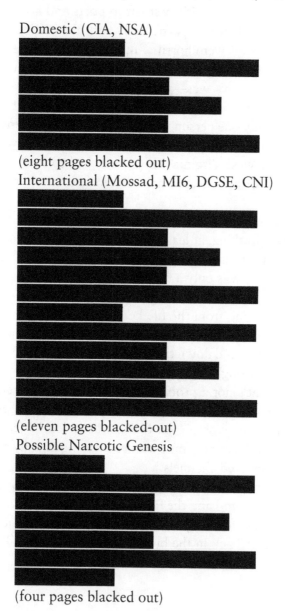

(eight pages blacked out)
International (Mossad, MI6, DGSE, CNI)

(eleven pages blacked-out)
Possible Narcotic Genesis

(four pages blacked out)

Web App Influence:

Third-party manipulation via Internet applications that control all/every aspect of user's action/activity including nutrition, sleep, belief/nonbelief, sex (both orientation/frequency), and unique behavior including criminality/altruism. Groups behind such apps still under varying levels of covert/overt investigation. Known baseline sources include: Virginia Believers of the One; Alliance of White Confeds; Conservative Men of Truth; Left of Center Knights (LOCK); The White Shirts; Freedom from God (Love of Life's Adventure); Face Time with God; Star Bound in Hollywood. Suspected source managers include: FSB, MSS, Mossad, Vatican, United Voice of Jesus, WMM, and New Alliance of al-Qaeda.

Wow.

That last section was the shortest passage and it had not a single blacked-out word, which probably meant the Big Brother workers with black magic markers believed it insignificant where Teagarden was concerned. He'd heard of the new cultural trend that allowed apps to govern many aspects of users' lives. They were called Life Guidance Apps, and PIMs (Personal Improvement Managers). His students mostly laughed at them and called them brain-based GPS, e-Binkies, and Babysitter Software for those who need help with questions such as "do I need to pee?" and "am I feeling hungry?"

So far as he knew, PIM apps consisted mostly of daily astrological advisers, exercise regimens, diet directives, and counseling to assist those afflicted with phobias and extreme anxiety. For the most part, they seemed harmless, and in some cases, as with diet apps, even helpful. But turning your life over to an app managed by something called "Star Bound in Hollywood" or "Conservative Men of Truth" sounded scary. Of the suspected app managers, he looked up three: FSB was Russia's Federal Security Service formally known as the KGB; MSS was China's Ministry of State Security, basically their version of the CIA; and WMM stood for Western Muslims for Muhammad.

He continued reading the official briefing:

Medical Theories: Bio-Terror Experimentation, Viral Schizophrenia, Audio Induced Psychosis, Etc.

(six pages blacked out)

Other: Dogmatic Theology, Paganism, Vatican Influence

(Seven pages blacked out)

Right or wrong, that was it, the entire file. Or at least, it was all the FBI allowed him to see.

They finally get around to something I can use for the mission they're sending me on, but their eyes-only rule prevents me from seeing it. Top Secret. Confidential. Hush-hush. Blacked-out. Classified. Restricted. Redacted. Why tease me with knowing it's there if I'm not allowed to see it?

I know the answer to that one. Because it's just more bureaucratic "tee hee" piety from Drakken. A big F-U for what I did to the FBI six years ago.

"I hope it's not a bad omen," he mumbled.

Teagarden reclined his seat and drifted asleep. When he awoke an hour later and maneuvered up the aisle to the WC, as it was labeled, the little window attached to the lock read "Occupied."

"It beats steerage."

Teagarden rubbed at his eyes and turned to the man in line directly behind him. "Pardon?" he asked.

The man gestured a thumb over his shoulder to the rear cabin. "Steerage," he said. "You know, third class, the huddled masses of wretched refuse."

"Oh, yes."

Teagarden recognized him as the business class passenger across the aisle. He'd been reading a paperback copy of *Starship Troopers* by Robert A. Heinlein—in Hebrew. He knew the title because it had the same familiar cover as the English language version he read as a teenager: a high-tech bug in crosshairs. The man was short but sturdy, noticeably condensed in flesh and muscle. Teagarden didn't turn to see the face because they stood uncomfortably close in line for the toilet where they were jostled by mild turbulence. He searched for a polite way to conclude the exchange.

"It's definitely more comfortable up here," Teagarden said, "but more expensive also."

"And worth every shekel. I was behind you in the New York queue when you upgraded at the gate. Smart move. I once read that there are five stages to enduring coach class: denial, anger, bargaining, depression, and acceptance."

He pressed a palm to Teagarden's shoulder and gave a hearty grip as though they were brothers at the local Elks Lodge. Though he read in Hebrew, his accent wasn't Israeli. It was a strange blend of Eastern European and some other odd dialect Teagarden couldn't place. Still half asleep, Teagarden guessed the man was waiting for him to laugh at the comment about coach class, so he tried to accommodate.

"Heh-hey," he puffed, managing a forced half smile. He caught a hard whiff of booze on the man's breath. "Yeah, you know, leg room is, uh, is always better than—"

"—Than *no* room at all back there in the meat packing district," the man said.

Teagarden nodded as politely as he could manage and was grateful the WC door opened at that moment. After emerging from the restroom a minute later, the man was no longer in line. Neither had he advanced to use the WC on the opposite bulkhead. Instead, he was back at his seat. He'd apparently finished *Starship Troopers*, because he'd opened a wrinkled paperback copy of *Stranger in a Strange Land*, also in Hebrew and also by Heinlein. His tray held a glass with ice and two mini-bottles of Kentucky-style bourbon. The glass and both bottles were empty. Besides making obnoxious comments, he also liked whiskey and classic science fiction. Back in his seat, Teagarden saw that his own reading material no longer existed on his Flexi-Flat laptop. The FBI memo had been automatically deleted, just as the warning promised.

That's like "this tape will self-destruct in five seconds." Except in the old "Mission Impossible" they say, "Good luck, Jim."

Hey, where's my good luck wish?

He decided it was more evidence of Assistant Director Drakken's enmity.

The transfer at Charles de Gaulle was a semi-controlled chicken run from one air crate to another. He intended to follow up on the suggestion in the FBI briefing by researching the Q

Document more thoroughly online, yet the promised airborne web connection wasn't working. Giving up and trying to sleep, his fitful slumbers were haunted by a pair of grim images: Wechter's terrified face before losing his grip on the balcony railing, and the consuming passion of the woman on fire just before Agent Utrillo shot her down.

# CHAPTER THIRTEEN

*Tuesday, March 18, 2025*

"Good morning, Professor Teagarden. This way, sir."

Introductions were unnecessary. Teagarden understood that the man waiting beside the Jetway control panel was Emmanuel Eveillard, his escort for the next forty-eight hours. Less than average height, with a middle-aged belly protruding under his cotton pullover and loose-fitting sports coat, he had a silken smooth obsidian skin tone. A ringer for a high school history teacher, he was ordinary in every respect, except his Haitian-Creole accent. That was unique. It was a baritone voice that held a musical inflection inherent in all Bantu languages.

"My associate will handle your bag," Eveillard said, with a small gesture. The other man who did not speak, was the exact opposite. He embodied all clichés of a macho bodyguard: tall, trim, alert eyes, and a ready bearing as though prepared to take extreme action with a microsecond's notice.

Walking as a group from the Jetway into Ben Gurion Airport, Teagarden realized a fourth man was keeping stride with them. No doubt about him: Israeli military. And his presence wasn't because of Teagarden. The nature of Eveillard's job required him and his backup to be armed while meeting Teagarden on the safety side of security. That meant having a uniformed Israeli military man escort the two Americans.

*Oh brother, this international secret agent thing is complicated.*

At immigration, the fourth man ushered them into a tidy side room. Eveillard and his backup displayed State Department IDs and passports with diplomatic stamps. Two bored men with churlish expressions posed them no challenge. Having no such clout, Teagarden anticipated rigorous questioning.

"What is the purpose of your visit?" asked the first.

"Research."

"Where spe-cif-i-cal-ly?" asked the second, pronouncing every syllable of the adverb in the manner of someone who speaks English one memorized word at a time. He officiously flipped through Teagarden's passport while the other made entries on a laptop. They both periodically looked up with a penetrating, almost accusatory gaze.

"Megiddo," Teagarden answered. "There's an ancient church there."

"Where do you stay?"

"I'm sorry?"

"Your hotel. Where do you stay?"

"Oh, I'm afraid I—"

Eveillard interrupted: "American Embassy," he said. "In our guest quarters." The men ignored him and continued with their questions.

"Are you Jewish?"

"No."

"Do you speak Hebrew?"

"No."

"Any friends or relatives in Israel?"

"No."

"Where in Israel is Megiddo, Professor Teagarden?"

"I'm uncertain. In a desert."

Uh-oh.

It was an obvious misstep that earned disapproving looks. He wasn't intentionally being a wise guy. He honestly did not know Megiddo's precise location. For him, it was the morning of the following day, which had arrived without a night of the previous evening. That's the way it is with long flights. After nearly twenty-four hours on airplanes and in airports, he felt sealed in a fog of jetlag. It was like having the flu without being sick. Teagarden guessed their sudden disapproval would crank the Q&A to a higher level; possibly send them all to another room for prolonged detainment, maybe even a strip search. Instead, one man exhaled a barely concealed sigh of disfavor and returned to making touchscreen computer entries. His companion tossed the American passport to the counter like a playing card.

"Professor Teagarden, more than half of this small nation is desert." He tendered a glance to Eveillard that indicated the Q&A was concluded. Then, still speaking to Teagarden, he added: "Megiddo is north of here, in a valley south of Galilee. There are many stones and building foundations there that date to the empires of Rome, Egypt, Mesopotamia, and before that to people of the Bronze Ages." He spoke the words "Bronze Ages" with a snippy flourish. "Contrary to what you may believe about us, we Israelis are proud of these things. And I think all of that equals considerably more history than your victory at Yorktown."

"Yes," Teagarden said. He picked up his passport. "It certainly does."

"Sir," the customs officer continued, "you are well known here. If you believe I am being intentionally unkind to you that is not my concern. This is my job. Listen to me. We in Israel respect your accomplishments in America. We were apprised of your arrival by way of our good diplomacy with your nation, and we are pleased that you are here. I ask you now, go up there to Megiddo and learn why Christians are making such a big problem for themselves. Then, kindly fix it before *we* get the blame."

Back in the tumult of the airport, Teagarden was glad he didn't get snippy in response. That immigration officer paid him a compliment by suggesting he was the man who could solve an internationally spreading mystery before it wrought more death. They paused at the down escalator leading to the baggage carousels. The Israeli commando gave a trace of a nod at Eveillard, then peeled off like a fighter pilot with such embellishment that Teagarden half expected to see a plume of smoke trailing in his wake. He had no checked luggage, so they continued to the curb where a large Ford SUV with smoked windows awaited.

"Welcome to Israel," said Eveillard once they were inside the vehicle. "Here's the most important rule: turn off your cell phone and keep it off the entire time you're here."

It was already off. He'd hoped to call his wife, or at least text, to let her know he'd safely arrived, but complied with the instruction.

"How long is the drive to Megiddo?" he asked.

"About an hour," Eveillard said. He opened his laptop. "But we're not going there."

They both sat in the roomy back seat, separated by a ten-pack carton of twenty-ounce water bottles. The silent security guard was in the front passenger seat. The driver of the eight-cylinder vehicle was a middle-aged man, possibly Hispanic, with hard-chiseled features and wraparound sunglasses, who also had nothing to say. Not only were they both uninterested in talking, they weren't so much as glancing at him.

"Okay, where *are* we going?" asked Teagarden.

"I received a text while you were in immigration with those two charmers. There's a new incident, happening right now. It's nearby and we need to check it out. We'll go to Megiddo afterward."

"Do I get to know where—"

"Jerusalem. The Church of the Holy Sepulchre."

"I'm no theologian, but isn't that where—"

"Yes, it is. That is the church built upon the site where the Roman Empire crucified Jesus Christ."

# CHAPTER FOURTEEN

Teagarden tapped into the Ford's Wi-Fi signal to quickly read up on their destination with his Flexi-Flat:

> The Church of the Holy Sepulchre is located in the Christian Quarter, one of four quadrants housed within the walls of the Old City of Jerusalem. Here, the most revered house of the apostolic faith is a short stroll from the Western Wall and Dome of the Rock, the holy of holies for the two other Abrahamic creeds. This close proximity has complicated history and acquainted the ancient cobblestones with periodic tides of religion-induced bloodshed.

On this day however, as Teagarden would soon learn, the carnage wasn't a crusade, jihad, intifada, or holy defense of Judea and Samaria. Instead, it was a public sacrifice of unknown purpose found terrifying to those witnessing it.

Twelve men and one woman were gathered at the main church entrance, an ancient courtyard on the southern side. After disrobing to nakedness, the men formed a circle around the woman and began chanting. Each of them held a knife of various shape.

"Parati sumus mori," the twelve men sang a capella. "Parati sumus mori...Parati sumus mori."

Alarmed pilgrims quickly yielded the space, though not all

departed. Some withdrew just enough to feel safe, then turned to become spectators. Within minutes the Israeli Defense Forces arrived, triggering the one woman in the group to chant a dithyrambic order to the men.

"Uno loco, ad mortem."

"Positus ad mortem," the men responded. Like trained military recruits, the naked protestors dropped to a defensive squat and positioned their knives at their own throats.

Switching to English for the gathered crowd, the woman warned the military: "Stay back or we shall commit mass suicide."

The ranking officer was not impressed. "זוז מהר!" he shouted.

His obedient forces moved fast, though not fast enough to prevent a chain reaction. One at a time, the squatting men began dutifully inserting their blades into their necks.

"I mori," said the first man.

"I mori," said the second, a moment after the first.

"I mori, said the third, a moment after the second.

Each thrust his blade deeply into his own neck, then yanked it hard to slice the soft flesh from left ear to larynx, causing each man to fall and twitch like a badly butchered goat. Stunned at the sight of so much blood gushing to the cobblestones at the final station of the Via Delarosa, the ranking officer made another decision. This time, he told his soldiers to stand down.

"תעמוד, תחזור!"

His unit retreated to a defensive line between the suicidal demonstrators and all remaining spectators. Now there were only nine naked men surrounding the woman, because three of them lay dead. Satisfied, they resumed the mantra:

"Parati sumus mori," the woman called out.

"Parati sumus mori," the nine responded in the monophonic tone of a Gregorian chant as they slowly paraded around her, knives at the ready. "Parati sumus mori...Parati sumus mori... Parati sumus mori...Parati sumus mori."

More spectators gradually fell away in singles and doubles. Still, several dozen remained to stare at the ordeal as though it were entertainment.

It was their stubborn presence that further irritated the IDF commander, forcing him to default to a second goal—that of removing the spectators. He barked another order:

"הסר את כל האזרחים."

But neither did that effort go well. As the uniformed men and women turned to forcibly escort all gawkers from the scene, a few resisted. A woman in a wide-brimmed beach hat objected by shouting: "Hands off, hands off, hands off." The naked woman in the courtyard heard and quickly responded.

"Leave them. Let them remain," she shouted. "The public shall remain or more of us will die."

Hearing her, the troops hesitated. They looked to their ranking officer who was in no frame of mind to stand down a second time. Such a thing wasn't in his playbook.

"להזיז אותם, עכשיו!" he said, gesturing for his troops to continue hustling the crowd from the perimeter.

This triggered another round of self-slaughter.

"I mori," said the fourth man to die by inserting his knife and yanking the blade with a grunt.

"I mori," said the fifth, who did the same.

"I mori," said the sixth.

Beaten and wanting to prevent more bloodshed, the IDF officer again ordered his troops to stand down. They retreated, which again halted the sequential suicide. That triggered a prolonged deadlock where remaining onlookers stood in place while nearby streets were blocked by backup IDF units to prevent additional entry.

It was during the stalemate that Sam Teagarden, Emmanuel Eveillard, and their silent bodyguard arrived. They had to leave the big Ford behind and squirrel past the entangled maze of meandering pilgrims, shops, and souvenir vendors. After Eveillard flashed his American ID to Israeli soldiers cradling Uzi machine guns and speaking to the ranking officer at the hastily erected barriers, they were allowed to enter.

By that time, six men were dead, their bodies lying where they fell. The remaining six men held position, knives at their own throats, prepared to kill themselves should there be another move by the military, or any other order found objectionable by their leader—the one woman.

The men, both dead and alive, were a variety of ages and body types. The youngest was about twenty, the oldest perhaps seventy. Those still living had the blazing eyes of zealots on a mission. As for the woman, she was approaching middle age, with long, perfectly straight black hair that draped to her waist. She was the only protestor who wore jewelry, a short silver necklace holding an emblem consisting of three overlapping triangles.

With her leading the chorus, they began chanting, as if in a trance:

"Afferte nobis Vulpes...Afferte nobis Vulpes...Afferte nobis Vulpes..."

"My God," Teagarden whispered to his escort, "it's the most degenerate spectacle imaginable."

"God has nothing to do with this," Eveillard said. "It's similar to the first event in Spain, except that particular bloodletting was done in privacy. These people actually *want* their deaths to be witnessed."

"Why?"

"I wish I knew."

"We must stop this," Teagarden said. His voice quivered with such dread that it dropped two octaves. "And we have to learn why they're doing it."

"Yes," agreed Eveillard. "Yes, we must."

"Afferte nobis Vulpes...Afferte nobis Vulpes...Afferte nobis Vulpes...Afferte nobis Vulpes...Afferte nobis Vulpes..."

"What are they saying?"

"It's Latin," Eveillard said. "I used to be good at it. I speak all languages evolved from Latin, so I should know. Right now, I'm brain dead. The only thing I can recall at the moment is 'Veni, Vidi, Vici.' By the way, did you know that proper Roman

pronunciation of those words was: 'weenie, weedie, weecee'?"
Teagarden gave Eveillard a cockeyed look. "We tend to imagine
Romans as being hard-asses. Truth is, they spoke like candy-asses."
"There're six dead men lying over there, and you're making
jokes about Roman elocution?"
"Sorry," Eveillard said. He looked around and exhaled hard.
"Stress humor. It sometimes helps on this job."
"I get that. You FBI types need thick skins."
"I'm not an FBI type. I'm a U.S. Embassy adjutant type. And
yes, since you're wondering, I will confirm it. That is coded
language for 'CIA'." He gestured to the silent bodyguard. "And
he's a second lieutenant in the Marine Corps type, which means
he's a trained killer type. And those people over there are 'psycho-
types.' And the Israeli soldiers over there are—"
"I get it. And I'm a math professor type." Teagarden had
suspected Eveillard was CIA. Now he knew.
As the standoff went unchallenged, all parties took a breath.
The IDF held position, ready to move fast if ordered. The six
kneeling men were ready to cut their own carotids if ordered. And
the remaining civilian spectators held their places ready to witness
more fanaticism if presented.
After a while, Teagarden whispered, "Why doesn't Israeli
security assault them all at once? There's enough of them for it.
Look, the troopers are just standing like rubberneckers at a high-
way crash."
"Two reasons," Eveillard said. "First, they've already tried it.
As you can see it didn't work because six are dead. And second,
in a word—Waco."
"Wacko?"
"No, the people prepared to kill themselves are wackos. It's
Waco that's holding back the military." Teagarden turned to
look into Eveillard's eyes with curiosity. "You remember," the CIA
man explained. "1993. The FBI stormed a Texas cult compound.
Seventy-six died, including twenty-five children." He bug-eyed as
he nodded at the crowd behind them. "If all the whack-a-doodles

punch their ticket, not only do the police get the blame, who knows how many more in this crowd are waiting to expose their birthday suit and begin act two of a public shit show."

Teagarden said nothing because he knew Eveillard was right. The explanation made sense. He turned to the six remaining men, now in a semi-circle, and the woman standing in the middle, all holding knives, all chanting the same Latin phrase:

"Afferte nobis Vulpes...Afferte nobis Vulpes...Afferte nobis Vulpes..."

And what knives they were. Teagarden recognized carvers, stabbers, and hackers. There was a switchblade, a couple of Bowie knives, a utility box-cutter, several antique daggers, a scalpel, a tile cutter, and a shortened curved scimitar like the one on the flag of Saudi Arabia.

Holy of holies. Who are these people?

It bordered on sick guerrilla theater. A real-life Greek tragedy penned by Euripides or Sophocles that concludes with debauchery, suffering, and everyone dying, including the children of Apollo and Zeus. Teagarden couldn't remember from his undergraduate world literature class at Chapel Hill—did the dithyrambic chant of the chorus always precede a total blood bath?

"Afferte nobis Vulpes...Afferte nobis Vulpes...Afferte nobis Vulpes...Afferte nobis Vulpes..."

The civilians in the crowd were entranced. They knew they were witnessing something that would make headlines. Perhaps they were the same faces of fear and fascination held by those who witnessed Lazarus rising from the dead, or witnessed men die in the Roman Colosseum. Unlike those spectators from an earlier age, each of these held their cell phones aloft, their video apps set to record.

"Afferte nobis Vulpes...Afferte nobis Vulpes...Afferte nobis Vulpes..."

Teagarden wondered if the IDF had mosquito-sized drones in their arsenal like the FBI. A batch of those little bugs would do the job nicely. The drones that attacked him in upstate New York in 2019 could be set to stun. He had no idea if it was possible to set bug-drones to stun.

"Afferte nobis Vulpes...Afferte nobis Vulpes...Afferte nobis Vulpes..."

"Uh-oh," Eveillard said. "Okay, here we go."

Teagarden saw it one beat after Eveillard. It happened on three fronts of coordinated attack, each moving with the efficiency of mechanized gears. First, a noise distraction came from a pair of klaxons stationed on a nearby rooftop that blasted a deafening barrage. Almost immediately after, soldiers poured from church doors directly behind the zealots, a lousy option for a surprise assault, but the best they had under the circumstances. Finally, there was smoke. It wasn't possible to know how it appeared. Thick clouds of opaque gray fog suddenly billowed everywhere, including between spectators and demonstrators.

Amid the pandemonium, Teagarden and his two companions tumbled to the cobblestones. Eveillard fell next to him while the silent American watchdog landed atop them both, shielding them. In the chaos, Teagarden saw Eveillard struggling to free his right arm to use his cell phone.

Really? At time a time like this?

Despite the blaring klaxons and noisy crowd panic, there was no suppressing the unmistakable sounds of grunting death. The chanting of "Afferte nobis Vulpes" ceased, replaced by the same ghostly voices speaking other words:

"I mori."

"I mori."

"I mori."

Each "I mori" was followed by an audible grunt, an exhale of pain, and a gushing of blood to the old stones. Then came the noise of blind struggle waged inside the fog.

"I mori. Ungh."

"I mori. Ungh."

"I mori. Ungh."

After a moment of breathless silence, the voices of masculine commands quickly filled the air. Military orders were shouted in Hebrew. Those directed at the crowd were shouted in Hebrew and English. The American bodyguard stood erect, then reached both arms to assist the men he'd intentionally knocked down. The smoke gradually cleared, and the bodies came into view. Some lay flat-out prostrate, others were curled, their heads tucked between their knees like sleeping dogs. Blood seeped from all wounds. It leeched into rivulets and finally into one common pool that drained down the natural gradient where it turned brown in the sun. Teagarden hoped that the absence of the woman and one of the men meant they'd survived.

"It just came back to me," Eveillard said as he and Teagarden coughed and rubbed delicately at hard-scraped knees and elbows. He cradled his cell phone in one hand, still talking into it. "Yes, confirmed," he said into the phone. "Op Five O'clock is safe. Yes, confirm, we are all witnesses."

"What just came back to you? And who are you talking to?"

"My Latin came back to me while we were kissing the blarney stones." He spoke again into his phone: "Affirmative. Op Five O'clock. We are prepared to assist. Advise." The phone squelched each time he pushed or released the talk the button.

"Is that some kind of secret agent phone?" asked Teagarden.

"Push-to-talk," Eveillard said. "The old analog phones are more secure." He returned the device to his ear. "Understood. Evidence of uploading? Okay. Monitor all usual channels including deep web. Unit One out."

"What was that all about?"

"Nothing." He dipped one shoulder with ambivalence. "Just the downtown office. Sometimes these cult groups live stream to MotherBoard and other social websites until Silicon Valley takes it down under pressure."

"That's sick," Teagarden said.

"You mean, that *too* is sick."

"Yeah, that's what I mean. So, back to the Latin. What were they saying?"

"It was you."

"What was me?"

"Your unhappy American adventure of six years ago. The media labeled you a 'smart fox.' Wasn't that it? You were called America's 'sly fox on the run.' Or something like that, right?"

"Yeah, among other hyped-up nonsense."

"Right," Eveillard continued. "That's what they were chanting. Afferte nobis Vulpes means, 'Send us the Fox.' The suicidal psychos knew you were coming to Israel. The show was in your honor."

"How?"

"It's called a leak. Nothing happens in this country without the IDF and/or the Mossad knowing about it. Either somebody leaked it or..." Eveillard shook his head and looked back at the eleven dead men..."or one of those dead psychos up there is, or rather—*was*—cleared to receive confidential U.S./Israeli communications."

Teagarden couldn't believe his ears. He'd been in Israel less than ninety minutes and already eleven people were dead because of his presence.

# CHAPTER FIFTEEN

*Tuesday, March 18, 2025*

"Time to go, gentlemen."

Righteous and unemotional, they were the first words spoken by the plain-clothed Marine bodyguard. Towering above them, he gestured with both index fingers, indicating that he wanted to see them do an about-face. It was his mission to protect them, and he seemed to be saying he'd endured enough challenge to that duty. "This way to ground-based transportation," he said.

The maze was more congested on their return. Pilgrims and tourists heard the chaos. Upon seeing the panicked crowd rushing from the Old City, local vendors and shop owners wanted to know what happened. Where was the danger? What was its nature? Was it intifada? Hamas? Hezbollah? PLO?

"No," "Non," "لا," and, "לא," came hastily shouted answers from the crowd, speaking English, French, Arabic, and Hebrew. "It was suicide." "At the church." "Mass suicide." "People killing themselves." "Crazy cult people!"

"المسيحيين؟," came several muted responses in Arabic. And from one Arab vendor of religious artifacts, the reaction was more than surprise. "Hah!" he barked with contempt, "حسناً، والسماح لهم الحصول على طعم منه."

Teagarden had no idea what the man said as he waddled back into his small shop, past rotating racks of postcards and tables filled with acrylic models of the Church of the Holy Sepulchre. It

79

didn't matter. Specifics were unnecessary. The souvenir dealer was delighted that—this time—it was Christians feeling the pain. Seeing that made Teagarden remember the passage he read on his Flexi-Flat explaining a "complicated history" that has made the "ancient cobblestones acquainted with periodic tides of religion-based bloodshed."

What a heartbreak, he thought. His own fledgling effort to get religion had taught him that sentiments like tolerance, forgiveness, and kindness were the way to go. Thinking about that shopkeeper made him wonder if he was naïve.

Yeah well, I'm probably as naïve as they come.

They were almost at the big Ford when Teagarden thought he heard his name being called from a distance. Vague at first, it came again, faint and shrill from the rear:

"...Miss-tah...Tea-gah-dunn..."

When he stopped to look and listen more keenly, it did not please the security guard.

"This is not a good idea," the Marine said. "We need to keep moving, sir."

"What is it?" Eveillard asked.

"Not sure. Someone back there is calling my name."

Then it came again:

"...Miss-tah...Tea-gah-dunn..."

"There it is," Teagarden said. He looked down the narrow street where a hubbub was advancing. "Look, a bunch of them are chasing us."

That sent the bodyguard into red alert. He gripped their elbows and tugged them into a shop where a few languid men sat, oblivious to the world as they drank tea and inhaled heavily on water pipes. It was small and there was no back door. There wasn't enough room for them to sit and pretend to be customers. Eveillard reached one hand under his sports coat to grip the stock of his firearm. The Marine did the same inside his suit jacket.

Seconds later, the owner of the tiny voice drew to a frantic halt at the entrance of the tea and tobacco shop. It was the naked woman, who was no longer naked. Having escaped her captors, she was clothed in military sweatpants and a long sleeve IDF shirt with twin horizontal hash marks denoting the rank of a corporal. Around her neck, she wore a pendant consisting of three triangles inside a circle, the universal symbol of a nuclear fallout shelter. Barefoot and wild-eyed, she dropped to her knees at Teagarden's feet, causing both Eveillard and the Marine to tighten down on their gun grips.

"Miss-tah Tea-gah-dunn," she shouted, "please, you must disclose it, proclaim it to the world like you did with the Dear John File in America." Her accent was classic Israeli. She glanced quickly over her shoulder. The pursuing soldiers were only a few steps behind. "Sir, I am IDF no longer. I renounce Israel. I renounce Judaism. I am now a global freedom fighter for FFG. When you obtain the document, we beg you with our lives, make it a gift to the world."

Seeing her military pursuers hurrying to catch up, the lethargic men inhaling sweetened tobacco jumped from their chairs as the soldiers pounced on the woman in a rugby-style pile-on. Between grunts and shrieks, the woman continued shouting to Sam Teagarden.

"Give it to the world. You must. Sir, we die for our cause. Please...help us..."

And it was over.

The final blow was delivered by a woman who'd likely given up her own shirt because above the waist she wore only an olive tank top. She silenced the woman's frantic cries with the heavy butt of her Tavor assault rifle. Once the limp body was carted off, the smoking men righted all overturned tables, took their seats, and resumed exhaling thick clouds of whiteness as though nothing had happened.

Teagarden wanted answers. Who was that woman? What was she talking about? How did she know he was in Israel? But he held his tongue, waiting for a better time. He didn't speak until they were all back inside the large American made SUV.

"Now do we go to Megiddo?" Teagarden asked.

"Yes," said Eveillard in the baritone accent of his native Creole. "Now we go to Megiddo."

# CHAPTER SIXTEEN

They were mostly in silent-recovery mode during the ninety-minute drive from Jerusalem. Eveillard used the time to work via cell phone and laptop, no doubt checking in with offices in both Jerusalem and Langley to relate details of the bloody incident at the Church of the Holy Sepulchre.

Teagarden used his Flexi-Flat to email his wife that he'd safely arrived but didn't mention the horror show he'd just witnessed. Instead he said that all was well and that he'd try to call later. After that, he and the stoic Marine bodyguard in the front seat mostly passed the time watching clumps of green agriculture alternate with stretches of brown desert. The engaged driver with a face that appeared carved from rock held silent as he commanded the vehicle like a fighter pilot. Teagarden guessed he was Mexican-American, about fifty years old. Behind his wraparound military-style sunglasses, he monitored all mirrors as though they were radar screens about to blip-up with bogies.

The dashboard really did have a screen that functioned as radar. Teagarden had heard of a new technology available to police and the military. During the short drive from the airport to the Christian Quarter, he'd thought it was a standard GPS with uniquely fancy colors. Now he realized it was one of those new security toys. The label at the base of the screen read "Immediate Ground Pulse." It obviously had an AI chip running an algorithm that color-coded potential threats. All nearby pedestrians, bicycles, drones, and motorized vehicles were scanned. Once detected, everything that moved or generated heat within a given range was graded. They received shades of green for safe, yellow for unknown, and red for potential danger. During the trip, there was only one intensely red blip caused by a Mercedes limo, which the driver and Marine intently watched until it exited Yitzhak Rabin Highway in the direction of Tel Aviv.

Teagarden awakened from a short nap just as they arrived at Megiddo. He'd slept only about thirty minutes, yet it was enough to shake the worst of his jet lag. The town was little more than a taupe-colored suburban enclave with one principal industry—a bulky maximum-security penitentiary housing enemies of the Jewish state. The ancient Church of Megiddo was outside its concertina-topped walls, yet inside the prison's outer boundary. Once discovered, the archeological site was allotted a secure plot bounded by a lemon field tended by prisoners. A guard perched on the nearest watchtower monitored the Ford's progress through the grove and into the narrow church compound. The dashboard GPS glowed deep red in the direction of the high concrete walls, then began blinking to emphasize extreme danger. In this case, the danger was tightly controlled behind the prison walls.

The road was noticeably void of signage except one posting which called it Megiddo Parish Lane and noted it was "Private." Two safari-style tents came into view, surrounded by excavation pits that varied in dimension. The parish itself hardly dated to the first century. That description was a misnomer. It was a single-story stone building nestled into the side of rocky hills and obviously built in the twentieth century, with renovations and modest bump-outs added sometime during the early twenty-first. The nearby pits however had tapped an ancient infrastructure. Walls and slate flooring were being exposed for the first time in centuries. Some asserted the foundation dated to the late first century when men took pen in hand to write Matthew, Mark, and Luke. Others, mostly scholars of history, disagreed. They claimed that, yes, these were the granite blocks of an early church, even a very early church, but one that dated to the third century of the Common Era. That debate was academic among theologians and archeologists and had nothing to do with Teagarden's status as a bargain-basement "interim ISR" agent on behalf of the American FBI.

Shears in hand, wearing bib overalls, Deacon Zaid Nasri was tending flower beds flanking the main church entrance when the Ford arrived. He departed his colorful blossoms to greet his visitors. Behind him, the only indication that the building was a place of worship was a small illuminated cross in a front window. Likewise, there was little to indicate that he was a man of cloth except a necklace with a mini-wooden crucifix.

"Deacon Nasri?" Eveillard called.

"Yes. I was concerned. Security forces advised me you would arrive earlier."

"We got sidetracked by another incident," Eveillard said. "In Jerusalem. It's all over the news."

"Thankfully, we don't follow much news here. But tell me, did it involve the Lord's subjects shedding their own blood?"

"Unfortunately, yes."

"I am sorry to hear of this. Now the madness has come to the Holy Land." He winced, closed his eyes, and appeared to pray for a moment, then wiped his sweaty neck with a hand towel. Behind a thin beard, Deacon Nasri had a broad, big-boned forehead with unusually prominent features, particularly his lips, nose, and cheek bones. It seemed more the face of a construction worker than a sedentary man of God. "Let me give you a tour of our excavation work. Then perhaps we will go inside where I have fresh chilled lemonade in the cooler. You have arrived during the height of the afternoon heat."

As in Jerusalem, the mute driver stayed with the Ford, though he did exit the car to survey the perimeter, a patrol that included a long and studious gaze of the nearby prison walls. The SUV was obviously his mission; therefore, it was his home base. Also, as in Jerusalem, the Marine accompanied Eveillard and Teagarden as they walked to the rear of the little church.

"These smaller pits are just exploratory sites." Nasri waved dismissively at the numerous square and rectangular holes in the ground. "So far we've found wells out here and a couple of latrines. Broken pottery is mostly what comes up. We hope to eventually excavate the entire hill. You know, to people of the faith, this hill is, well, let me tell you, English is not my best language, perhaps the closest word is—'important.' This hill called Mount Megiddo is *important* to all Christendom."

A sturdy man, the deacon walked with the determined gait of a leader on a mission. Hastening behind him, Eveillard and Teagarden glanced into the pits, each dug to precision with perfectly vertical walls. Some were shallow, some deep. At their base, each had string carefully suspended in crisscross patterns to mark every square foot of soil.

"Where are all the workers with little spoons?" Eveillard asked.

"They break in the middle of each workday. For the heat. They are students from America and Europe. Even with these heat reflective tents, they're not so disposed to enduring the sun of the Holy Land. Digging begins shortly after sunrise. They break to return to air-conditioned barracks in town and come back in the afternoon to work until nearly sundown."

Teagarden considered interrupting and asking Eveillard to explain why they were in this place. What was the point? He was spending spring break freelancing for the FBI, separated from his wife, and had just endured the horror of watching a suicidal cult jam blades into their own necks. Before he could say something, Deacon Nasri did the job for him.

"So," he said, "as I understand from the security forces, the purpose of your visit is the discovery made by Dr. Pablo Zurbarán a few weeks back." He crossed himself at his own mention of Zurbarán and added, "God bless his soul during his eternal rest."

Teagarden looked to Eveillard for an explanation but received nothing in response.

"The site of the professor's work is under the second of the two large tents. First, let me ask, do either of you have issues with claustrophobia? No?" He looked carefully as each man shook his head. "Very well, then. Let us go there, and I will show you the place of Dr. Zurbarán's remarkable discovery."

The deacon took the lead and they walked behind him in single file, zigzagging around the exposed open pits to the larger of the two safari tents. Under it was a rectangular hole that ranged from twelve to twenty-five-feet deep. At the surface, the edges were surrounded by worktables and shelving units filled with pottery shards and artifacts encrusted by hardened mud. Inside the pit was a multilevel series of ramps, stone-arched doorways, excavated rooms with slate flooring, and short flights of steps leading from one elevated platform to another. It reminded Teagarden of the M.C. Escher poster on the wall of his dorm room at UNC-Chapel Hill depicting optical illusion staircases that led nowhere except back to the beginning.

"Do you see that tunnel entrance at the far end of the pit?" the deacon asked. Eveillard and Teagarden nodded. The Marine didn't like it but said nothing. "That is where we shall go. It is also where we shall emerge after our excursion. That opening is, for now, the only entrance and exit. As you see, the ladder is here. I shall descend first. Please follow me carefully to...umph, umph, and umph." He made a series of hand gestures to indicate moving up, down, and around the M.C. Escher chasm. Again, Eveillard and Teagarden nodded agreement. Deacon Nasri tucked the chain holding his small crucifix below the neckline of his bib overalls. "Right," he said, "here we go."

The Marine stepped forward. "Sir, are you certain there is no one down there?"

"Yes, my son. I can assure that the site is unoccupied."

"Are there forward exits or alternate entrances?"

"As I already explained, no. All tunnel chambers are complete dead-ends."

Suspicious, the Marine gazed into the pit. He stepped back to survey the rear of the small church building. From that position, he could see the Ford parked at the front of the parish building where the driver stood still looking at the prison walls that loomed beyond the lemon orchard.

"What say you, Lieutenant Cole?" Eveillard asked, respectful of the Marine's concern.

"Sir, I believe it's best if we summon Master Sergeant Sanchez from the car. He can stand guard here while I descend to accompany you. That prevents a visual separation. Sir, a visual separation is a violation of my orders."

Not only was the silent Marine now speaking, but Teagarden learned his name, as well as that of the driver.

Eveillard took command. "I am comfortable with Master Sergeant Sanchez watching the church front and the approach from the highway, while you remain here Lieutenant Cole. There's no boogeyman down there." He looked at Deacon Nasri. "If there were, the deacon would have spotted him long ago and exorcized the devil." The deacon gave a semi-agreeable nod. "And besides, I may be a short, Brooklyn-raised, Port-au-Prince born, Haitian-American, but just as the Marine Corps taught you a few tricks, so did the Company do the same for me." He patted his left armpit.

Teagarden absorbed the new data. His CIA escort was a New Yorker of Creole heritage and capable of self-effacing humor, a personality attribute that psychologists claim denotes intelligence.

Lieutenant Cole acceded to the man who outranked him. "Very well, sir." The bodyguard didn't like it. But in the end, he turned back to Deacon Nasri with a go-ahead nod.

"Right, then," the deacon said. He picked three sturdy flashlights from a worktable, keeping one for himself and handing one to each of his visitors about to become spelunkers. "It's routine for the Americans to sing during their descent into this pit. Their lyrics go something like, 'heigh-ho, heigh-ho, it's off to work we go.' It quite amuses them when they do this."

"You shall not hear me doing that," said Eveillard.

"Nor I," said Teagarden.

"Good," Deacon Nasri said. "And by the way, there is no

danger of a cave-in so long as you stay with me. Just the same, it is best if we speak only in quiet voices. The engineers warn that sound waves can pose danger."

The Marine watched from the edge of the pit as the three men clamored down the long ladder propped at an angle. The deacon went first, stepping upon each of the twenty-five rungs with careful familiarity. Eveillard followed with less confidence. Then Teagarden descended, keeping the pain of the snap and crackle inside his knees to himself. At the bottom, they maneuvered through the carved-out spaces, step units, ramps, and platforms of the open pit.

At the stone-arched tunnel entrance, they stooped and entered in the same order, disappearing from Lieutenant Cole's sight.

# CHAPTER SEVENTEEN

The heat quickly fell away as three shafts of handheld light waved helter-skelter in the darkness. It wasn't a tunnel arbitrarily bored into an old hillside for scientific research. Rather, it was an excavation of a previously constructed underground corridor. The walls were made of ancient stone, reinforced with two-by-six planks where excavators found it necessary. The ceiling had the same vaulted design as the entrance, with each perfectly cut stone held in place by gravity in a manner typical of Roman architecture. Except for maneuvering around recently installed support columns, the original design was still doing its job, still holding back twenty-five feet of earth.

It was, however, uncomfortably narrow. The tunnel width was too cramped for Teagarden to extend his elbows without scraping them. There was no need to stoop-walk like hominids, yet Teagarden, being the tallest, needed to keep his head tucked to avoid bumping support rafters. As the shortest, Eveillard was able to stand fully upright, making it probable that he was about the same height as the people who constructed the passage twenty centuries earlier.

Low-wattage blue lightbulbs hung every fifty feet from a wire running along the top of the sloping ceiling. Deacon Nasri explained that blue light was less harmful to the delicate stonework. Teagarden thought them useless until his eyes adjusted.

"Ignore those side channels," Nasri said after they'd trudged along for a couple of minutes in single file. "They haven't been

reinforced, and the engineers warn they're unsafe for passage."
Teagarden saw that he was referring to two separate tunnels, one
to the right and one to the left. "Also, the electric line is not strung
through them, so there is no illumination."

The entrances to both side tunnels were blocked by small red-
and-white-striped sandwich boards that posted the word "danger"
in five languages:

DANGER
ACHTUNG
DANGEREUX
סַכָּנָה
خطر

"What was the original purpose?" Eveillard asked.

"Unknown. The early Christians were Jews who had some
well-documented problems with Roman authorities. We suspect
this may have been an escape chamber."

Eveillard seemed impressed. "Will it lead to an opening?"

"Uncertain. As I said, we've not fully excavated. It is slow going.
There was a cave-in during the early going. No injuries, fortunately. Still, we must take great care."

"Any idea how far it goes?"

"Not yet," Nasri said, "but we'll see soon, once it's fully
excavated."

"There is no forward exit?"

Their advance stopped dead. The lead flashlight clicked off.

"Sir," the deacon said, "so many identical questions." His
voice strained to maintain a courteous tone. "Do you believe I
lied to your Lieutenant Cole? Do you suspect that I have brought
you here for reasons other than your request for assistance?"

Silence followed. Eveillard's flashlight also clicked off.
Teagarden kept his on though he held the shaft pointed down
and away. They stood halfway between the two nearest low-
wattage blue bulbs. He too wondered why Eveillard repeated the

same basic question. He doubted it was a mistake, not with his calculating CIA-trained mind. The deacon broke the silence. Instead of ending the awkward moment, he upped the ante.

"Mr. Eveillard, I am assisting you in response to a formal request posed by the government of Israel. Do you understand that?"

"Yes," said Eveillard.

"The Vatican closely follows everything pertaining to these underground stones. Do you know that?"

"Yes," said Eveillard.

"And Vatican officials have signaled agreement for cooperation. Do you also understand that?"

"I do," said Eveillard.

Teagarden heard in the exchange an answer to his speculation about Eveillard's repetitive questions. He was probing, being intentionally irksome to learn what reaction it wrought or what information it gleaned.

"Sir," the deacon continued, "please do not needle me. I do the work of God both on and under the soil of this ancient and sacred hillside."

"Yes, of course," Eveillard said again. "I apologize, Deacon. Perhaps I have a touch of claustrophobia that I was not aware of. Tell me, is it much farther to our goal?"

"We are getting close," the deacon said.

The uncomfortable exchange ended, the two flashlights clicked on again and they resumed their slow parade. Two minutes later, Deacon Nasri stopped and clicked off his light once more.

"Have either of you ever toured the catacombs of our great Christian cities of Rome and Paris?"

"No," said Eveillard. "When in Rome I never do as Roman tourists do."

"Never have," said Teagarden.

"It is a moving experience. The bones are stored along the walls in a visually artful display. In the not-so-distant past, Paris needed real estate. As it expanded, they dug up the cemeteries. Ah, but what to do with all the bones? Well, they found a convenient answer. They shifted them from graves to an old underground mine. Gentlemen cast your lamps upon both walls as we walk the next few steps."

A short stretch on, the narrow channel was lined with human bones stacked floor to ceiling: skulls; humeri, radiuses, and ulna bones from the human arm; femur, tibia, and fibula bones from the human leg. They numbered in the thousands, which meant they comprised the bodies of hundreds of people. The design varied. In some sections, they were arranged in tic-tac-toe hashmarks. In others, it was concentric diamonds, herring bone, and zig-zag optical illusions. In one design, Teagarden recognized geometric theories made with judiciously placed skulls: Euclidian spheres, Pythagorean triangles, and the circles of Archimedes.

"Who are they?" asked Teagarden. He corrected himself, "I mean, who *were* they?"

"Also, not clear," said the deacon. "We believe them to be the earliest worshippers of the faith. Men who risked their lives to improve the world with the power of prayer made in the name of the Son of God. For all we know, the bones of St. Paul himself lay here before us."

He muttered a short prayer to himself in a language that sounded like Greek. Eveillard crossed himself. For his part, being a newcomer to regular attendance at his wife's protestant church, Teagarden admired the artful arrangement that seemed like early pop art with geometric imagery embedded within the larger composition.

For two minutes their three light shafts crisscrossed the walls of bones like beacons searching the night sky. The shadow effect was eerie, particularly on the eye sockets of skulls that seemed to stare back at the intruders as if protesting the trespass of their eternal repose. In defiance of Eveillard's earlier instruction, Teagarden turned on his cell phone. There was no signal, but the camera worked fine.

"Gentleman, would you please train your lights upon the geometric designs in this section, so I may photograph them?"

They complied. While aiming and clicking, he felt a chill

coming on. When it morphed into a full shiver that ran through his body, he wondered if it was the tunnel temperature, or something else. Seeing the bones made him understand that, for the Vatican, this site was more than mere archeology. It was a voice from two thousand years ago. He guessed the Papacy was hopeful about making a great discovery to undergird the faith of resurrection. It did not occur to him that the Pontifex Maximus might also *fear* what was found here.

"Would you gentlemen be willing to take a selfie with me?" Teagarden asked.

"Very well," said Deacon Nasri. "I am told the flash should not be used, though I will make an exception for you."

"I'll pass on being included in the photo," said Eveillard. "But I'll snap the shot if you like."

After Eveillard took the final photo, he returned the phone to Teagarden who powered it off just as the man of cloth issued a dramatic curse and jumped in panic.

"Oh, damn it all!" the deacon shouted in English. His light shaft trained on a narrow gutter where it caught a large black rat, pattering deeper into the tunnel. Judging by its direction, it must have passed directly under them all. "That devil tread upon both my feet," he exhaled with dread.

Eveillard and Teagarden stepped back and cautiously aimed their lights to the drainage trench cut into one side of the stone floor. Like floodlights in the prison yard, they scanned both directions, searching out a feared tsunami of plague-carrying vermin.

"Sorry, gentlemen," Deacon Nasri said when recovered and there was no tsunami. "There is little that frightens me more than those beasts. No matter how hard we try, we cannot seem to rid ourselves of them. We have not yet found their home nest."

"Sir!" came a distant voice. "Mr. Eveillard, speak to me, sir!"

It was the voice of Lieutenant Cole calling from the tunnel entrance. They couldn't see him because the corridor curved slightly, yet his voice rang with booming clarity through the chamber.

"Stand easy, Lieutenant," Eveillard responded. "We're fine."
The Marine was not satisfied. "I heard a cry of alarm."

"Yes, Lieutenant. Caused by the passage of an uninvited guest.
A rat! Nasty creatures, those rats. No harm done."

"And Operation Five O'clock is secure?"

"Yes," shouted Teagarden. "I am fine. Thank you for asking."

That satisfied him. There was no further response. Teagarden
wondered if the bodyguard walked back through the M.C. Escher
pit to the surface edge of the pit or remained at the tunnel entrance.
If he was near the portal, it violated Eveillard's instruction to
keep a visual on the church grounds and the Ford at the front of
the church.

Deacon Nasri directed his light at a recess in the tunnel a few
steps past the bones. "Beyond this point, the excavation is not
adequately protected against cave-in. That's fine. We needn't
continue. The reason you are here, and unfortunately the probable
reason some in the apostolic flock are finding the need for self-
slaughter, was found inside that niche."

It was a tiny room on the right side of the tunnel directly beside
one of the blue light bulbs. Deacon Nasri focused his light shaft
over the threshold where lettering was carved into the gray stones
of a much smaller archway. Eveillard and Teagarden also raised
their flashlights to illuminate the words:

προειδοποίηση
αν και αν

"It's the only engraving we've found," he continued. "We
believe it dates to the mid-first century." Their three lights
scanned the chiseled words like laser beams.

"It's neither Latin nor Aramaic," said Eveillard.

"True enough," the deacon said. "Professor Teagarden,
would you care to try?"

"Thanks. I'm no linguist."

"I see neither of you speaks Greek," said the deacon.

"Greek!" Eveillard echoed. "Well, it does make sense. The original Gospels were written in Greek. What does it mean?"

"The top line means 'warning,' or, 'danger,' or perhaps, 'beware of.' The second translates quite neatly as, 'if and if.'"

The trio went quiet while staring at the engraved words in the semi-darkness. Eveillard exhaled a slight whistle of astonishment. Teagarden mouthed the word "whoa." Deacon Nasri remained silent to let his guests absorb the curious message posted nearly two thousand years in the past. After a long pause, Eveillard spoke.

"I get 'beware of.' It's a warning, like King Tut's tomb had a warning to violators. And the epitaph on Shakespeare's tomb is still doing the job because no one has opened his grave. Something about 'cursed be he that moves my bones.' But what does 'if and if' mean?"

"Unknown," said Deacon Nasri. "We're working on it. We have a Biblical student here who theorizes one explanation. He believes it refers to a passage from Luke that reads, 'If your brother sins, rebuke; and if he repents, forgive.'"

"Works for me," said Eveillard.

"And how does that student explain the warning?" Teagarden asked.

"Exactly," replied the deacon. "He cannot explain it. Which is why I'm not convinced it's from scripture. And I am equally unconvinced that 'beware of' is a warning about the discovery of ancient texts found in this tunnel."

Eveillard beat Teagarden to it. "If the word for warning does not literally mean warning in this usage, then what could it possibly mean?"

"It may be a reference to something we do not yet understand," the deacon replied. "We shall see. If not in my lifetime, we'll come to understand in the next lifetime, or the next. After all, like these stones, time is something that we humans have plenty of."

A moment later, the already cramped tunnel became more confined.

# CHAPTER EIGHTEEN

"This way, gentlemen."

The deacon guided them into the rounded alcove not much larger than an old-fashioned phone booth. Once inside, the three of them stood shoulder to shoulder against walls of smaller stones, some of which were dislodged below eye level, creating a shallow secondary recess.

"Thanks to the work of Professor Zurbarán of the University of Santiago de Compostela and use of ground-penetrating radar, we learned of this hideaway cavity. Very interesting and useful equipment for this sort of work."

"Do you believe what Dr. Zurbarán found here relates to the suicides?" Eveillard asked.

"Quite possibly."

"Do you also believe it relates to the reason Zurbarán was murdered in Spain?"

"I fear it is so."

"You knew him well?"

"Very well. He was a man of faith and a scientist."

"I'm sorry," said Eveillard.

"Is that hole in the wall where the document was discovered?" asked Teagarden, changing the subject.

"Yes." The deacon focused his light onto the carved-out shelf. "We found an urn of antiquated pottery there. A type of ancient amphora. The scroll was inside."

Eveillard pressed his host: "Where is it now?"

"The Vatican Antiquities Lab, along with the urn. Unfortunately, the pottery cracked about a thousand years ago, which caused the contents to decay. Like the Dead Sea Scrolls and the Nag Hammadi codices."

"Has the Vatican done carbon testing on the parchment?"

"If it hasn't already, I'm certain it will."

"How much was legible?"

"Seventeen scraps. A few were several pages. Some were quite short. Sadly, everything else was dust."

"Was the language Greek?"

Teagarden remained silent during the exchange but noted that Eveillard's tone grew more dogged with each question. The deacon gestured that he wished to step back into the tunnel where it was less claustrophobic. This time, Teagarden expected the deacon to show irritation, yet when he resumed speaking, he sounded more conciliatory than ever.

"Gentlemen, my presence at Megiddo is a delicate matter. I am here at the direction of one government—the Vatican—and the tolerance of another government—Israel. Several days ago, another group of Americans visited. They were, as you say in America, 'feds.' After a brief tour of the grounds, I met with them in the church."

"Why didn't they receive a tunnel tour?" asked Eveillard.

"The same reason they did not view photos of the documents: Vatican prohibition."

That explained Klassen's sunburn and directive to drink plenty of water. Teagarden wondered why an FBI agent was sent to investigate an international crisis. The answer came a moment later.

"Does the Vatican not respect that those men were investigating mass suicide on American soil? Investigating mass suicide in other nations? And that their findings might assist in resolving the wider global crisis?"

"Mr. Eveillard, as I said earlier, please do not needle me. This has nothing to do with distrust of America." He regarded

Teagarden while continuing to speak to Eveillard. "You see, priorities changed when it was learned that Professor Sam Teagarden would participate in America's second investigation of this horrible matter. Doors opened. My instructions from the Vatican are to be helpful to a point. In Italian, the phrase is 'Custodisci il nostro mistero.' It means 'guard our secrets.' The office of His Holiness is advising that my patronage must stop shy of complete release. Israel, however, has made it clear that *all* allowances should be made in the effort to end this madness. I interpret the Jewish state's instruction to mean 'full cooperation.'"

"And which government do you choose to obey?" Eveillard asked.

"I choose the third."

Teagarden understood immediately. It took the American-trained spy a moment longer.

"Oh," said Eveillard. "You mean God."

"I do indeed. Suicide is a violation of the will of God. The faith is not tolerant of this abomination. It must be stopped. If I may contribute to stopping it, then I must do so. In any manner at my disposal. I have no choice on that."

"You have photocopies of the documents?"

"On my desktop PC in the church. Again, thanks to Professor Zurbarán. And I also have some ice-cold lemonade there. So that shall be our next stop."

"What about—"

"The Vatican?"

"Yes, Deacon. I too am Catholic," said Eveillard. "I wouldn't want to be on the receiving end of the Holy See's displeasure. When he learns that you have violated his explicit instructions—"

"Thank you for those considerate words," the deacon interrupted. "As a man who represents Washington, you must be familiar with something called bureaucracy." Without looking at him, Teagarden could practically feel Eveillard nodding in agreement. "Tell me, are you here on direct orders from the American president, or even from the director of the CIA?"

"No, Deacon."

"Right," he said. "We all live within our own boundaries of authority." He gestured toward the tunnel entrance.

"We certainly do," agreed Eveillard.

For Teagarden, it was an uncomfortable exchange. He spoke little while they stood in the darkened, chilly space, using flashlights to peer into a secret, well-hidden hole that once held something, and which now held nothing. He wondered why they didn't merely hear about the tunnel while looking at the photographed copies, instead of what they were doing, which was hearing about the documents while looking at the tunnel.

But the exchange between Eveillard and Nasri sparked a larger question. Why him? Why was he present? Why didn't he just stay home in New York with an FBI bodyguard, instead of traveling all the way to Israel to meet up with a CIA agent and Marine bodyguard? He was incapable of offering much help. He was no linguist, no historian of the early Judeo-Christian narrative, and he was certainly no expert in antiquities.

The answer to the mystery dropped with a thud into his cerebellum as they walked back to the tunnel entrance.

Question: why him?

Answer: bait.

That's it. It has to be.

It was obvious. He was the worm on the end of the hook, the "Going Out of Business" sale sign in the store window. In fact, Nasri just said it. When they learned of his participation, "doors opened."

It made sense. He was the world-famous man who made unkind truths from America's past become public knowledge. Both Republicans and Democrats urged him to run for office. And those who didn't love him, and even those who *really* hated him, still had to live inside the new reality he helped force into existence.

This is as ugly as ugly can get.

In short, with his name on the marquee, the CIA could grease diplomatic angles in Washington, Israel, Rome, the Vatican, and anywhere else. They had only to assign an agent to accompany him to ask all the questions, as Eveillard was doing to the point of annoying their host. That explained why the briefing provided to him on the plane was so deeply redacted. He was a mere PR patsy. They didn't want him to know details, because they didn't want his input, and didn't expect him to provide any.

Hi, remember me? My name is Sam Teagarden. I'm a famous whistler-blower who changed American history, so you know you can trust me.

There was still one compelling reason for him to be tolerant of the whole ruse. The CIA really *was* trying to learn why people were killing themselves, so the killing could be stopped. The government of Israel was doing the same. That meant they were at least trying to do the right thing.

Okay, so maybe using me as window dressing is acceptable.

"I repeat my question," the CIA agent said when they were halfway back to the tunnel entrance. "In what language was the document written?"

"Greek," Nasri said, "like the overhead inscription. There is, as you say in America, 'a catch.' Some of the fragments are encoded."

"Yes, I have heard reports of that. But tell me," Eveillard pressed, "is the document what they say it is?"

"Sir, I *do* intend to share the photographs with you. God wishes it. Israel wishes it. However, I cannot and will not relate in any *official* capacity exactly what that document is. No one here can do that. The true identity of the relic can only be determined by the Vatican Antiquities Lab."

Eveillard was not dissuaded. "Yes, I get that. What do you *think* the document is—*unofficially?*"

"Well, let me pass on what my students call it. They are from America, Britain, and Germany and are working on advanced degrees in archeology, anthropology, and biblical studies."

"Okay."

"They are young, so naturally they believe they know what was found in the wall." He sighed. "I, however, have learned that youthful confidence should be considered with aged prudence."

"Understood. So what do they say?"

"They say it is the Q Document."

# CHAPTER NINETEEN

There it was again.

Nasri's statement was the third citing. The first was by FBI Agent Klassen from his hospital bed as he passed into drug-induced darkness. The second was a brief mention in the laughably redacted FBI briefing.

Whatever the Q Doc was, it was obviously linked to the contagion compelling cult leaders to host self-death parties. Even stranger, the same uncovered parchment also encouraged atheists to public displays of death by their own hand.

That's weird.

Believing there was a connection didn't explain why. Why were so many willing to stick blades into their own necks? And not one of them bothered to leave a note.

Back at the tunnel entrance, Teagarden and Eveillard squinted and tilted their heads against the radiant glare of the afternoon sun.

"Oh, wow," and "Whoa-wee that's bright," complained Eveillard and Teagarden as they shielded their eyes.

Being familiar with the discomfort, Deacon Nasri looked down and away from the open tent flaps, patiently allowing time for his engorged pupils to adjust. "This is one situation where you should not look at the Lord's light," he said.

"Left my shades in car," Eveillard said.

"Left mine in New York City," said Teagarden.

"You are better without them," the deacon warned. "Sunglasses only trick the eyes into believing they are safe in sun."

They were halfway across the myriad earthen platforms and excavated step units in the M.C. Escher pit when it became apparent that something was amiss. Their eyes were sufficiently adjusted to see that Lieutenant Cole was not stationed at the upstairs edge of the pit. Eveillard gestured for the single-file jaunt to halt, then put one index finger to his lips.

Really? The CIA agent put a finger to his lips to indicate silence. Wow. Just wondering here, did they teach that in spy school?

When there was no answer, Eveillard handed his flashlight to the deacon and reached under the loose sports coat just as he'd done at the tea and tobacco shop in the Christian Quarter in Jerusalem. This time he withdrew his Glock. He glanced around the pit. Nothing. He glanced back at the tunnel entrance. Nothing. He gestured for Teagarden and Nasri to remain where they were while he went ahead.

They watched him complete the path to the base of the ladder, which he slowly ascended. At the top rung, he eased forward, weapon at the ready. Apparently seeing nothing worrisome, he clambered over the edge and disappeared.

Nasri and Teagarden listened, waiting for an "all clear." When it didn't come, Teagarden gave voice to the question they were both wondering.

"What do you think could possibly be happening up there?"

The deacon shook his head. He slipped the two flashlights in a bulky hip pocket of his overalls. "I do not understand. This is peculiar."

"If there were trouble, wouldn't there be—"

"Noise? Voices? Sounds of struggle? Gunshots?"

"Right, there's none of that. I tend not to believe in time warps, so they haven't been teleported."

"Are you armed?" Nasri asked.

"No," Teagarden said. "I wish you were."

"I usually am. Unfortunately, my AK-47 is in the office."

Teagarden broke from his squinting focus on the surface to look askance at his companion. Nasri addressed the question etched in Teagarden's face.

"Professor Teagarden, this is Israel. I am a Lebanese priest of a church not six hundred meters from a maximum-security prison housing two thousand Muslims willing to commit terror against the Jewish state. That means the men behind those walls would happily kill me and my students and destroy this historic parish without a moment's hesitation." He put the wooden crucifix to his lips and kissed it. "I am sorry to say that my weapon is as necessary as my cross."

"Right," Teagarden said. He thought of apologizing but changed his mind.

"The cult that tried to kill you last week in New York City is also a terror group," Nasri continued. "Even when believers spill their own blood. In the eyes of God, that too is a form of terrorism."

"Unfortunately, their motive is unknown."

"Not really." Again, Teagarden was surprised. And again, Nasri answered the question without being asked. "They are frightened, Professor Teagarden, both people of the faith and people without faith—frightened."

"Frightened of what?"

"Two things. First—you, entirely because of your reputation."

That reaffirmed what he'd already concluded: that he was a front man for the CIA to conduct the mission.

"And the second cause of their fear?"

The deacon exhaled and looked away. "The unknown," he said as though it should be obvious. "That document may bear challenge to the faith for some, or affirmation of the faith for others. It likely also has a powerful influence for those without God in their lives."

"But—"

"Shh," said the deacon. "Too much talk. It is close to the time for my students to begin their second shift. I must check on their safety and retrieve my AK-47."

He kissed the wooden crucifix again, tucked it away, then

moved to the base of the ladder and ascended. Near the top, he eased higher to peer beyond the edge. Seeing nothing out of the ordinary, he did exactly as Eveillard. He scaled the final rung, stepped over the edge of the pit, and disappeared.

Teagarden looked for signs of movement, including any shading of the sun's glare. There was none.

It was like one of those horror movies where dim teenagers enter a haunted house one at a time and never come out again.

He listened intently for sound. Any sound. Distant conversation. Muffled noise of struggle. Blowing wind. A panting dog. Still nothing. He powered up his cell phone. Nothing there either, except for the last photo Eveillard snapped of him and the deacon. There was still no cell signal, and outside of the Ford, he had no Wi-Fi capacity. Still, on the worrisome assumption that it could be traced by the unknown powers that be, he prompted the phone to power off.

The sun's harsh dazzle held steadfast at the top of the ladder.

I'm not just going to sit here and wait for it to come to me, whatever "it" is.

Teagarden opted for Newton's Third Law of Motion: for every action, there is an equal, but opposite, *reaction*. He turned to navigate the dirt path back toward the tunnel. Perhaps it would be safer for the time being. If nothing else, they (whoever *they* were) would have to go to the inconvenience of searching for him instead of him simply walking into their hands. Inside the tunnel, he pulled the flashlight from his hip pocket and clicked it on.

# CHAPTER TWENTY

With elbows tucked in, and despite his arthritic knees, he managed a fast gait. At the intersection where the two additional tunnels branched off, he continued straight to the wall of bones, then paused to listen. The last time he stood in that spot, Lieutenant Cole's voice piped in like a stereo speaker, so he knew he'd easily hear anyone following.

Nothing.

A nearby low-watt blue bulb aided his limited vision. The alcove beyond the If and If Arch was a few strides farther on. He shined the flashlight beam across the hundreds of skulls and thousands of bones on both sides. The thought nagged at him again, something about the display tugged at his mathematical instincts. Somehow it seemed a tribute to Archimedes, Euclid, and Pythagoras, the Greek geniuses who paved the way for Copernicus, Galileo, Newton, Tesla, Hubble, and Einstein. The deacon spoke of duty to God, but for Teagarden, God lived in the many fields of study that forced the universe to keep some secrets and yield others.

He listened again for any sounds coming from the tunnel entrance. Still only silence. He moved on to the arch with the overhead engraving:

προειδοποίηση
αν και αν

If his freshman students saw it they'd take to MotherBoard to

107

make snarky comments and attach emojis, while his older grad students would ponder its link to the mysterious Q Doc. If that document did pose a threat to the faith, why had ancient men of faith hidden it under the first church where future generations could find it? Why not simply destroy it?

The wording was vaguely familiar. Looking at it now made him think of an ordinary logical syllogism, an example of deductive reasoning so masterfully used by Sherlock Holmes:

if a = b...and b = c...then a = c.

In this case it would be:

if Q = Panic...and Panic = Suicide...then
Q = Suicide.

It made no sense. No matter what Nasri just said, he saw no reason to explain why an ancient script would initiate an international cult of hari-kari. Neither would it inspire suicide if the document really were the truthful word of God.

Or would it?

He stood under the arch. Still, there was no sound in the echo chamber. He turned off his light to look for flaring illumination in the direction of the tunnel entrance. There wasn't any. He turned the light back on and scanned the arch engraving, left to right over the alcove threshold:

προειδοποίηση
αν και αν

He had an idea. Deacon Nasri said cultists were jumping into fire and swallowing ricin and vodka chasers because they were "frightened." Atheists, too. They were all threatened by the unknown. That was the word he used: "threatened." He didn't mean physically threatened. He meant *spiritually* threatened. The "aha" moment was such a logical bullseye that Teagarden wondered why he hadn't thought of it earlier.

He modified the syllogism:

if Q = Doubt...and Doubt = Spiritual Death
...then Q = Actual Death.

For some of intense faith, sudden bankruptcy of that faith would spark such despair that jamming a ten-inch blade into their own neck may seem the only viable alternative. It was still only a theory. Meantime, there were other important things to think about.

Teagarden took a breath, shined the light ahead, and walked beyond the alcove. Here, nothing was reinforced by timber planking, confirming Deacon Nasri's warning that it wasn't safe. After a few strides, the tunnel curved, sharply at first, then more gently until it straightened for a spell where the grade descended, then twice ascended. The drainage gutter wasn't constant. Because of erosion and other shifting forces of gravity, it was absent for long stretches.

When the narrow culvert reappeared at his feet, he saw the occasional rat using it like a toboggan track to scoot one way or another, causing Teagarden to stay clear. There were periodic drippy leaks. Sometimes it was a semi-thick liquid, sometimes a dry sprinkling of sandy dirt.

"Urmph-h-h."

He stopped short, almost bumping the dark impasse. That was it; he'd reached a dirt wall dead-end. At its base was another small red-and-white-striped sandwich board warning of danger in five languages. While he stood there, two rats pattered along the narrow gutter. Seeing him, they squealed and dove into a hole the size of a bottlecap.

How?

Okay, they weren't huge rats like those in New York that think they own the subway system. Yet neither were they small.

Their rotund bodies seemed way too large to fit into the aperture. Yet they were the proverbial pudgy square pegs adroitly squeezed into a small round hole. They disappeared just as Eveillard and Nasri did after climbing the ladder. He watched the hole for further action, but there wasn't any—no poking whiskers with little sniffing nostrils and no whiplashing tails. He turned and shined his light behind him. Neither were there more coming down the sluice.

He didn't hate and fear rats, though he understood Deacon Nasri's phobia. His problem with rats was just the opposite. He felt sorry for them. It was a sentiment that stemmed from his undergraduate days at Chapel Hill in Psych 101 when the class had to run white rats through a maze on lab day. He learned only one thing from the experience: rats are smart yet receive no respect.

His flashlight was beginning to dim. Though there was no cell signal, his phone would suffice temporarily if the flashlight batteries expired. He turned and walked back. This time, there was a vague flash of shadowy illumination from beyond the curve.

Then came a sound, an echoing footfall of more than a single pair of legs advancing slowly. Eveillard and Nasri? Maybe. But wouldn't they call out?

Yes, they would.

He clicked off his light.

Now what? Where to run?

The alcove was too obvious and the tunnel behind him was a dead-end. He could go forward, but if the people coming from that direction were part of the same team that tried to kill him in New York, well—

"Professor Teagarden!"

His own bones stopped like a dead man beside the wall of bones. He didn't recognize the voice. It certainly was not Eveillard with the dreamy cadence of his bass-baritone Creole. Neither was it Deacon Nasri, who spoke English with long open-ended vowels and hard-hit consonants like all speakers whose native tongue is Arabic or Hebrew.

"Professor Teagarden, we know you are here, and we know there is no escape. Come forward. Return now to the open excavation pit."

And neither was it an American accent. That ruled out Lieutenant Cole. He'd never heard Master Sergeant Sanchez utter a single word, but it stood to reason it wasn't him either. Then came a second voice alternating with the first.

"We will get you, Professor Teagarden. That document is not your document. It is ours, and its translation must not be made public by you."

"Not by you, not by anyone, not ever."

"By the way, Professor Teagarden, we are not suicidal."

"We are not part of that madness. We are just the opposite. We will never lose our faith and we will always defend it."

"Indeed, it would be suicidal for you *not* to come forward."

The two distinct voices grew louder and closer with each swollen boast. In a snap, Teagarden realized his only option. He must hurry *toward* the intruders, then duck into one of the side tunnels that Deacon Nasri said were unsafe dead-ends. If he was lucky, perhaps there would be a boulder, a pile of dirt, or a hole in the ground he could squeeze into and hide, like the rats. It was risky. He had to arrive at the branch tunnels before they did. Worse still, he had to do it in the dark.

Do foxes ever race straight toward the hound dogs?

He doubted it. Foxes were too smart for that. Although, if it's the only smart choice, well—

He tucked in his elbows and bolted as fast as his painful knees would carry him while delicately feeling his way along the stone wall and lumber abutments. At the junction where there was nothing for his fingertips to touch and low-level blue lighting provided just enough illumination to see the void to his left, he turned, felt for the small red-and-white-striped sandwich board, stepped over it, and dropped flat. Done. Silent. No breathing. The fox made it to the den ahead of the dogs by mere seconds. Now to hold perfectly still.

Once at the transverse, the men ran their flashlights down each side tunnel as he and Eveillard had done when they first passed.

"Nein ausgang," one voice whispered. "Das ist gut. Elad hat den Eingang verdeckt."

"Gut. Diesen Weg," whispered the other as they moved on without detecting him lying prone in the side tunnel.

Teagarden exhaled after they passed.

Germans? Really?

"Professor Teagarden, be advised that the tunnel entrance is the only exit. It is covered by our man." In addition to menace, Teagarden heard in their voices the tone of schoolyard braggarts. "There is no other way out. We know because we work here as students."

"Yah. And our man covering the exit at the excavation pit is named Elad."

Silence.

"But that is not his real name. We do not know his real name."

Silence.

"That is because he was with the Mossad before."

Silence.

"Now he works for us."

Silence.

"Elad, say hello to Professor Teagarden."

"Yah-h-h," came the distant response. "Hello, Professor Teagarden. This is Elad. I am here, awaiting your exit from the fox's lair. There is only one path for you. That is, straight to me."

"By the way," said one of the two Germans, "I believe you two have met. Isn't that right, Elad?"

"Yes-s-s," shouted Elad from the open pit. "Professor Teagarden, you know, there are five stages to enduring coach class—denial, anger, bargaining, depression, and acceptance."

Oh shit!

The man on the flight who drank Kentucky bourbon and read Robert A. Heinlein in Hebrew. He was the ex-Mossad agent, part of the team that tried to kill him in his office at Columbia, nearly killed Supervisory FBI Agent Bernard Klassen, and did kill Special Agent Wechter.

"Professor Teagarden, while you were in the WC, I got a look at your official briefing on the laptop which you foolishly left exposed. Ha! They blacked out everything useful. Do you know why? Because they don't share data with a patsy they fully expect to be eliminated."

Oh, shit!

# CHAPTER TWENTY-ONE

He waited until the Germans moved on before standing.

Don't make a sound. Don't kick a stone. Don't bump the wall. Don't click on the flashlight. More important—don't drop the flashlight!

This wasn't going to be easy. He slowly worked his fingertips in search of a hiding spot where loose walls posed the threat of a cave-in. Worse, he had to do it with the silence of a fox.

It would be easy for a real fox. Real foxes see in the dark and move with the stealth of a ghost.

Like the main tunnel, the side-shafts were made of ancient stone, though there were many gaps and the passageway was narrower, requiring him to turn sideways. Every few feet he nearly tripped on debris from centuries of dribbling dirt and mini cave-ins. Twice the ceiling bowed so low he bumped his head and had to stoop.

Then came the rats.

While squeezing around a protruding stone at chest level, it dislodged and tumbled with a soft thud between his feet. The result was the opening of a swarming home nest. They bolted in sudden terror, grazing his shoulders and arms. When they reached the blue light in the main tunnel, he could see a vague silhouette revealing their number to be in the hundreds and making him fear being carried off atop a wave of black fur.

It was mid-stampede that one particularly large rat latched onto his chest and held there instead of using it as a springboard like the others. Sensing this was the boss, Teagarden offered no resistance, but only tightened his lips and squinted as hard as he could. A moment later, the creature opted against combat. Instead of drilling into Teagarden's eyelids, it leapt to join the others in their panicked streak, allowing him to quietly exhale with great relief.

Once in the blue light, the swarm encountered another challenge that reset their frenzy. Instead of continuing their flight, it was as though the boss rat delivered telepathic orders:

Cease retreating...stand and fight!

And they did. No longer content to mindlessly stampede, they assaulted the two German men blocking their escape path with drill-bit teeth and front-loader claws. Like the rats themselves, the men panicked.

"Achtung, ratten!

"Gottverdammt."

Blam...blam...blam...blam...blam.

"Do not shoot!" It was Elad calling from the entrance. "Do not shoot," he ordered, his voice growing closer as he ran into the tunnel. It did no good. The horrified German students continued firing and crying with dread. From his narrow chamber, Teagarden listened to the noises of surreal combat.

Blam...blam...blam...blam...blam.

"Lauf, diesen weg...nein...achtung...scheisse...töte sie... gottverdammt...yaiii, töte sie..."

Blam...blam...blam...blam...blam.

"Stop shooting. Stop shooting. Hold your fire!"

"Gott, bitte...halt...lauf...nach hinten..."

Blam...blam...blam...blam...blam.

The cave-in was quick. It was caused by the bedlam of angry rodents, two panicked men shouting in German, a third man shouting in English, two guns firing, and three pairs of madly stomping feet. Advance warning of the event was vague. There was only a slight shuddering. That was followed by a heavy slump of dirt and stone to the floor of the main tunnel shaft. Then came total darkness and complete silence.

Teagarden felt the residual impact in the side tunnel. A wider portion of the rat nest loosened and gave way, causing his footing to sink, like when a riptide causes the sandy floor to shift. He felt for the narrow walls with his arms and backside. When his fingers searched for the opposite barrier, it wasn't there. More surprising, his nose inhaled a scent of fresh, cold air.

Yes. It makes sense. Rats need oxygen too.

He listened. Judging from the dull sound, the collapse happened between the wall of bones and the bottlecap-sized rat door at the end of the main tunnel. If that were really the case, he could return to the main shaft, turn left, and safely exit at the excavated pit—providing Elad was also buried. He held still. He listened. First, there was nothing. Then came coughing. He, too, gasped and hacked for air when the dust cloud reached him. For several alternating rounds, whenever he caught his breath and momentarily stopped, the coughing in the main corridor resumed. Finally, the voice spoke again.

"Professor Teagarden, you are a clever and lucky man. That silly adventure in America six years ago was quite a streak of beginner's luck. We have an expression in Israel: 'As long as the cow can be milked, it will not be led to slaughter.'"

Shit! Elad!

"Well, your teats are dry, and your time is up."

Elad, the Mossad agent turned hired killer, not only survived the cave-in, he'd entered the narrow side tunnel. Silence being no longer paramount, Teagarden ceased all caution. He clicked on his flashlight to examine the wall and floor where he stood.

"By the way," Elad continued, "did you know these tunnels form the shape of a cross? You are now in the transverse, from which there is no exit. Did Nasri explain that?"

With the light beam, Teagarden could see that the opened cavity was more than a dead-end berth for rodents. Because of the rats, it was possibly a way out. The dirt was dry and loose. When he pushed at it with the end of the flashlight, it easily crumbled. At the top of the cavity there was a small aperture that seemed to be the source of fresh air. When he pushed harder, the gap widened, creating a welcome breeze.

"The only exit is the entrance," Elad called out, continuing his monologue between hacking coughs while getting closer to Teagarden's position. "Is that existential? It certainly sounds existential. *No Exit*, and all that French crap. In your case, it means the fox is trapped. Your teats are dry. You luck is over."

Teagarden dug furiously. The dirt gave way so easily that within seconds he could make out the source of the illumination.

"But you are not trapped like a fox. It was in America where you were a sly fox. This time you are trapped in Israel."

Teagarden could see natural light. Sunlight! That could only mean one thing. The rats created a crawlway between the narrow transverse and the wider excavated pit.

Fresh oxygen.

"Just so you know, I do not wear the armband. These fools may kill themselves all they wish. What do I care? I only take their money. When they kicked me out of the Mossad, I was told I could become a bodyguard for important people. Politicians. Maybe movie stars."

And heat. He could feel the furnace effect of the Israeli sun burning into the excavation pit.

Teagarden dug like a hound dog on the scent.

"Ha—bodyguard! I make more money working for these religious kooks than any Mossad agent ever imagined. Plus, I do what the Mossad trained me to do. I was part of Kidon. Did you ever hear of that? It is the first to kill. As a Kidon Mossad agent, I tracked and assassinated people on assignment for religious Jews. Now, as a for-hire, ex-Kidon Mossad agent, I track and assassinate people for religious Christians. Ironic, don't you think?"

Between bouts of coughing, Elad laughed with delight at his own story while Teagarden dug and scraped at the cavity. The deeper it stretched, the more natural light spilled in. He could only hope the still settling cloud of dust would prevent Elad from seeing this new source of illumination.

"I went to America to kill you. It should have been simple. Okay, I ended up killing that FBI boy. I almost killed the other FBI man. He got lucky. He got off a shot that grazed a rib, and your dog bit my arm. Did you know that?"

So, Klassen struck his target after all. And he was right about Coco Too, who also drew blood.

Teagarden tried to recall Elad's face but couldn't. The only memory was that he was comparatively short and built like the proverbial brick shithouse. Trying to suppress more coughing, he kept digging while Elad kept talking as he grew closer.

"I should not talk now like Blofeld or Goldfinger closing in on a doomed James Bond. You are certainly no 007. They made us read all the Bond books in Mossad training. Also Graham Greene, John le Carré, Robert Ludlum. Silly stuff, really. I prefer science fiction. That's where the real truth can be found. Science fiction is the future. Don't you think so, Professor Teagarden?"

Silence.

When Elad paused talking, Teagarden paused digging.

C'mon, start talking again.

"I like talking to you. I seldom have the opportunity. And with you, it is a privilege. Besides, I am my own boss now. The Mossad wanted to demote me, but I told them to, as you Americans say, 'take this job and shove it.' So, they fired me."

Silence.

"Do you know why the Vatican hired me to kill you? It is simple. They anticipated your involvement before the FBI hired you. They wanted to prevent the man who altered U.S. history from any involvement with the Q Document. They fear that old parchment will verify that their faith was formulated only by men instead of by God. Of course, mortals invent all the religions. Did you know that ancient Egyptians believed the Sun God Ra masturbated and deposited his seed upon the Earth to fertilize it? That is how *they* explained the beginning of the world. So much more practical than our own Judeo-Christian Genesis which sounds like God had a magic wand. Well, as Heinlein once said, 'Never underestimate the power of human stupidity.'"

Judging from his voice, Elad was more than halfway along the side tunnel where Teagarden was frantically digging free. Once the hole was large enough and there was sufficient sunlight, he turned off the flashlight. With both arms, he swept dirt behind as he scurried forward. Elad hacked and spit.

More silence.

Teagarden heard him make a series of snorts, like a sniffing dog on the trail of his prey.

"Okay, so you got away from me in New York. That sort of failure does not happen to me. It was a first. I respect you for that. Of course, you had some help from your FBI friends and their miniature air force. That was clever. But we are here now, on my home ground, where I will finish my job. Then, the zealots in Rome will pay me a lot of money. Not the Pope, himself of course. I deal with what you Americans call 'the middle man.' You know how your favorite soda-pop gets from the factory to the store? The *middle* man. That is how."

Teagarden wormed *inside* the hollow.

"Of course, they don't *all* want to kill you," he said. "Those crazies in Jerusalem, for example. That woman who called herself FFG. They're atheists. They're on your side."

Yes, of course Teagarden remembered. She called herself a global fighter for FFG. He had no idea what it meant and neither did he care. The light grew brighter as he army-crawled through the tight culvert.

"They actually *want* you to find the document, decode it, and release it to the world. They know of it because of Zurbarán. I got to him about one hour late. Too bad the atheists didn't hire me. If they had, I'd be protecting you now instead of killing you." He inhaled again with a snort. "Which I am about to do."

Teagarden suppressed his gag reflex caused by flying dust.

"Don't you find it interesting that not too many years ago the Muslims were killing themselves with suicide bombs and now it's the turn of Christians and atheists? As you say in America, 'what goes around, comes around.'"

Once fully inside the chamber, Teagarden folded into a fetal position to use his legs for thrust.

"Of course, it's only the cuckoo people who kill themselves. Not that I mind. It's called God's pruning fork. The cults, crazies, and crackpots can't handle news that the Q Doc bears proof that you-know-who wasn't really the son of you-know-what."

Teagarden dug with both hands and both elbows.

"By the way, as I mentioned, this tunnel is shaped like a cross. That was my weapon of choice for killing Zurbarán. A cross. Wonderfully ironic, don't you think? I had it custom made in Malta while I was with Mossad. Quite a lovely weapon. A long, double-sided razor with the point of a needle. And beautiful. The outside is inlaid with Italian coral and mother of pearl. I will use it on you if you like at the conclusion of our talk."

One last hard push and Teagarden broke through a loose barrier of dirt and stepped out into the M.C. Escher excavated pit. From there, Elad's voice rang with stereo clarity from the main tunnel entrance *and* the newly opened culvert behind him.

"You have stopped coughing, Professor Teagarden. And you must be using a flashlight and cell phone to light your way in the dark, which means you are panicking. This tells me I am close now. He made another series of snorting noises. "Yes, I am so close I can smell you. It is the smell of fear. Did you know that when humans face imminent death, they emit a unique odor? It is the smell of ammonia with a touch of cheap perfume, like that of a fresh cadaver."

Despite his knees, Teagarden's pumping adrenaline helped him navigate the platforms and staircases to the ladder which he quickly scaled. Nothing seemed amiss. Knowing the seconds were ticking down, he ran as fast as he could manage to the front of the church where he ventured a furtive glance into the window with the illuminated crucifix.

Nothing. More lost seconds.

The big SUV was still parked at the front. He looked inside. Nothing. More lost seconds.

He scanned the entrance road within the wider prison grounds and its menacing walls topped with razor wire.

Also, nothing unusual. And still more valuable seconds wasted. What? What to do? Where to run? Where to hide?

By now, Teagarden guessed that Elad had discovered the crawlspace to the pit and was racing to catch up.

He turned again to the prison that loomed beyond the lemon orchard in full bloom. It was distant and forbidding. There must be a gate. Maybe a door. Running to that penitentiary wall was his only option. Shout. Bang. Make noise. Desperately plea for assistance to the man in the watchtower. A few hurried steps toward the goal, he stopped in disregard of the ticking clock.

They were there.

No.

On the far side of the church.

Oh, God. No.

All of them.

Oh, please God!

All of them. Not only Eveillard, Nasri, Cole, and Sanchez, but a half dozen others that Teagarden guessed were the deacon's American, German, and English students. The sight was unbearable. Necks were broken. Jaws caved. Skulls crushed. The bodies were arranged semi-neatly in the shade.

The nearest corpse was the silent driver, Sanchez. The holster on his belt still held his Glock. His broken arms were pulled behind his back and up to his ears like a twist tie. The car's key fob still dangled on the thumb of his stiffened hand where it protruded unnaturally behind his head. At that moment, it was human flight instinct that ruled Teagarden's state of mind. Consequently, he ignored the Glock, snatched the key fob, and ran to the Ford. He quickly cranked the engine, causing clouds of dry desert to fly. Before completing the turn, the human killing machine appeared like an apparition in the side mirror, flanked by twin minicyclones spitting behind the rear tires. Teagarden panicked. He gunned all eight cylinders, causing the SUV to fishtail in the sandy grit and spin out, giving Elad all the time he needed to rush. Sensing it was best, Teagarden released the accelerator. He recovered control, straightened, and rocketed past the lemon trees of Megiddo Parish Lane as the back windshield deflected a nine-millimeter fusillade. On the dashboard, the Immediate Ground Pulse flashed a bright red blip at the rear.

# Chapter Twenty-Two

He drove west only because the nearest highway entrance was a westbound ramp. In Haifa, he mindlessly drove city streets, then up and around Mount Carmel which had a panoramic view of the waterfront.

He wondered if it was symptomatic of his fragile state that he imagined his wife was sitting next to him. If it was, well, that was too bad because there was nothing he could do to interrupt the fantasy.

(Cynthia)
Wow. Just wow.

(Sam)
Wow, what?

(Cynthia)
Wow what? Are you kidding? Wow—you! That's what. Tunnels, rats, outsmarting a super villain, driving a fancy escape car. Whoa, there. You're a regular 007, Jason Bourne, and Jack Ryan all rolled into one math professor named Sam Teagarden.

(Sam)
Oh, that.

(Cynthia)
Yeah—that (small laugh). That little performance
you gave back there.

(Sam)
I guess I did all right for a math teacher.

(Cynthia)
I'd say so.

(Sam)
(Starting to cry) But c'mon, Cynthia. Did you see
what else happened back there? There was, there
was so much—

(Cynthia)
Sam, knock it off. I know what else was back
there. Listen to your partner's advice: think, then
do. 'Think' means be careful. 'Do' means, after
thinking, choose the right action for the maximum number of people. Not just you. Remember,
there are more people than just you involved here.
You can do it. I know you can.

(Sam)
I'm trying.

(Cynthia)
Good. That's all you can do.

It worked. His budding emotional breakdown halted before
tears began to flow. From Haifa, he turned south to Tel Aviv,
then veered for the Negev Desert in the heart of Israel's center of
gravity. There is a tough beauty to the desert where only the most

stubborn life forms abound. It seems to happen through hard-learned adaptation. Here, all that breathes or is verdant must negotiate with barren cruelty in exchange for survival.

Is there a life lesson in that? Something about tolerating the intolerable until evolution reveals a work-around?

He tried not to think about it. It sounded like something meaningful and the last thing he needed to think about was *meaning*. There couldn't be meaning to the two events he'd witnessed in a single day. The police feared flash-mob suicide was catching on like a new extreme sport. Problem was, adrenaline-rush stunts like skyscraper climbing and subway surfing only *risked* death. For these people, dying *was* the rush.

As for Elad, it was the act of killing that he enjoyed.

Try to find meaning in that.

It was because of the Q Document. That much he knew. Still, he had no idea if it was authentic, or as mythological as the Golden Fleece, the Ark of the Covenant, and the Holy Chalice.

Maybe there was meaning out there in the desert where the death of one creature equaled life for another.

On this day in Jerusalem and Megiddo, there wasn't any.

All those good people. All dead.

Meaning?

He couldn't see any.

The night drive in the desert was cathartic. He found something poignant in the dead landscape. It was a window on the past, exactly the way the world looked two thousand years earlier when humanity sought comfort in the face of Roman oppression. Stubborn life sprouted in the sand. Patchwork green and brown vegetation survived amid the inexplicable hardship of nature. Perhaps, like the stars and planets, they too found an algorithm, a trial-and-error formula, a syllogism to foster survival. If so, like the stars, these life forms also held close the secrets of their survival.

Smart. I wish I had one of those work-arounds.

He continued driving aimlessly. When the road ran its course, he turned and retraced his route, then turned and retraced it again. He wasn't tired, didn't need sleep, and had no appetite. He was still wearing the same slacks and shirt he put on in New York. After flying halfway around the world and crawling through ancient tunnels in northern Israel, his clothes felt like a soiled onesie. He didn't care. The only thing he really wanted was to think of nothing, to push the day far from his mind.

For that purpose, the Negev served nicely.

# CHAPTER TWENTY-THREE

*Wednesday, March 19, 2025*

*Think, then do.*

It was not until the sun began to rise that his mind seemed to improve in small increments. As his brain came around, his body resumed speaking to him about thirst, hunger, and the need for a restroom. And finally, the Ford needed gas.

The twenty-four-hour roadside mini-mart in the middle of no-where was called Shimon's Eleven, a play on words that made Teagarden inwardly smile. It was a ramshackle sandwich shop, mini-grocery, and gas station that could be airlifted to any rural crossroads in America where, except for the name, it would fit perfectly.

The slow-moving clerk accepted cash for petrol and took his food order. He seemed to size up Teagarden as an odd duck: a lone, distressed-looking American in messy clothing and driving a luxury SUV. Though stooped with age and arthritis, the man's eyes were quick, like those of someone who'd seen enough to be troubled by the sum total of everything. Waiting for his food, Teagarden readied himself for conversation filled with probing questions, yet the man said nothing, which increased his overall paranoia index. When his order was ready, instead of sitting at one of the rickety indoor tables near the dirty front window, he took his food to the car. As with every mini-mart the world over, the two egg sandwiches were greasy, but tasty. He washed them down with a large, American-style coffee. Gas cost the equivalent of twenty-five dollars a gallon and filling up the huge tank ate three-quarters of the Israeli shekels he'd converted before departure.

The begrudging contract approved by Assistant FBI Director William Drakken did not allow for an expense account since he was supposed to be managed by an escort during his short stay. It would have been smarter to charge the gas, but his still reassembling brain knew that was dangerous. A credit card would make him blip up on everybody's radar: FBI...CIA...Mossad...Vatican... Christian suiciders...FFG suiciders...and—Elad!

No thanks.

Some of them wanted to kill him, while some wanted to prevent him from being killed. He figured that as long as he could get by on shekels and dollars in cash, it would be more difficult for Elad to trace him. Unfortunately, it also meant Agent Klassen couldn't trace him either. Once Klassen learned about Megiddo, Teagarden assumed he'd summon the cavalry. That too was dangerous. None of them understood what they were up against. After Eveillard, whoever the CIA next sent from the American Embassy would be easy pickings for this specter that kills Marines without breaking a sweat or making a sound. Because of it, Teagarden was as committed to preventing more collateral death as he was to avoiding his own passage into the afterlife.

The bodies had probably not yet been discovered by Israeli police. With the sun rising, and Eveillard not checking in with the home office, they would soon be found. That meant the Americans would use satellite-based surveillance to learn the SUV's location.

Okay, it's time to think, then do.

Teagarden verified that his cell phone was powered off. Still parked at Shimon's Eleven, he made certain the arthritic counter clerk was minding his own business, then began a thorough search of the Ford from engine, to cab, to rear cargo space. He was looking for the car's GPS tracer. More importantly, he was searching for anything that would aid his survival.

Based on all he'd read and all the spy-trained people he'd

spoken with since his previous adventure, he knew the exterior was where private detectives placed cheap GPS tracers when hired by suspicious spouses. Indeed, that's where he found it. Smaller than a pill box and with a dangling wire, it was a disposable unit powered by a single AAA battery under the rim of the rear bumper. Odder still, it was attached to the inside of the bumper with chewing gum.

No! There is no way the CIA would put a cheap GPS on its own spy car in such a manner.

He finished the outside search then moved to the interior where he found what he expected. About half the size of a deck of cards, it was plugged into a series of USB ports next to the fuse box under the steering wheel. The model was called V-Trak Ping 3000. He unplugged it and securely wrapped both GPS units with the two sheets of aluminum foil saved from his egg sandwiches. He slammed the package twice against the inside door, then turned it and slammed it twice more. Afterward, he lowered the driver side window and heaved the tinfoil wad into the nearby dumpster.

The glove box was locked but easily opened with one of two keys looped to the ring with the ignition fob. Inside were pens, pads, a small multi-tool, breath mints, lip balm, rubber bands, a few business cards, and a pair of sunglasses with particularly thick lenses and a fat frame. It was the stuff of every ordinary glove box the world over, including his own Subaru. He examined the business cards. One was for a dermatologist in Tel Aviv. Another was for a CNN producer stationed in Jerusalem and Washington. A third was for a psychologist in Haifa who specialized in "Job Stress, PTSD, Depression, Drug & Alcohol Abuse, and Suicidal Thoughts."

Great.

He wondered if the cards belonged to Eveillard, Cole, or Sanchez. They were probably Master Sergeant Sanchez's since the car was his responsibility.

Perhaps he too had seen more than he cared to see and was struggling with his own relentless trauma.

Teagarden felt another wave of regret, combined this time with a rising sense of nausea that churned the egg sandwiches in his stomach. He reached for one of the bottles of water in the back and chugged half, then returned the cards to the glove box. While waiting for the queasiness to pass, he withdrew the card for the network news producer a second time. The name on it read Moira Gray. He tucked it into a slot in his wallet.

Why not? Power of the free press, and all that. You never know.

He felt under the front seats. There were holster slots for handguns that were empty. If the door panels had secret compartments, he couldn't figure how to open them. And the back seats yielded nothing. It was the rear cargo area that proved the most fruitful.

Wow, this is like 007's tour of the lab where Q (no pun intended) demonstrates the latest fashion in gadgets for survival, murder, and deception.

There were four overnight suitcases, including his own and one for each of the other three Americans, which he opened one by one. The contents were perfectly normal: underwear, socks, toiletries, and fresh shirts. Each one also yielded personal insight into who those three men were.

Master Sergeant Sanchez had an unopened box of condoms, a flask filled with liquid that tasted like good scotch, and his passport. Born in Oxnard, California, in 1975, he was fifty years old. His full name was Mateo Sakonnatayak Blackhorse Sanchez.

Wow!

That explained his stone-carved features and complexion. His heritage was Native American and Hispanic. He was both Old World Indian warrior and a New World Latino. Unfortunately, he was also an American Marine stationed in the Mideast on a plain-clothed security gig, which was the reason he was now deceased.

Looking at the passport photo, Teagarden was struck by his own resemblance to Sanchez in the general shape of his head and face. He withdrew his own passport and compared them. Eyes, nose, and mouth bore similarities. He held the Sanchez passport aside and moved on.

Eveillard's suitcase had two boxes of 9mm ammunition, each with fifty rounds, and a coloring book where each vibrant page was signed in a child's hand by someone named "Aimee." In the book's center was a double-page image of brightly colored trees on a mountainside with a meandering path. It was signed, "For you, daddy."

Lieutenant Cole's bag also held his passport. His full name was Joseph James Cole, from Virginia. There was a small photo book filled with snapshots of him and another happily smiling man at various tourist attractions in Venice, Florence, and Naples. On the Spanish Steps in Rome, there was a close-up selfie of them kissing in the fading light of evening, the twin towers of the Trinità dei Monti church in the background.

Oh, God! I'm sorry. To all three of you, I am really sorry. You men are the reason I cannot contact Klassen for help. I will not be the cause of anyone else losing their life.

When a white Fiat zoomed into the adjacent parking space, he waited to lift the hinged cover of the lower storage compartment that held the spare tire. Gazing only with peripheral vision, he saw a lone, long-legged female wearing a beige safari hat with the brims folded up, a military style T-shirt, and jeans. Seeming perfectly mindless of him, she squished out her cigarette butt on the asphalt with her sneaker and hurried inside the mini-mart.

Lifting the secondary storage cover, he found a cache of true military armament and spy paraphernalia. There were two assault rifles labeled M4, each wrapped in clear plastic and each with half a dozen magazines of ammunition. A bright orange sticker on an army green box read "F92 Stun Grenades, 12 Non-Lethal Flashbang Explosives." A soft rollaway satchel unzipped to reveal two sizes of binoculars, a Japanese-made satellite phone, and a selection of mini-cameras variously shaped like a light switch, cell phone charger, and ballpoint pen. The final two containers were identical, about the dimension of standard cigar boxes, made of solid aluminum, and locked.

So—real-life spies actually have little doohickeys in case they go into peeping-tom mode. Not to mention plenty of firepower.

There wasn't anything in the guns or gadgetry that interested him. He kept Sanchez's passport and the two locked boxes, lowered the hinged cover, shifted the luggage back to the storage compartment, and closed the rear hatch.

Back in the driver's seat, he dropped his own rollaway luggage to the passenger side floor and transferred the two aluminum tins to the seat next to him. While thinking about his next move, he sipped his coffee and watched the sun grow sharper as the temperature quickly rose.

Take a chance on calling the American Embassy?

No good. It was apparent that Elad had informants everywhere, including the two German students who died in the tunnel collapse. Deacon Nasri obviously did not know that he'd been compromised.

Head for the nearest airport and book a flight back to New York?

That would require purchasing a ticket and having security agents scan his passport in the little beep-beep machine. After that, Americans and Israelis would be on him in a matter of seconds, with Elad following in a matter of minutes.

Call his wife and ask her to work it from her end?

No way. Sure, FBI Agent Utrillo was protecting her at the house in Bethel, New York. But that wouldn't mean a thing if Elad's allies learned his wife was actively assisting.

Okay, how about going undercover?

That option made sense. If he could pull it off, perhaps he could hold out long enough to get a look at this mysterious Q Document. That would mean getting to Berlin on his own for the World Judeo-Christian Council Conference where Klassen would be waiting. If he succeeded, maybe he could even analyze the document and go through with the scheduled presentation on Sunday. The problem was, what did he know about how to go undercover and travel all the way from Israel to Berlin?

*I did a fair job of it back in August 2019, didn't I?*

The answer was—yes, which was the reason he was now in this mess. It was his global reputation earned during that run for his life which caused the CIA to co-opt him as window dressing.

The leggy driver of the white Fiat sauntered back to her car with a large cup of coffee and a red-and-white pack of Marlboros from which she removed the cellophane wrapping and tapped out a fresh cigarette. She was tall, thin, muscular, and strutted with a don't-fuck-with-me gait. Her longish brown hair protruded in a messy curtain around her face. Watching her light up made him want one. The sign in the mini-mart window read "Cigarettes, All American Brands: $32."

*Whoa, how does anyone afford the habit these days?*

When he stopped smoking, they cost three dollars a pack in New York.

The woman dropped her key chain ahead of climbing into her Fiat and stopped to pick it up, which flipped his caution into red alert. If she bounced up with a weapon, he'd have to rely on the Ford's bullet-proof glass to save him. At least he knew it would work because it saved him from Elad's fusillade.

*How many bullets will bullet-proof glass deflect before breaking?*

He had no idea.

When she popped up two-seconds later, keys in hand, she jumped into the Fiat, cranked the engine, and sped off into the desert. Headed for her job most likely, which made him wonder what she did for a living.

*Maybe a waitress or factory worker. Possibly some sort of back office clerk.*

Whatever it was, he guessed her breakfast routine amounted to coffee and two or three rapidly inhaled cigarettes.

After she departed, he returned to thinking about keys and locks, which sparked a brainstorm. The two locked boxes sat on the passenger seat. The ring with the ignition fob also held two other keys. The small one opened the glove box. The other key was odd looking, with a plastic collar and indentations that shifted up and down like tumblers. The lettering read, "Magneto Transponder, Do Not Duplicate."

I wonder.

He picked up one of the aluminum cases, found the recess, and inserted the strange key. It was a perfect fit. He turned it one full circle to the left and opened the box.

# CHAPTER TWENTY-FOUR

At first it was difficult to identify the contents. There were two dozen parts, all medium-gray in color, each individually wrapped in clear plastic. It resembled a toy model of the sort his father used to buy him at the local hobby shop: the monster in the *Alien* movies, the USS *Theodore Roosevelt* aircraft carrier, and the Starship Enterprise. The components all came in slate gray plastic, to be assembled with airplane glue. Decals and paint were the last to be applied.

He dug for instructions in the metal box. Something that would say "attach side panel 'A' (right) to side panel 'B' (left)." There were none.

What the hell is it?

After ripping off and discarding all plastic wrapping, the shape of the two largest pieces and the five smallest made him realize its purpose.

A plastic gun!

Assembly wasn't difficult. He fit, snapped, and inserted all parts without instructions. It was shaped like a semiauto without a magazine. Five white plastic .22 caliber bullets, the smallest pieces, fit neatly into a chamber above the trigger.

Okay, let's check box number two.

The same key opened the other lock. This time the contents required no guessing or snapping together. It was filled with money. There were stacks of cash in dollars, shekels, and euros. The dollars and euros were all in denominations of twenty, while the shekels were in hundreds. He tried to count the total value of the dollars but stopped at twelve thousand, about halfway through the wads of fresh Andy Jacksons. If there were equal amounts of euros and shekels, it meant the box held about seventy-five thousand in cash.

The discoveries in the Ford made him recall his favorite novel, *Robinson Crusoe*. On the morning after Robinson's first night as a castaway, the storm had passed, and he was trying to figure his next move when fate, or God, or luck, showed the way. Looking out to sea, he beheld the wrecked ship precariously perched upon a distant rock. If he could build a raft and retrieve the vessel's storehouse of tools, food, clothing, guns, powder, and all the other essentials—*he might survive!*

Robinson's destiny was to be stranded on that island for twenty-eight years. After the mass murder at Megiddo, Teagarden figured he'd be lucky if he had twenty-eight hours. Still, with the cash, he had a chance to survive without charge cards until reaching Berlin.

And once there, maybe, just maybe, he could prevent Eveillard, Cole, Sanchez, and all the others from dying in vain.

He transferred wads of dollars, euros, and shekels from the aluminum box to his various pockets. He put the balance in two stacks, tightened them down with rubber bands from the glove box, and tucked them into his rollaway luggage.

Then there was the plastic gun. He had no use for all the firepower in the cargo hold, but a .22 caliber pistol that could breeze through metal detectors was a different animal. That might come in handy. Of course, it could also get him arrested, yet so would all the cash. And if he was arrested, there was no reason to fear he'd really be in trouble. One call to the American Embassy in Israel, or to the FBI in New York, and he'd be off the hook. Or so he hoped.

In the end, he dismantled the .22 and stuffed all parts into a side compartment of his suitcase. Still feeling dehydrated, he chugged the water bottle. When empty, he tossed it into the garbage dumpster to join the pair of aluminum-wrapped GPS trackers.

With the morning sun climbing on his right, he cranked the Ford and headed north, back to the city of Haifa where he'd seen ships in the busy harbor before sunset the night before. There were navy cruisers, private yachts, sailboats, fishing vessels, tourist sightseeing boats—and two cruise ships.

Teagarden hadn't fully sorted out how to go about it. He could try bribing a boat owner to ferry him to the nearest reasonably safe country along the Mediterranean. Or he could simply buy a ticket on one of the cruise ships. Like the airport, that would mean having his passport scanned. Perhaps a bribe could prevent that. He certainly had enough cash for bribery, although waving money around was not something he had much experience with. Neither was he experienced in secretly traveling around the Mideast with zealots hunting him like lions on the savanna.

No, wait.

The proper comparison was not a lion on the veldt, but a fox in the field. He'd done that one before.

It was midmorning when he arrived back in Haifa. It took another forty-five minutes of circling to find a pay-per-day lot near the port. After parking, he tucked the empty aluminum boxes under the front seats. He took Sanchez's oversized sunglasses from the glove box and his luggage. Knowing it was useless to him, he left his Flexi-Flat behind, locked the Ford spymobile, and walked to the attendant's booth. His intention was to abandon the SUV. That meant doing whatever was necessary to draw as little attention as possible to the vehicle for as long as possible. Teagarden tapped on the little window, interrupting the cashier's study of *People* magazine in English.

"I'd like to pay in advance," he said when the glass partition slid open.

"How long?" the man asked in a thick Israeli accent as air-conditioned coolness rushed outward. He was a young man, nineteen at the oldest, and clearly bored. It was a natural guess that he was a college student working a part-time job. Yet there was something about him that was too rough edged for scholarly pursuits. Before Teagarden could answer, the man said, "It's sixty-two dollars a day or two hundred twenty shekels." His tone was both distracted and irritated.

"Well, I'm going on a trip."

"Are you on Blue Voyager? That is the next ship to depart. It is with the Tricolore Line." Again, Teagarden looked perplexed. Misunderstanding his confusion, the attendant shrugged as though he didn't care one way or another. "Look," he said, "I am only trying to help you. If you booked with that ship, you will want to do what others do."

Teagarden's eyes lighted with relief. "Yes, yes. I will be, or that is, I hope to be on the Blue Voyager."

"Okay."

"What do others do?"

"Most others pay for all ten days. Or, sometimes, because they know the ship opens the throttle to reach Venice in two quick days and some people get sick, they pay for two weeks in case they need to get off and stay for a while in Venice to recover."

"Good idea. I'll pay for two weeks."

"That means you get a discount. The total is seven hundred seventy U.S., or twenty-seven thousand Israeli." Teagarden was ready. He paid in shekels and walked away. "Wait," the attendant called, "your ticket."

The attendant watched him depart with an expression that Teagarden felt was either suspicious or aggravated. He hoped it was the latter but feared the former. Then, paranoia being a self-fulfilling prophecy, he felt the creeping sting of paranoia about being paranoid.

C'mon, knock it off. Stay focused.

Once on the sidewalk, he tossed the parking receipt and the Ford's key fob into the nearest public trash bin. He had no idea what time the Blue Voyager sailed for Venice, but missing the boat was a risk he'd have to take because more preparatory moves were necessary.

Within a few blocks, he found a drugstore where he purchased motion sickness medication, a beige makeup base labeled "Medium 22," an eyeliner pencil, a bottle of liquid shoe polish with a spongy applicator cap, and an adhesive lint roller.

Almost there.

He needed a couple of minutes of privacy to apply a thin layer of pancake base. A hotel lobby bathroom would be best. A restroom in a library or movie theatre would do the job, though he'd have to pretend to be a patron. He passed a coffeehouse that could work nicely. Unfortunately, there was a problem with the name over the entrance: Ilan and Elad's Books & Roaster Café.

Oh brother.

He shuddered with revulsion and moved on, then one block away, he reconsidered. The fact that the café had several laptops affixed to flexible arm mounts did it for him. He swallowed the PTSD related to the name of the man with supernatural killing powers and entered the café.

In the restroom, he again compared the Marine's passport photo to his own image. Sanchez was fifty but appeared older. Teagarden was fifty-five but appeared younger. They had the same hair style, were both in the same weight class of about a hundred seventy-five pounds, and, at five feet eleven inches, exactly the same height. A quick glance by a ticket agent or cruise ship official, and he just might pass. On the other hand, if examined closely by any trained security guard, it would be obvious that it was not a photo of Teagarden. The big difference was complexion. Teagarden was whiter than white. Sanchez was Latino and Native American Indian.

There's nothing to do but try.

He applied base to his face, neck and hands. Too much would be a dead giveaway. Too little, and the ticket agent for the cruise line might take a closer look. After the base, he delicately drew thin semicircular lines around his mouth and chin to accentuate his own wrinkles and imitate Sanchez's stone-carved, dog-faced look. Again, there was the problem of too much/too little that would cause him to be shifted to a little side room like the one at

Ben Gurion Airport. Only this time, the interview wouldn't enjoy preclearance arranged by the CIA.

In the end, he opted to err on the side of too little makeup. Using toilet tissue, he patted the base and liner to blend. He looked at Sanchez's photo, then at himself in the mirror, then back at the photo. It was neither good nor ridiculous. The fact that he hadn't shaved in thirty-six hours helped conceal obvious dissimilarities to the jawline. He gave his shoes a quick liquid polish, brushed his hair thoroughly, and tidied up his clothing with the lint roller.

When he exited, a tattooed girl with blue hair and a face bejeweled with silver studs was waiting her turn. He watched for any sign of a double take. There wasn't one. Neither was there a curious stare from the barista when he ordered a double espresso.

So far, so good.

At a private counter space, he tugged the café computer mounted on a flexible arm into reading position. The start-up screen was a photo of Ilan and Elad, two slender men holding hands at the entrance to the Brooklyn Bridge. The caption read "Locations in New York, London, Paris, Rome, and *everywhere* in Israel."

That's not the Elad I know—thankfully.

Using the public login posted on the overhead menu, he checked the departure time for the Blue Voyager.

> Depart Haifa 1:30 p.m. Total ten days. For the first two days enjoy a luxurious, romantic cruise on the Mediterranean followed by stops at Venice, Syracuse, Malta, Athens, and back to Haifa on the morning of the tenth day.

He checked his watch. Twelve thirty p.m. It had been nearly twenty-four hours since he escaped Megiddo. If the police had found the bodies, they'd be watching for his passport or credit card to blip up—*not* the passport belonging to Master Sergeant

Sanchez. But that window wouldn't last long. They'd eventually figure out that dead men don't book cruise tickets. With a little luck, perhaps he could get all the way to Venice, then bail from the ship and find his way to Berlin.

A mistake on timing would mean being easy pickings because foxes can't run if they're caged. Cruise ships are large and have plenty of burrows, but they're all dead-ends. That means all passengers are captives.

While sitting there, he thought again of trying to get a message to his wife in upstate New York or his daughter in Key West, but decided against it. Not only would it defeat the purpose of masquerading as Master Sergeant Mateo Sakonnatayak Blackhorse Sanchez, it would put *them* at risk.

(Sam)
That's unacceptable.

(Cynthia)
Stop worrying about us. Remember—

(Sam)
I know, I know—worry about the maximum number of people. Think, then do. Right?

(Cynthia)
That's the idea.

(Sam)
Okay, I can't call you, but I can imagine your voice. And I can follow your advice.

(Cynthia)
I love you, Sam.

The café's generic login was BKLYN. He entered it and went

to PaisleyBird, his preferred online encyclopedia. Elad, who called himself a Kidon Mossad agent, was first up:

> Kidon (From Hebrew, literally: tip of the spear.)
> One of eight divisions within the Mossad, the Israeli National Intelligence Agency.
> Considered elite, they are the most highly trained, highly skilled unit with a specialty in preemptive assassination. The number of Kidon agents is a closely guarded secret, as is the nature of their missions.

How nice.

The woman who ran up to him in Jerusalem called herself FFG, which Elad repeated while taunting him in the tunnel. He looked it up:

> FFG (Freedom from God)
> Activist global alliance of atheists connected by a common cause of ridding humanity from what it calls the god mythology.

Now it clicked. He first saw the words "Freedom from God" in the briefing report he read during the flight to Jerusalem. It was in the shortest passage and the only one with no blackouts, which meant it wasn't on the FBI's or CIA's radar.

He refocused on the website and read on:

> FFG claims a principal goal is peaceful negotiation to allow non-religious options for all, particularly in nations designated as religious states. Despite its claims, FFG is widely suspected of anti-religious terrorism resulting in the murder of scores of ecclesiastics, primarily in Islamic nations. Some international monitors allege the group to be a reactionary

counterpart to Islamic terror organizations.
Their list of religious states includes:
- Islam: Iran, Saudi Arabia, Iraq, Egypt, Pakistan, Afghanistan
- Buddhism: Thailand, Myanmar, Sri Lanka, Cambodia
- Judaism: Israel
- Roman Catholic: Argentina, Costa Rica, Bolivia
- Protestant Christianity: Denmark, Iceland, Norway, Finland

Members also actively campaign against state-sanctioned references such as "In God We Trust," the official motto of the United States.

That FFG woman in Jerusalem said she wanted the Q Doc to be published. Great. Now I'm at the center of dueling terror groups pitting religious zealots against anti-religious zealots.

Next: Zurbarán:

Pablo Zurbarán, PhD
Professor of archeology and papyrology at the University of Galicia, and Director of Antiquities for the Cathedral of Santiago de Compostela. Noted for his extended excavation of Roman ruins at Italica near Seville, Spain where he discovered preserved homes of affluent first century Roman citizens and...

Teagarden skipped ahead.

...found murdered in his private office below Santiago de Compostela's famed cathedral on February 22, 2025. No arrests have been made and Spanish authorities have not revealed a suspect...

Yeah, well, I can reveal a suspect for you. His name is Elad.

> ...motive remains unknown. Police suspect the crime may relate to a recent ecumenical assembly in Dallas, Texas where Zurbarán made a controversial presentation pertaining to discovery of an ancient parchment called the Q Document.

That was a natural segue:

> The Q Document (Q for quelle, from German, literally: *source.*)
> The Q Source was a term first coined around 1900 by Johannes Weiss, a German biblical eschatology scholar who claimed to find evidence of two sources for two of the three synoptic gospels (Matthew, Mark, and Luke) through study of the church's early oral traditions.
> Mark is known as one source for Matthew and Luke. The other source remains missing. Idea for the double source tradition is widely supported by both faith-based and secular scholars. Today the Weiss theory survives in common vernacular as The Q Document.

That public access website held more information than Count Drakken allowed him to see in the official FBI memorandum. But what the hell does eschatology mean?

> Eschatology: (Greek eschatos for "last" and -ology for "study of.") Theological study of human fate variously called "end of time," "end of days," "the final battle," and "Armageddon." Some Christians believe the site of the final battle will take place on the field of Armageddon, a hill in Israel known

by the translation from the Latin word Armageddon to the Greek: Megiddo.

That meant he'd just escaped his own personal Armageddon at the site of the *real* Armageddon.

"I—am—one—lucky—man," he said without realizing he was speaking out loud.

In the shock of the moment, he leaned back on his stool, accidentally jostling the customer behind him, causing her to slop coffee to the floor. It was the tall, tattooed, blue-haired girl with a face full of silver studs.

"Sorry," he said. "I was startled by something I read."

"Are you leaving?" she asked, ignoring his apology.

"Yes."

She slid her long legs atop the stool before he could clear his own legs from under the counter. Outside, he turned toward the Port of Haifa.

Still speaking out loud, he said: "Time to get the hell out of the Holy Land."

# CHAPTER TWENTY-FIVE

The dirty white ship loomed at the far end of the wharf.

Check-in was handled in stages, each with tighter security than the previous. At the main front desk, ungoverned queues bulged with impatient passengers dropping luggage for the embarkation obstacle course. Harried clerks verified passports and processed credit cards at the first line. The second stage was managed by a throng of surly men scanning bags with bomb sniffing dogs and randomly opening a select few. Cabin numbers were assigned so that every bag could be separated from its owner and carted away for X-ray before shipboard delivery. The photo session was next. Every man and woman stood for a snapshot, followed by issuance of room key cruise cards labeled "YOUR PASSAGE TO MAGIC."

But not all were in the security gauntlet. That parking lot attendant was correct. At the far side of the crowd, out of earshot of those who'd already paid, was a row of hagglers looking for last-minute deals. There, clerks behind a portable counter did a lot of head shaking and making universal gestures that said, *It's the best I can offer, I'm afraid that's simply not possible*, and finally, *I'll tell you what I can do.*

Teagarden considered turning and trudging back to Ilan and Elad's Roaster Café. What was he thinking? Two full days at sea? It would make him the clichéd "sitting duck." Plus, they're only taking credit cards. He thought of retooling the whole plan. Was it possible to take a train from Israel to Europe? He doubted it. Just as he doubted he could drive a rental car north through

Lebanon, Syria, and Turkey. With all his cash, maybe he could charter a small plane.

"May I help you sir?"

Teagarden noticed him when he first approached the wharf. He stood aloof in his blue blazer with brass buttons, hands behind his back, eyes intently watching everything.

"What's the casino's limit?"

It was a clever question processed so quickly it surprised even Teagarden. The man's lips twitched with interest.

"Ten thousand American on a single blackjack bet," he said. "On roulette it's twenty thousand, and there is no limit on Texas Holdem. The other games vary a bit depending on certain—"

"—Certain details like how much I'm winning or losing." The man in the blue blazer nodded slightly. "Those limits are good," Teagarden said. "Comparable to Vegas." He scanned the crowd with disapproval. "It's my first cruise and I'm a little wary. Maybe I should just head back to Ben Gurion Airport. I can gamble in Cannes where I already have an account."

"You're not yet ticketed?"

"No, and that's another issue. I'm a cash-only person. I do it that way to keep myself on a daily limit—at the tables and in life." He paused for effect. "It helps with the bad days. You see, I tend to get carried away with an Amex or MasterCard. So, tell me, does your company offer—"

"Cash accounts?"

"That's it."

"What limit, sir?"

"Five thousand American per day. I was thinking an initial deposit of twenty thousand should work."

"Right this way, sir."

Inside the small wharf office, Teagarden became a VIP. While the blue-blazered manager checked his passport, Teagarden distracted him by laying out a pile of shekels that equaled twenty-two thousand American dollars. In exchange, he received a ticket, a large VIP stateroom with a double balcony, guest passes for two

Swedish massages, clearance to the casino's private poker room, dinner for two at the Maltese Falcon steakhouse, plus complimentary champagne and cigars (to be sent to his cabin). The final step in the security gauntlet was to hoist his single piece of luggage onto a conveyer belt.

"Mr. Sanchez," the man said to Teagarden, "here is your Magic Pass. Use it to pay for all onboard services. You will find a scanner on the interior wall near your stateroom door. All you do is swipe it to summon your personal porter who serves only our four VIP suites of the Sicily Deck. His name is Theo, a fine young man from Greece who speaks fluent English. I am confident he will provide any assistance you require. Also, here is your passport and my business card. My name is Benjamin Adoram. I will not be with you on this cruise, though I am constantly in touch with the ship. It is my responsibility. Should issues arise, do not hesitate to contact me here in Haifa."

Teagarden gave him an overly generous tip of five hundred dollars in shekels.

"By the way," Adoram continued, "your cabin is The Taormina Stateroom. It is the finest of the four."

"Your accent is not Israeli."

"It is Hebrew that I speak with an accent. I'm American born. Queens, New York. The Mets are still my team."

"Yankees for me. I'll bet your dad took you to the eighty-six World Series."

"One of the finest moments of my life. I was six years old, in nosebleed seats behind first base for game six when poor Bill Buckner reaffirmed the Curse of the Bambino."

They smiled like brothers-in-arms as Adoram tugged Teagarden's bag from the conveyor belt after it briefly departed his sight for scanning. He placed it on the floor and flipped up the handle.

"I'll call a porter to handle your bag."

"No thank you. I prefer to go solo."

Teagarden was intuitively concerned about Adoram but knowing why would have to wait. There was too much going on. He had to think only of safely reaching his cabin.

Though solid, the ship was old and bulky. The décor was upscale Mafia, though everything was a bit dog-eared. The name Blue Voyager reflected the color scheme of all common areas. The walls were light blue, the carpeting medium blue with dark blue borders. His cabin was spacious: galley kitchen, large sitting room, bedroom with king-sized bed, balcony that ran the length of both rooms, and a bathroom with soaking tub and shower large enough to fit two comfortably.

(Sam)
If only you were here with me. Shower. Sex. Sleep. And a cruise on the Mediterranean. How's that sound?

(Cynthia)
Hmmm.

(Sam)
Maybe soon.

(Cynthia)
I've never taken a cruise.

(Sam)
Neither have I.

(Cynthia)
How about the Caribbean in the fall?

(Sam)
Yes, let's do.

He shut the balcony curtains, hung out the do not disturb sign, double-locked the door, found the remote, and powered up the large-screen television. After repeated clicks, the first English-language news channel he found was the BBC. Two more victims of the New York attack had died of their injuries, bringing the total dead to sixteen. The newscaster also had an update on seven-year-old "Little Girl Blue." Doctors said her condition was "extremely dire," though she was still "clinging to life with massive internal injuries."

"I'm sorry, for all of them," Teagarden said to the television screen. "I hope that little girl pulls through."

The newscaster on the Beeb moved on to the weather, first the British Isles, then the continent where northern France could expect heavy showers followed by unseasonably pleasant temps. While listening, he examined his luggage, which was only briefly out of his sight during X-ray screening. Everything was where it should be. The cash was wrapped in rubber bands and tucked inside his toiletry kit, and the dismantled plastic gun remained tucked into a side pocket.

Satisfied, he again spoke aloud, "Time for a hot shower." He wondered if talking to himself was symptomatic of extreme stress. "Well, if it is evidence of PTSD, that's why God invented hot water and chilled scotch."

Under the four pulsating heads, the Medium Base 22 makeup and eyeliner quickly washed off. He watched the beige coloring circle the drain between his feet, making him wonder if it was even necessary. His conclusion was—maybe not. So far, there'd been only two factors aiding his escape. The first was a pure run of luck in the tunnels at Megiddo, aka Armageddon. The second was the universal language—cash. Like Robinson Crusoe's rock-wrecked ship, that box of money was a gift. And like Robinson, he intended to make certain it was a gift that kept on giving.

While luxuriating under the powerful twin showerheads, a man's face suddenly bubbled from his subconscious, appearing as a spectral image, like an omen. Ironically, it wasn't any of the dead men. Neither was it any of the suicide victims, or the mysterious master killer, Elad. Rather, it was the face of the Queens-born

Israeli-American, Benjamin Adoram. And Teagarden knew why. He'd told Adoram that the Yankees were his team. But at the time, he wasn't Teagarden, he was Sanchez. And Sanchez was from Oxnard, California, which Adoram saw on his passport, therefore he would almost certainly be an Angels or Dodgers fan.

Oh, crap!

He was still trying to shake the voices of self-blame when he heard, or thought he heard, his own name being spoken by a man's voice. It made everything else between his ears go silent.

He dog-listened for further utterance that sounded like a human voice speaking the words "Sam Teagarden." When it came again, it was softer and more distant. And this time, it was a female voice.

He pushed the silver lever topped by a knob of cubic zirconia to shut the hot water. The television droned in the background. When the voice speaking his name came a third time, he realized *that* was the source. His name was being spoken by reporters on the BBC.

Bracing himself for news about the dead at Megiddo, he walked naked and dripping wet from bathroom, through the bedroom, to the main sitting room, where he stood in shock. It was *not* about Megiddo. The network was airing a full-court presser at the White House. The lower-third graphic read, "LIVE PRESIDENTIAL NEWS CONFERENCE."

"Look," the president of the United States said, "all I can tell you at this point is that our various intelligence agencies are lending all possible cooperation to our allies to figure out what's going on with these horrible suicides. And we're—"

"But Mr. President," the camera cut to a female reporter in the audience, "my question was, 'What has been learned so far from that cooperation, and what was the strategic reasoning behind dispatching Columbia University math professor Sam Teagarden to Israel?'" The camera cut back to the presidential podium in the West Wing Briefing Room.

"Well, ha, now listen, umm, that's a very clever, you know, question." Noticeably uncomfortable, POTUS looked away to gather his thoughts. "I don't know where you get your information, Ms. Ellison. I never said that Professor Teagarden was in Israel. And if he was, I wouldn't confirm it. What I can confirm, and all that I will confirm at this particular point in time, is that the man widely respected for decoding the Dear John File a few years back is now providing valuable assistance to our intelligence services and lending a hand on this horrible matter."

No fewer than a dozen voices suddenly shouted, clamoring to be the next recognized questioner. Teagarden heard words and phrases like, "abroad with the CIA," "seen in Jerusalem," "recent bloodshed," "Church of the Holy Sepulchre," "next destination," and "atheist movement." The president affected a casual glance around the boisterous gathering and pointed to a disheveled man holding a reporter's pad in one hand and a ballpoint pen in the other.

"You're my next victimizer," the president announced to a smattering of polite laughter. The lower third identified the reporter as Paul Rittenhaur of *The New York Times.*

"Sir, is CIA assistance from a civilian known for his decryption skills an indication that, yes, an ancient document has in fact been uncovered that relates to the whole matter of the suicides, and that, yes, that document is encoded?"

The president smiled. "No, that is not an indication of any particular 'yes.' And, no, I did not cite the CIA in particular as investigating anything at all."

The next reporter named Sheila McGovern, from *The Los Angeles Times,* changed the subject to the February terror attack in Manhattan. She wanted to know if there was any truth to a rumor that the FBI had discovered a domestic terror group retaliating against the recent national ban on assault weapons.

"The FBI is hard at work in all metropolitan areas," the president said, avoiding a straight answer. "They're tracking down every possible clue and are cautiously optimistic that they're making sound progress. Meantime, Ms. McGovern, it's important for all Americans to be cautious on this issue, while conducting business as usual and not let these fears disrupt their normal routine."

The press corps didn't like the answer and again began shouting for more specificity. Teagarden didn't like the answer either, but instead of shouting, he turned off the television and spoke quietly to himself: "Unfortunately, there's nothing normal about my current business routine."

He downed his sea sickness pill and took two swigs of lukewarm scotch from Master Sergeant Sanchez's flask. Without returning to the bathroom to towel off, he pulled back the comforter and sheet, fluffed the pillow, and climbed in. It was obvious that details of the dead at Megiddo had not yet filtered through the news machine. When he woke, the murder of three CIA operatives, Deacon Nasri, and a dozen archeology students would probably be a banner headline. He could only hope against hope that his presence onboard the Blue Voyager would not be part of the story.

"As Scarlett O'Hara once said, 'Tomorrow is another day.'" He clicked off the light. In the dark, he spoke again. "That was weird. Why am I quoting *Gone with the Wind*? Lord, I hope I'm not cracking up."

# INSIDE THE CRISIS BUBBLE
## CHAPTER TWENTY-SIX

*Thursday, March 20, 2025*

He slept straight through to the next morning, which his mind and body desperately needed. Another shower and fresh clothing helped make him feel reborn. Tuning the television to the BBC again, there was still no mention of mass murder at Megiddo. The major headlines focused on Manhattan's terror attack in February. The rumor that the bomber was linked to a wider domestic terror group was apparently nearing official confirmation. There was also a follow up on Little Girl Blue who was still clinging to life but "according to doctors, showing modest signs of improvement."

"That's a good omen," he said to the television screen. "Hang in, Little Girl Blue."

Needing to clear his head from such a long and deeply anesthetizing sleep, he visited the ship's uppermost deck, picking up coffee and a buffet breakfast roll along the way. Once on the Sky Deck, he found a glorious new day waiting. The ship was headed due west and the still-rising sun was chasing the stern. He stood at the railing, eating buttered bread, sipping hot coffee, inhaling salt-sea air, and feeling the warm spray rise and fly into his face. Under differing circumstances, he would have indulged in the moment with great enjoyment.

Score another truth for the parking lot attendant in Haifa.

That bored young parking attendant was correct about the throttle being opened for a hard bolt to Venice. It wasn't the weather causing the ship to pitch and yaw. It was the speed. Off the bow, the horizon visibly rose and fell as the ship rolled on its main axis. That young man was also bang-on about people getting sick. The proof was directly behind him where two men were sprawled in recliners, their jaws gaping and eyes bulging, wishing they could vomit their vertigo from body and brain. At that moment, a woman staggering like a drunken sailor dropped into a heap on a lounge directly behind him. She looked as though she'd prefer death to the misery she was suffering. From the other direction, a porter approached. He toted towels and a tray holding ice and a water pitcher. The two men waved him away. The woman who'd just arrived spoke loudly enough for Teagarden to hear:

"Been looking for you."

"Sorry, ma'am. I am here now."

"More prescription-strength Dramamine, please. Tell Niccolò it's for me. He knows me and will respond quickly."

"Yes ma'am. I'll summon Dr. Almonti right away." He placed his tray on the nearest table and withdrew his cell phone to send a text. "Your appointment is confirmed," he said afterward. "The doctor will come here to the Sky Deck immediately. Meanwhile, would you like some water or a towel?"

She raised just enough to give a languid head shake, then flopped back to the pillow. Not wanting to stare, Teagarden turned away. He looked again at the rolling sea. He once suffered seasickness and knew it to be a cruel combination of vertigo, hangover, and stomach flu. That experience was the reason he knew to purchase plenty of OTC medication in advance.

"Mr. Sanchez?" It took Teagarden a moment to realize he was being addressed by the same young porter. Teagarden looked and nodded. "Sir, just to advise, Dr. Niccolò Almonti will be passing this area very soon if you require any medication for the rough sea."

"No, thank you," Teagarden said. "I'm fine."

"Very good sir. And, just to let you know, a delivery of cigars and champagne has been made to your cabin. Compliments of my supervisor, Mr. Adoram. I waited until your do not disturb tag was removed to make delivery. I hope you enjoy, sir."

Like all Tricolore employees, he wore crisp khaki slacks and a turquoise pullover with three bright stripes on one sleeve: red, white, and green, the colors of the Italian flag. On him, however, the outfit was more than a uniform. He wore it uniquely well, like a dancer, like Gene Kelly in *An American in Paris*. This young man's demeanor made a statement to the world that said he was gay, proud, and unencumbered by any troubles about the advertised message. Teagarden checked his name tag: Theo Kanakaris.

"Thank you, Theo. Mr. Adoram spoke of you. You handle the four staterooms on the Sicily Deck."

"Yes sir. It is my job to assist. I am on call twenty-four-seven. My number is on your cabin phone, listed as 'Porter on Call.' Or you can simply swipe your cruise card on the e-pad just inside your door. My own studio cabin is between Syracuse and Palermo, which means I am close. I am one of the few ship's employees allowed to reside on an upper deck among the guests."

Teagarden was impressed by the young man's natural confidence. "I'm guessing you're between college semesters," he said.

"Yes sir. I resume graduate studies in September, thanks to what I earn here. I have one more year to finish my diploma."

"Where?"

"I stayed home for my undergraduate work at the University of Athens. I am proud to say I am now between years at Oxford. After finishing there, I hope to become a professor of Hellenic studies, which is my heritage. Perhaps I will eventually work at home in Greece. Maybe Italy or Great Britain. Now I am very happy to be with an Italian company that travels the Mediterranean from Israel to Gibraltar. For me, it is exciting to see and explore the same lands once trod by my pioneer ancestors."

Hellenic studies. Oxford. Wow.

"Right. Thanks for delivering cigars and champagne. I'll catch up with you." It was Teagarden's signal that he'd tip him later.

"Of course," Kanakaris said. "Also, there was a package, a last-minute delivery before departure."

"A package?"

"Yes sir. A large envelope. I left that in your cabin as well. On the cocktail table, sir."

After a pause, Teagarden said: "Did you notice who dropped it off?" He tried not to seem alarmed, though he was.

"I regret to say I do not know. I can assure you however, Mr. Sanchez, that it was screened for safety in our ship's mailroom."

The porter had picked up on his concern but misunderstood its nature. Teagarden wasn't worried about anthrax-laced envelopes or package bombs. He was worried about someone else knowing he was on board.

After exchanging a few more words, the porter departed. Teagarden wanted to hurry back to inspect this mysterious package, but fearing it would reveal his anxiety, he remained a while longer. He turned again to the rail and the vast sea to consider the facts. It was apparent that cruise supervisor Benjamin Adoram had briefed Theo, not only on Sanchez's VIP status, but also on his generosity when tipping. Because of it, Teagarden expected to encounter more shipboard servitude during the next two days. But—

A package?! Okay, settle down. Probably nothing to worry about.

He looked to see if anyone was eyeing him. The sick men were still there, still limp with the agony of vertigo. A man wearing a white tunic was sitting at the foot of the woman's recliner. He leaned in to speak softly to her. Clearly this was Dr. Niccolò Almonti. Other than that, no one was around.

He decided the package was probably another gift from Adoram after he saw his tip. Most likely an additional welcome with excursion tickets, perhaps a complimentary gondola tour of the Venetian canals. If so, it would be for two. The thought of it made him think again of his partner. If she were with him, they would enjoy the cruise and all port calls.

(Sam)
I miss you, Cyn.

(Cynthia)
And I you.

(Sam)
This is not what you imagined for me when we kissed goodbye in New York, is it?

(Cynthia)
No, I'm afraid not.

(Sam)
Is it okay that I'm imagining you're here with me? Talking to me? Helping me?

(Cynthia)
Yes. It's fine, Sam. We'll solve this thing together.

(Sam)
I'm glad. Still, it's a little worrisome.

(Cynthia)
Don't be concerned about it. You're only trying to cope.

In between the rolling swells, he caught sight of another cruise ship heading in the same direction. It was pacing the Blue Voyager and appeared to be a twin, probably another Tricolore vessel that departed Tel Aviv at the same time the Blue Voyager departed Haifa. Once in Italian waters, he guessed they alternated port visits. He'd been to Italy before. If there was any nation on Earth that had the industry of tourism down solid, it was Italy. Unfortunately, the restaurants and shops that depend on tourism tend to take vast hordes of travelers for granted, and the Italian citizens are so jaded with roving masses of Japanese, English, Germans, and Americans, they don't seem to notice them on the streets. Still, he considered it a great and romantic land.

Uh-oh. Don't get too relaxed. Remember, this is not a leisure trip.

At that moment, his math students were probably in places like Key West, Miami Beach, West Palm, or maybe the Caribbean. All, that is, except Aken Okeke, who said he was going to his home country, Namibia. And how was the mathematics professor spending his spring break? Answer: running from dueling terrorist groups, one pro Q, the other anti Q.

So far, it appeared that he'd be safe for these two days at sea. That meant he could rest and clear his mind. Though he needed to get a message to his wife, and by extension, to Supervisory Special Agent Bernard Klassen, who would be out of the hospital by then and recuperating at home. If the FBI and CIA were smart, they'd have arranged some sort of confidential messaging system. Unfortunately, they weren't, because he was only window dressing, and therefore they hadn't.

He decided the best way to get out a message was to have someone on board send an email to a neighbor in the Catskills, then ask that neighbor to print the message for hand delivery to Blair. That's one way to get around the challenge posed to spy agencies when it comes to monitoring global Internet communications.

Yeah, right. Who can I trust on board this ship?

His answer: no one.

Okay, enough waiting. Time to go.

When he turned, the two seasick men were still in their respective recliners, still suffering miserably. The woman, however, was gone. Dramamine doesn't act that quickly, so he assumed the doctor escorted her to the infirmary or back to her cabin.

# CHAPTER TWENTY-SEVEN

In his main sitting room, the champagne was chilled in a free-standing bucket. The box of a half dozen Cuban cigars sat on the side table with a note boasting "hecho a mano" quality. The package in question was on the coffee table between the two couches, a large manila envelope nearly two inches thick. There was no postage, which meant it was hand-delivered. In elegant lettering, the address read:

Mr. Sanchez
Taormina Stateroom

He opened the securely taped envelope and withdrew a second envelope with a wide metal clasp. Inside he found many pages of photo-quality paper and spread them out on the table, couches, and side chairs. Each was labeled Fragmento followed by numbers spelled out in Spanish: "Fragmento Uno," "Fragmento Dos," to the final page, "Fragmento Diecisiete." It didn't take a linguist to know that there were seventeen remnants. Neither was there any question as to why they were labeled in Spanish. It was because they originated with Dr. Pablo Zurbarán of the University of Santiago de Compostela, whom Elad boasted of murdering. Nor did Teagarden have to call upon his PhD in advanced mathematics to know that he was looking at reproduced images of the original Q Document uncovered at Megiddo.

"Holy of holies," he muttered, glancing from one thick

photocopied page to the other.

All of them were images of preserved scraps of ancient text. The first thirteen ran on for multiple pages. Many had preserved passages of text in paragraph form, while the majority held only fractions of copy, a few lines of lettering on disintegrated parchment, like the Dead Sea Scrolls. The seventeenth was not only the last, but also the shortest.

He picked them up one at the time. He couldn't be certain of the language, though guessed it was ancient Greek like the If and If arch in the tunnel. He held up the first photographed page of the first remnant to the brilliant light pouring into his stateroom from the balcony. It was clear from the image that the originals were fragile. The black ink was faded, and the paper, or papyrus, had decayed to a yellowish brown. Even without being able to read a word, the letters themselves stirred a sense of awe, like gazing at the stars on a clear night.

"Yeah, but *suicide?*" he whispered to the pages. "Why do you inspire cult barbarity around the world?"

That was his mission. He was assigned the job of examining these documents to discover an explanation for mass suicide made cultural trend with the goal of helping end the self-destructive bloodletting. That enigma, he knew, could be solved only with translation. And because the words were encrypted, they'd have to be translated first, and decrypted second.

"Nuh-uh," he murmured. "I am not the man for this job. I speak only one language."

The folly of the FBI's casting him as window dressing for Operation Five O'clock and sending him to hook up with the CIA was now more apparent than ever. He doubted they'd ever admit their screw up, which meant flash-mob suicide would continue around the world. That, in turn, meant Elad would continue trying to kill him and anyone who came to his assistance including agents of the FBI and CIA.

Whoa.

That's when it dawned on him. Even if they knew he was on

board, there was no way the package was from Klassen. The FBI would never send him the Q Doc package. Neither would Elad, the Vatican, nor any other religious group want him to receive a copy of the fragments.

Therefore, it had to come from the one other faction he knew owned a horse in the race: FFG, Freedom from God.

"Great. They may be on my side, but that's nothing to brag about."

So, how'd they know I'm on this creaky ship?

That was the new mystery. Who among the FFG movement knew he was on the Blue Voyager and using the name Sanchez? And where were they at that moment?

He sat on the long balcony that spanned the length of his state-room. With the photocopies stacked in his lap, he flipped through them again and again while running down possible candidates who knew of his whereabouts. Of those he'd encountered since deciding to buy a cruise ticket less than one day earlier, there was the parking lot attendant in Haifa; Benjamin Adoram, the American-Israeli boarding supervisor on the dock; Theo Kanakaris, the porter on call; and Niccolò Almonti, the ship's doctor. As for all others operating in the background, the list was truly endless. He'd read that new GPS chips could be as small as a grain of rice. Something that tiny could easily be slipped into a pocket or dropped into a pants cuff. Hell, it could even be secreted into someone's food.

Knowing it was silly, yet unable to resist, he stood to search all pockets and cuffs. Nothing. As for food, he'd mostly lost all appetite. There had been only coffee and a buttered roll that morning and those greasy egg sandwiches the previous morning. It was unlikely that the cautious clerk at Shimon's Eleven was on the payroll for the FBI, Vatican, FFG, or Mossad.

On the other hand, that guy *was* in Israel. It's not unfair to say that Israel is peopled by the most intensely cautious population on Earth. And the clerk who took his food order did take a pro-longed measure of his appearance. Consequently, he wondered how long a mini-GPS, once ingested, would remain in the system. Enough!

Maybe he wasn't being unduly paranoid. Still, being so distracted only made him more vulnerable. In the end, he settled on Benjamin Adoram as the likeliest suspect. As ticketing supervisor on the wharf, he was clearly a smart man. He could probably size up the motives of any passenger with a glance: gambler, tourist, carouser, even terrorist. And there was that screw-up about the Yankees. Still, the theory didn't explain how an employee of the Tricolore Line, FFG member or not, would come to possess a copy of the Q Document.

He turned back to the pages. The letters were carefully inked by a steady hand with minimum spacing between words. The lines of copy were well formed and perfectly straight from side to side. Where the pages were nearly whole, there were one-inch margins all around. He wondered if it read from left to right like English, or right to left like Hebrew and Arabic.

As for penmanship, the words did not have the cursive rush of scribbled lines that, to the untrained eye, made Hebrew and Arabic resemble abstract art. He considered that proof that the language was Greek. Then again, it could be Aramaic, the language widely believed to be spoken by Jesus.

It didn't matter. Once the language was determined, how could he decode it without being able to read or speak it? It was impossible. It would be like asking him to solve a word puzzle in complete darkness.

Here's a pencil. Here's the London Times crossword puzzle.

And-d-d...lights out! Get to work. Chop, chop. We'll be waiting outside. Hope it doesn't take long. It shouldn't. After all, you're the legendary Sam Teagarden.

Yeah, right. Good luck to me.

Below his cabin on the port side, the sea churned under the speeding hull. The pacing sister ship was on the opposite side and couldn't be seen. In the distance, there was only the deep, grayish-blue of the Mediterranean. Farther on, the coloring changed to consistently darker shades of gray until, where the water met the horizon, it was black.

He studied the shortest photographed text, Fragmento Diecisiete, which held only a few words. Among them was the line:

Επιλέξαμε αυτόν τον εργάτη

Somehow, the characters felt drawn from something he'd seen before, even something he could understand, where all other pages inspired only blankness. Perhaps with a computer he'd have beginner's luck, but he dared not log on as Teagarden, and he doubted the ship provided a publicly anonymous login like the café in Haifa.

Back inside, he tossed all pages to the table, couches, and chairs. This was spooky. So spooky, he feared it could be bait for another purpose. Against all odds, he'd made it safely aboard the Blue Voyager, yet now it seemed supernatural that some unknown actor was aware of his presence and playing him like a marionette.

What if it wasn't FFG, but someone pretending to be FFG with the motive of luring him to a private corner of the ship's railing where he'd disappear overboard? It happens all the time on cruise ships where there is no law, no police, no governing jurisprudence. Who would investigate his MIA status—the Israelis? The Italians? The FBI didn't even know where he was. The thought of moving about the ship's decks chilled him. He closed the balcony doors and pulled the drapes, then secured the internal dead bolt on the main door.

He picked up the pages.

He plopped into one of the cushy chairs in the parlor to study the Q Doc from a different perspective. It occurred to him that the secret might exist visually, rather than linguistically. Instead of translating the words from the original language to English and then decoding the puzzle, perhaps he could solve the mystery if it lay in patterns of characters and spaces. It's been done before with braille, semaphore, basic computerized binary, and even Morse code. It may be farfetched for a document dating to the first century, but it was worth considering.

Working to eliminate that as a possibility, he scoured every page of the Q Doc with such meticulousness that his eyes went blurry and his shoulders tensed with cramps.

# CHAPTER TWENTY-EIGHT

Hours later, an out-of-place noise made him snap from his daylong obsession. It was a soft scraping sound from the entryway of his cabin that sounded like footfall on the carpet.

Someone else is inside this suite with me!

He froze with red alert, the type of universal caution known to every sleeper who awakens in the night when an unfamiliar noise reverbs through the house. He listened intently, waiting for it to repeat.

There was plenty of ambient sound. The balcony doors were tightly closed, yet the rush of wind and rolling sea was audible. The ship's old motor churned at top speed, causing a mechanized strain in the bowels that could be heard everywhere as a distant growl. The snail-shaped tubes inside his inner ear also felt the pitch and yaw wrought by twin propellers grinding hard in the ancient waters of the Mediterranean Sea.

Well?

He waited. The photographed pages were now scattered across the two couches. A long slit of crepuscular light passed through the crease where the drapes were pulled shut. He knew from the quality of the glimmer that it marked the end of daylight, what movie makers call the magic hour.

In the opposite direction was the foyer where, if someone was standing, he'd know it. He'd feel their presence.

Wouldn't I?

In his heightened state of alert, he'd probably hear their heartbeat.

Yes, of course I would.

He leaned forward to peer into the bedroom where he could see the outline of his luggage on the rack and which held the dismantled firearm.

Never mind that. What am I going to do, tell Elad to wait a moment while I snap my gun together?

He gave it another minute. Then two. Then three.

(Cynthia)
Really, Sam?

(Sam)
What? I'm thinking, I'm thinking. When I'm done thinking—I'll do.

(Cynthia)
(Sigh) Don't overthink it. And don't put so much faith in that silly firearm. You're Sam Teagarden. You don't outshoot villains. You outsmart them.

(Sam)
Sure, but don't I have to think before doing?

(Cynthia)
I think the time has come to do. You're on a ship, Sam. A ship at sea is a wonderful metaphor. Don't you agree?

(Sam)
So, it's time for me to act within a metaphor? Shall I be a verb or an adverb?

(Cynthia)
Oh, Sam, stop. A ship at sea is a journey of life, a whole world traveling though the cosmos. By

being smart and taking action, this is your opportunity to alter the course of that world.

(Sam)
I love you.

(Cynthia)
Be smart, Sam. I love you too.

He clicked the lamp from low illumination to medium, to high, then stood and walked to the foyer.

*There's no one here but me. So why am I embarrassed?*

The noise was caused by an envelope slipped under the tight space at the bottom of the cabin door. It made the same scraping noise when he tugged it free. It was addressed to him. He opened the flap:

Mr. Sanchez,
As our special guest, you are cordially invited to join us in the private Cielo Blue Room of the casino. Complimentary drinks, buffet, and other amenities are yours to enjoy.
Best wishes,
Sicily Deck Steward, Theo Kanakaris

*They do want me to gamble, don't they?*

It was understandable. Sleeping all night then disappearing to his cabin all day meant he'd been a casino no-show. To Benjamin Adoram's way of thinking, he was overdue. The entertainment end of the cruise business wanted him to lose the twenty thousand he had in their bank, then kick in with another twenty.

Teagarden decided that spending some time at the tables could work to his advantage. If the messenger who delivered the Q Doc was on board, he or she would see him there and likely initiate contact. That might lead to a working partnership. On the other hand, what if the package was delivered by Elad with the motive of making him panic and do something stupid?

He wouldn't kill me in the casino, would he?

The answer was—yes. If sociopaths were movie stars, Elad would be an A-list box office draw tapped straight from the Middle Ages. He'd kill everyone on board if he had to. Yet it seemed a chance Teagarden had to take. He couldn't hide in his cabin until the ship reached Venice. Besides, if Elad really were on board, he'd figure a way to get to him no matter where he hid.

Teagarden reassembled the Q Doc pages into the manila envelope and locked it in the cabin's safe. He set the combination to 7777, which he'd easily remember because the letter Q was assigned the number seven on the phone dial. He withdrew the sports jacket carefully packed by his wife inside the luggage side flap designed to prevent wrinkling. It was a stylish brand from a boutique shop she purchased the day before his departure. He put it on for the first time to find it a perfect fit. She knew his clothing size better than he did.

"Thanks, Cynthia. For you, I'll even wear socks today."

He reached into the luggage and withdrew the plastic bag filled with gun parts, then sat on the bed and snapped the gray interlocking components together. Never a firearm enthusiast, he found something oddly exciting about watching it come together: two internal rods and two thick springs that had to be inserted into half a frame, short barrel, two-piece frame, three-piece handle, boxy-shaped bullet chamber that toggled back and forth for loading, trigger guard, and finally a durable trigger. After full assembly, the only remaining task was insertion of five light gray missiles.

He dropped the weapon to the pocket of his sports coat. Next, he retrieved the sunglasses taken from the Ford's glove box and one cigar from the complimentary Cubans.

All right, let's go play sitting duck and lose some money.

# CHAPTER TWENTY-NINE

The casino's exclusive Cielo Blue room was for high rollers in a galley cut off from the main crowd. That didn't work. He needed to hide in plain sight. He needed to see and be seen. It was such a necessary tactic it made him wonder if it was part of the FBI curriculum at the training academy in Quantico and spy school at Langley. Both towns were in northern Virginia, where his friend Stuart Shelbourne and his son were murdered by a black ops FBI team in 2019.

That's an ugly memory. Stop thinking about the past.

With each passing minute he regretted accepting this new job. He again contemplated breaking his silence to contact Agent Klassen in New York with a resignation notice.

Hey Klassen, people are getting killed and I'm coping with full-blown PTSD. You come over here and deal with Elad. He's more than ex-Mossad. He's the sorcerer of assassination.

He stopped his rumination with the same ugly reality. If he alerted Klassen, it would mean more bloodletting. More murder. More suicide. So long as Teagarden was alive, Elad would do his job.

No way. Never again. There will be no more Megiddo-style attacks. Just do what you're in this gambling den to do—gamble!

Back in the main casino, he cruised the perimeter. Though small, it offered a wide choice of currency options. Each table played chips pegged to a particular currency. If you bought your chips with shekels, you played at a shekel table; with dollars, at a dollar table. Even at that early evening hour, all table games and slots were jammed elbow to elbow with players. Some slot machine gamblers were so intently focused on their machine they appeared to be break-dancing to the rhythm of rolling tumblers, clinking payouts, and the clamor of universal *kah-chinking*. Teagarden wondered if the noise wasn't prerecorded special effects blasted by hidden speakers to influence the crowd with manufactured excitement.

Looking for the best game to suit his needs, he took a close look at the geography of men and women hoping to exchange small amounts of money for big amounts of money. Blackjack was no good. Players of that game perched in high chairs around semicircular tables facing only one direction. That would restrict his study of the wider crowd and limit his ability to judge eyes and gauge body language. Baccarat, with a similarly shaped console, presented the same problem. Craps was a better option because gamblers stand and shuffle around a communal table, making it easy to keep a steady watch on players and onlookers. Problem was, he had no idea how to play craps. Nearby, another crowd gathered around the smaller roulette table, a game so simple even a PhD in advanced mathematics could grasp it.

All right, American dollars at the roulette table it is.

He decided to make his effort noticeable by withdrawing the full twenty thousand. He presented his cruise card at the house bank where he asked for ten one-thousand-dollar and a hundred one-hundred-dollar chips. The one-grand chips were a rich shade of yellow, like gold doubloons; the more common c-chips were reflective black. At the table, the colors of his stacks earned immediate regard from the players and sluggish croupier.

Okay, that's cool. Gold and black were my high school colors in Rockland County, New York. Maybe it's a favorable omen.

He broke them into stacks of ten, each held tight by finely cut grooves at the edges and each standing a mere one and a half inches. After betting two blacks, the table earned visits from the pit boss, crew boss, and floor manager who eyeballed him and his chips. Seeing nothing improper, they retreated to positions that allowed tag-team supervision with a pretext of indifference.

It didn't take long for the other gamblers to animate. He had a run of beginner's luck they greeted with raucous cheering. His twenty grand became twenty-five, then thirty. The other players followed his lead by stacking their chips atop his. Every time he won, the dealer presented the winnings with praise: "Congratulations, Mr. Sanchez," "Very nice, Mr. Sanchez," and, "Nice decision, indeed, Mr. Sanchez."

Instead of asking if he'd like to order a drink, the cocktail waitress brought him a tray crowded with a selection of freshly prepared beverages. "Mr. Sanchez, please help yourself, compliments of the house." She pointed to each glass as though describing a dessert tray. "Here I have Jack Daniels on the rocks, this is Johnny Walker Double Black, then Murphy's, and Balvenie. Over here, these are Ketel One and Grey Goose vodkas. And finally, for bourbon, I have Maker's Mark and Knob Creek."

Ah, yes—booze. After human stupidity, it's the casino's best friend.

Every player watched him. The waitress had a plunging V-neck bodice revealing generous cleavage, but her outfit was not as tasteless as Atlantic City. Instead of short-shorts or a miniskirt, she wore black slacks.

"Or," the waitress continued, "if you prefer any other cocktail or fine wine, I can—"

"I'll take them all."

He expected her to be annoyed. Instead, she gave an agreeably wide smile and a nod as she passed each glass to him, one by one. After accepting each drink, he moved it on to another gambler.

"Thank you, here you are. Thank you, here you are."

He said it nine or ten times as his arms worked like a production line. When all "thank you's" stopped and all drinks were passed, Teagarden put a black chip on the waitress' tray.

"Thank you, Mr. Sanchez." She dipped her cleavage as she stepped away.

The dealer flicked the ball into the circular groove, causing a low whirring noise that started everyone reaching arm over arm to place bets. In between, Teagarden placed a single thousand-dollar chip of golden yellow onto seventeen black, and a second of equal value on a side bet for one to eighteen.

They both lost.

As the croupier collected losing bets and paid out small gains to the few winners, the other gamblers eyed Teagarden while he eyed the surrounding crowd. There was nothing of interest. Not one person drew his attention.

Okay, let's do that again.

"Place your bets," the croupier called.

This time, Teagarden chose red number one and a side bet of nineteen to thirty-six for his bet of two bright yellows. The jumble of crisscrossing arms followed his lead as gamblers dropped coins of colored plastic atop his selections and elsewhere with the randomness of pop artists placing paint.

Again, both bets lost, which put him down four thousand dollars. If it were his own money, it would hurt. Because it wasn't, he enjoyed it. As the crowd thickened, he lost view of the wider room, forcing him to concentrate on only the closest faces. Still, nothing caught his attention, not even vague recognition.

"Place your bets, ladies and gentlemen."

As the wheel spun, and interlacing arms weaved in and out, he finally spotted a suspect. She'd paused earlier at the back of the crowd where he caught a brief sidelong glimpse, though he saw nothing familiar about her at the time. Now, she reappeared at the front edge of the crowd, where she took an interest in the game. Her face was attractive and intelligent, with large brown eyes, high cheek bones, and short, light brown hair. Something about her sparked a sense that he'd seen her before. But that something was so remote he knew he'd never be able to name it.

Okay, now for some tactical action to back up my strategy.

On the next play he bet bigger. He placed one-thousand-dollar chips on six separate numbers, which made the crowd fall silent.

The droning hum faded as the circling ball slowed.

The croupier gave a limp arm wave. "No more bets, ladies and gentlemen."

Just ahead of the steel marble tumbling from its channel, the woman in question looked away from the spinning bowl to steal a glimpse of him.

Yes!

That did it. She was the one. No question. The timing verified it. No one, not even a thorough non-gambler, would remove their eyes from the ball at that moment. Not with six yellow doubloons on the table. There was no way she was in that casino for anything related to gambling. She was there for—*him*.

When the steel marble settled into a numbered compartment, the crowd exploded with excitement. Red nineteen! It was one of his six straight-up bets which paid thirty-five to one.

"Congratulations, Mr. Sanchez," the dealer said when the noise settled. Her eyebrows rose as high as they could possibly go on her forehead. She paid other winners first, then counted out his thirty-five yellows and pushed one straight stack nearly five inches tall toward him.

"Thank you," he said to the dealer. He tipped her two blacks and departed the roulette table to the frosty silence of the disappointed crowd, croupier, and pit boss. At the bar, he took a stool near the outdoor promenade where the final glint of the setting sun was still visible. When he turned to search the casino for the woman in question, she was nowhere to be seen.

# CHAPTER THIRTY

Maybe she's outside on the promenade.

He thought of stepping out to patrol the deck and indulging in the fine cigar he brought along.

Better not. Ms. Big Brown Eyes knows where I am. If she's the one, she'll be back.

He ordered a vodka martini straight up with an olive. When it arrived, he turned around to take the first sip while eyeing the crowd. There were lots of people, but no tall lady with searing mahogany irises.

He did, however, notice something he'd failed to spot earlier. Most gamblers were elderly females. The next demographic was elderly men. Non-elderly gamblers were equally divided among young and middle-aged, male and female. He wondered what it meant and if there was a formula to explain it. If there was, it was a certainty the cruise/casino industry knew the code and used it to maximum exploitation.

He also saw that most staffers were watching him. It wasn't constant. They weren't holding unbroken stares. Yet when not dealing, shuffling, or raking dice, the eyes of the croupiers turned repeatedly to check on him at the bar. It was the same with pit bosses, cocktail waitresses, and even the bored security guards posted at both entrances. All gazes habitually wandered back to him as if verifying, however briefly, that he was still there.

Could they all be FFG or Elad allies?

Yes, they could.

He took another sip of the martini.

Wait. There's another perfectly obvious reason.

It's the tip money. They all knew that for this loop around the Mediterranean, he was Mr. Moneybags. They knew it because Adoram told them. Not only that, but his winnings totaled nearly fifty grand, and they want to be in the gratuity line when he says "thank you" for services rendered.

Well, I hope that's why they're watching me. Either way, this paranoia is doing me no good. I've got to get off this roller-coaster ride and get home to Cynthia and my math students ASAP.

"How's your martini, sir?"

"Fine." He spun the barstool to place a black chip on the bar. "No change," he said to the bartender.

"Thank you, sir." The bartender slid a bowl of cashews closer to Teagarden. "Let me know if you need anything else, sir."

When Teagarden resumed his study of the casino, he had no trouble spotting her. She was perched two stools away, digging in her purse with distraction. In that moment, he recognized her.

Holy crap, the seasick lady!

She was the suffering woman escorted from the Sky Deck by the ship's doctor after begging for more Dramamine. Clearly, she was no longer ill.

"Excuse me," he said, "I just won enough money to buy an Italian sports car. Let me buy you a drink."

She nodded agreement. When the bartender stepped closer, she pointed to Teagarden's martini to indicate that he should make another. She wore a sleeveless black dress that displayed pronounced biceps. Her large eyes held a sexiness despite, or perhaps because of, sleepy lids that highlighted glints of copper in her brown irises. Small talk followed.

"Feeling better?"

"Yes. Dr. Almonti gave me a pill and a medicated patch." She raised her chin and pointed to an oversized band aid on her neck.

"Ah, I only took a pill," he said.

"I did too, but it wasn't enough. Niccolò gave me extra-strength tablets and patches. I felt better right away. If you're still having trouble with this two-day sprint to Venice, I have a couple of backups with me."

"Thanks. My one OTC pill worked fine." She nodded acknowledgment of his good fortune at skipping the misery of seasickness. "You're on a first-name basis with the ship's doctor. Have you taken this cruise before?"

"Yes, often. I live in Bern and am mortally frightened of aircraft. If you do frequent business in Israel as I do *and* have a fear of flying, this cruise line is the best option. From Venice, it's a tolerable train ride to Switzerland."

"It's good to see that you're feeling better. You were *really* suffering."

"Desperately," she said. "I'm uniquely prone to vertigo and always need medication. Unfortunately, I had to board without enough. Then once the sickness kicked in, my job required me to go to the Sky Deck where the ship's rocking is worse on the inner ear."

"What sort of job prevents you from stopping at a pharmacy and then compels you to go where vertigo worsens?"

"The job of following you, of course."

He was surprised only by her candor. After the bartender served her martini, she waited for Teagarden to assimilate what she said.

"How long have you—"

"Been following you?"

"Yes."

"Since Tel Aviv. I'm FFG. But you already know that."

"Yes."

"That was an FFG protest writ in blood yesterday in Jerusalem. One of two. We staged another in Rome at St. Peter's Square. From Tel Aviv, we followed you to Megiddo."

"The blue Mercedes limo?"

"That was an FFG vehicle, though I was not in it."

He listened to the slot machines rattling with *kah-chinking* sounds and the din of gamblers hoping to get lucky. In between card deals and dice tosses, the eyes of staffers continued to gaze his way. Now, in addition to minding his whereabouts, they studied him with a touch of *Aha, now there is a woman.* He imagined they were thinking that a bit of romance would follow.

"Megiddo was, was—"

"I know," she said. "Ugly."

"How do you know?"

"It's called the news." She withdrew her cell phone, the latest model manufactured by the Wutang Company of China named a DRAGON-II with an oversized foldout screen and 3D video. "Normally I rely on LOLA for my news, but you'll probably be more trusting of a mainstream source. So-o-o..." She keyed in a few strokes to pull up a site for the *Jerusalem English Dispatch* and handed him the DRAGON II. The time stamp on the article was less than one hour old. The headline read:

More Christian Bloodbath

It was just as he'd figured the night before. It took several hours for the police to find the bodies and another half day before it was released to the international networks. Teagarden put his elbows on the bar and scrolled the glass screen with his index finger to glean the basics:

> Another scene of mass death has been discovered at a place of Christian worship—this time inside the Jewish state.
>
> At least twelve bodies were found last evening piled at the side of Megiddo Church in northern Israel where a long-term excavation has been taking place. The body count is uncertain because more human remains are believed buried in the collapse of a nearby archeological tunnel. Among the dead are students from the U.S., England, and

Germany, as well as the local deacon, Father Zaid Nasri, a native of Lebanon.

Unlike other recent events of mass death at churches, authorities say this one does not appear to be exclusively suicide, though authorities believe it is somehow related.

...includes murder...

...motive unknown...

...follows yesterday's suicide carnage in Jerusalem at the Church of the Holy Sepulchre and simultaneously at St. Peter's Square in Rome's Vatican City.

...some victims may be foreign intelligence agents... no identifications yet released...

...unknown if anyone escaped...

...Corrections officers at nearby Megiddo Prison cannot help investigators as they saw nothing suspicious.

...Megiddo is believed to be the site of the first, or one of the first churches ever built...is buried on a hillside once named Armageddon, where some Christians believe the end of times will be initiated.

The only good thing was that he wasn't mentioned. Not that it mattered. After last night's presidential news conference, the whole world knew he was on the job. What the world didn't know was that he wasn't really on the job—that he was only window dressing for others who were *supposed* to be on the job but who were now dead.

Teagarden shook his head. "I'm a lucky man," he said.

"Yes. If I believed in God, which I most certainly do *not*, I would say you are more than lucky. I would say you're blessed."

"There's a hired killer named Elad. He's the Megiddo killer."

"Uh-hmm, ex-Mossad. Very dangerous." She sucked the red pimento from the olive and irritably plunked it back into the martini. "Red and green," she said. "I hate that color combo."

"You've crossed paths with Elad?"

"Not personally. We know he was hired by the Vatican to prevent decoding and publishing of the Q Document."

"If Freedom from God is such a wide network, how did Elad get past all of you to enter the compound at Megiddo?"

She sighed hard with impatience. "Simple. It was a certainty that you would go there, so he arrived ahead of us. He likely hid among nearby hills and waited for your oversized Ford with smoked windows and American license plates to roll in like the Batmobile to the rescue." She gave a mirthless laugh. "You Americans are so predictable."

When he returned her big-screen cell phone, she cleared the news article. Her default screen was a yellow circle with three black triangles, the same design on the necklace of the suicidal woman who chased him in Jerusalem. There was a difference however. This image was captioned by three words:

Freedom from God

"So, you're part of this FFG thing," he said, looking at the symbol.

Her brown orbs flashed with anger: "FFG is no mere *'thing.'* It is my life's passion and the life passion of many around the world. Your meeting will be in Berlin. Our own convention will be a week later in Rome, the home of god incorporated."

"I meant no disrespect."

"Good." She looked with affection at the symbol. "In the olden days, it was the symbol that marked radiation fallout shelters. We adopted it as the flag of the Global FFG Party because belief in God *is* radiation of the soul." She logged off the DRAGON II, folded it, dropped it into her purse, and took another sip of her drink. "You know, we stand at the precipice of the complete undoing of religion."

"All religion? As in—"

"Oh, yes, as in all of it. The Tanakh, Koran, Shruti…and every other excuse for mass murder."

"Were you at the Sepulchre courtyard?"

"I was. I videotaped the whole protest and uplinked it. That was the first time you saw me." He struggled to remember. "It was when the soldiers tried to evict spectators." He nodded with vague awareness.

"Were you the lady wearing a blue hat who shouted, 'hands off'?"

"Yes. That was my signal to Mara that we were being forcibly removed. I knew she would hear and recognize my voice."

"Who is Mara?"

"The woman at the center of our blood protest. Mara Baker-Mann. She broke free of the soldiers to chase you. She also happens to be the love of my life."

Incredulous, he turned toward her. "She's your partner? And you were prepared to watch her die?"

Instead of answering, she cocked her head at him; her twin lazy-lidded browns again flaming at the edges. Only when she saw the minute muscles of his face react with genuine repugnance did she respond.

"You must try to understand. We are in a vitally crucial moment. A true turning point."

"We?"

"Yes, we—*we*—the human race. All of us on this planet. We may finally, in *our* time, be able to rid our species of this madness called worship of God. I do not want to die by my own hand. And I certainly do not want that for my dear Mara. But we are FFG warriors prepared to make that sacrifice for the survival of the species."

"Just like the Christians who're doing the same," he said. "Just like all the Muslims who've been suicide-bombing innocents for the last seventy-five years. And now you're videotaping mass suicide and uploading it?"

This time, an expression of repugnance come over *her* face.

"I thought you were smarter than that. The whole world respects you for what you did in 2019. That took great courage. Now I see much of that is mere public perception. You need to toughen up."

"If willingness to commit suicide is your idea of being tough, no thank you, I will pass on that."

She sighed. "We do what we must. Do you have any idea how many have been murdered through the ages in the name of this relentless need to believe in mythological drivel?"

"A whole bunch?" He immediately regretted being snarky.

"Yes, a whole bunch," her own voice bled with sarcasm. "Well over two hundred billion people and counting."

That was a nice round mega number. He wondered what percentage two hundred billion was out of the total sum of people who ever lived. He didn't ask because she likely had an answer and he didn't want to hear her prattle on about numbers as though they proved her assertions. He knew numbers to be a zealot's best friend because they're impressive to an audience while seldom proving core assertions. Besides, real numbers were *his* thing, though he'd never done much work with metadata. His specialties were algebra, calculus, trig, geometry, advanced number theory, and, alas, encryption/decryption. To him, metadata was the domain of Madison Avenue gunslingers hired to wring more dollars from the American consumer, and of spies hoping to fix elections by rigging jillions of posts on MotherBoard and all the older and more passé social media sites.

"So, Jerusalem was the first time I saw you. And this morning on the Sky Deck was the second."

"Mmm, this morning on the Sky Deck was the fourth. The second was at Shimon's Eleven. I drove a white Fiat."

"The GPS on the Ford's bumper was yours."

It wasn't a question, but she answered anyway. "Yes. We attached it at Ben Gurion. When you destroyed it at the mini-mart, I moved in and planted another before you departed."

This time, it really was a question: "When you dropped your keys?"

She shrugged to indicate that it was easy. "The third time you saw me was at the coffeehouse in Haifa. You departed that PC while still logged on to the Tricolore website. You should be more careful."

"The girl with the blue hair."

"I washed it out last night and got a new cut in the ship's salon." She ran the fingers of her left hand through her hair.

"The tattoos were fake?"

"Not all of them. Maybe I'll show you the real ones later. And before you ask, the studs were totally fake, except one."

It was a pickup line, which he ignored.

"You're good at disguises."

"Very," she said. "Unlike you. You looked ridiculous in that makeup. I worried that you'd be spotted and pulled out of line. Fortunately, Israeli security in general is not as great as its rep. Now that we're here, the good news is that this ship is safe for the time being."

"Just to confirm, FFG means me no harm?"

"What?" She gripped his forearm. "Why do you think I sent you the package? We have no intention of harming you. We need your assistance with decoding the portions of the Q Document that're encrypted. And we have a deadline. The World Judeo-Christian Council opens tomorrow night in Berlin. FFG makes a presentation Sunday afternoon, directly after yours."

"Thank God you don't want to kill me."

"God has nothing to do with it."

"I'm not sure I can help."

"Listen, you may not care for our methods, but it's important for us to work together. We're both too far into this to turn back now. The Vatican will kill us both just as they killed everyone at Megiddo and Dr. Zurbarán in Spain who first decoded it."

"You're certain Elad was hired by the Vatican?"

"Oh, yes." She laughed. "We have informants deeply embedded there. When the time comes—"

"Hold on," he interrupted. "Did you say it's already decoded?"

"Yes, of course. Why do you think some Christian groups are killing themselves and the Vatican is trying to kill you? It's because they've seen the decoded truth with their own eyes. They know what it contains and do *not* want the wide world to know."

He slumped with frustration. "Then why do you need me?"

She looked around to make certain no one was close enough to eavesdrop. The bartender was at the other end speaking quietly to the same cocktail waitress who served drinks at the roulette table. No one was within easy eavesdropping proximity, yet she wasn't satisfied.

"I've been doing this too long to assume anything. May I ask you to turn and face the bar? I will lean in and speak quietly."

"Yes, all right." He decided her personality was either manic-depressive, or obsessive-compulsive, or both. Either way, she was as fired-up a zealot as he'd ever encountered. "There," he whispered, "I'm facing the bar."

She leaned toward him.

"It is obvious that your CIA and FBI allies have not fully down-loaded the basics to you. Therefore, I will now perform an info dump to your RAM load. Are you ready?"

"Yes."

"Here goes: a new codex was discovered in February inside the main tunnel at Megiddo by Dr. Pablo Zurbarán of the University of Galicia. It was written in ancient Greek, just like the so-called New Testament. But he found that a portion was encoded. He made photostats, sent the originals to the Vatican, then decoded the copies himself. After that, and naïvely believing it was in the best interest of all humanity, he emailed his work around the globe to an interdenominational group called The Ecumenical Apostles."

When an elderly gambler slowly walked behind them, she stopped speaking. After he passed, she scanned the casino. "Have you heard of a new vision and hearing technology nicknamed 'God Glasses?'"

Teagarden remembered Klassen mentioning it when using his monocle. "No," he lied. "What is it?"

"It's rumored to be a pair of eyeglasses that allows the wearer both Superman vision and Superman hearing."

"The only nifty toy I've seen so far is a GPS that color codes danger of nearby vehicles and even pedestrians."

"Right," she said, "I've seen that one." After another protective survey to detect eavesdroppers, she appeared satisfied and returned to business. "As I was saying, the professor in Spain emailed copies to a global ecumenical group that claims to be tolerant of all religious faiths. Ha! Good luck with that." Her upper lip sneered at the thought. She took a small sip of her martini. "The idea of religious tolerance among religious people is a folly that will kill us all, which is why we must kill all religion."

Teagarden steered her back to the subject. "And what did Zurbarán learn from his decryption?"

"We believe it verifies that the world's most populous religion is based on complete fraud."

"You believe? That means you're uncertain."

"The facts speak for themselves. As word of Zurbarán's work spread, believers began killing themselves. They saw the decoded Q Document with their own eyes, believed it to be the truth, and it simply hurt too much. It killed their faith, which killed their reason for living. *That* is what I know. *That* is why they committed suicide. And when *you* decode it, we will all know—for certain."

If she was correct, it explained everything. It explained the suicides among Christian-based cults, why the Vatican hired Elad to kill him, and why she wanted him as an ally. Teagarden remembered his syllogism: If Q = Doubt, and Doubt = Soul Death, then Q = Soul Death. In this case, for many cult-minded persons of faith, soul death equaled requisite suicide.

"Is your info dump finished?"

"Yes. Now you're fully downloaded."

They went silent. When the bartender cruised them again, he ordered two more martinis and again tipped with a black chip. In the interest of maintaining lucidity, he had no intention of consuming more alcohol. If it further loosened her tongue, it was fine with him because the more he learned, the better his odds of survival.

Once again, she sucked out the pimento and tossed the olive back into her cocktail glass.

"I've got to ask. What's with hating the combo of red and green?"

"They're the colors of *EX*-mas," she said with disgust.

Staring into her brown eyes, Teagarden gave an involuntary head shake. "God almighty," he whispered in disbelief.

"Don't look to him for any help," she said.

# CHAPTER THIRTY-ONE

He almost laughed when she told him her name: Gretta Wharron. It sounded like "Get a War On."

Listening to her rhetoric made him think of two lines from his favorite poem, "The Second Coming," by William Butler Yeats:

> The best lack all conviction, while the worst
> Are full of passionate intensity.

Maybe she wasn't the absolute worst, but she was so full of passionate intensity that she was scary. The only good part about making contact was learning that FFG meant him no harm and that he was safe until the Blue Voyager docked at Venice.

*At least I can breathe easy for one more day without fear of Elad the Impaler.*

Their conversation continued intermittently on the promenade where she requested they go for an e-cigarette break. She indulged in several quick pulls on a device shaped like a battery-powered nose hair trimmer that smelled of vanilla, marijuana, and burning plastic. He lit the cigar, his first tobacco indulgence in years. The lights of the pacing ship glowed in the distance.

"That's the Blue Horizon out there," Wharron said. "The company's sister ship. I've been on it. It's a duplicate of this one. It will separate at the heel of Italy and go around the toe to Naples, while we shoot straight up the Adriatic to Venice."

"I saw it earlier and figured it was another Tricolore ship."

They inhaled their respective smoking stimulants in the salty semi-darkness while he learned the basics of her life. She was Israeli born, studied philosophy in Jerusalem, theology and more philosophy at NYU, worked as a copyeditor for academic publishers, lived in Israel, New York, London, Paris, and Switzerland. Fluent in Hebrew, English, Spanish, Italian, and French, she was happily married to an English-born woman named Mara. And the fact she most wanted him and the world to know—she was prepared to die in the name of eradicating religion for the salvation of humanity. All religion. When she got going on Judaism, she was just as venomous as she was about Christianity, Islam, and all the others. She spoke of FFG as though it were a startup tech company, boasting that its membership gained more in the last five years than Christianity gained in its first five hundred, or Judaism in its first two thousand. She possessed a fast intelligence and was capable of epic run-on monologues, stopping only to briefly consult a software app called LOLA.

"Wait," he interrupted, when she mentioned it a second time. "LOLA is an app?"

"Oh, yes. It's a Personal Improvement Manager patented by FFG. It stands for 'Love of Life's Adventure.' It's owned by FFG's parent company called True Song Software, headquartered in Bern."

"I think I've heard of it."

"Sure, you have. LOLA is everywhere. It's second only to the most used PIM made by the Vatican called LoL."

"I think I've heard of that one too.

"Of course." She laughed. "That one stands for 'Love of the Lord,' which makes FFG members 'laugh out loud.'"

"I wondered."

"Most LOLA users don't even know it's related to FFG. And if they know about True Song, they don't care. They're nonbelievers without knowing they're nonbelievers."

"And LOLA really controls—"

"Everything? Yes, everything. We key in every aspect of our

lives. In return we're told what to do and when to do it. All for our own good, of course."

"Of course," Teagarden said, trying not to sound sarcastic.

She keyed-in her time spent vaping and the two martinis. In response, LOLA spoke in a softly sweet feminine voice.

"Now Gretta," it murmured, "you've reached your maximum nicotine, marijuana, and alcohol consumption for a week. Because of your recent mission progress, you are certainly entitled to bonus indulgences, to be repaid in the future through moderate self-restraint. BTW, you should consume one laxative tablet before retiring."

"Thank you, LOLA." She turned to him. "You should try it. She manages everything for me. Weight control. Cholesterol. Hydration. Sleep. Even aesthetic stimulation and orgasmic needs."

"Sounds like submission to a substitute supreme being." Again, he tried not to sound sarcastic. Still, she took offense. "Sorry," he said. "I'll keep LOLA in mind." Tiring of the cigar, he tossed it to the sea and watched the fiery tip extinguish in the mist long before it disappeared.

"Well now, back to the subject at hand," he said. "If the goal is to decode the document, the encoded version must first be translated. And that's a major complication because, as I've told you, it's quite literally Greek to me. I envy polyglots such as yourself. Unfortunately, I speak and read only one language. English. In that regard, I'm as American as they come."

It was surprising news for her and had the effect of pushing her mute button. They did several loops on the promenade in silence while she pulled harder on her e-cigarette filled with pot in violation of LOLA's instruction. When she paused to gaze at the waxing moon and contemplate the new glitch, he ducked into the casino to exchange most of his chips for euros, though he retained a handful of plastic coins for tipping.

Wharron was still absorbed in planning, smoking and stargazing when he rejoined her. They strolled past other smokers, kissing lovers, and running children playing tag on the teakwood floors.

One level up, a wedding party was dancing to "Hava Nagila." Wharron's pace fell into a vague rhythm with the song. She half-sung a few lyrics under her breath while thinking about the obstacle of translating the Q from ancient Greek:

> Hava neranenah
> Hava neranenah
> Hava neranenah ve-nismeha

Finally, she stopped and gave a nod at the distance. "You know, it's too bad I don't speak Greek, but Greece isn't so far from here."

"Don't even think it," Teagarden said. "If we transmit that document by any means to anyone, we become sitting ducks on this ship. We'll both be dead before we get a glimpse of the Grand Canal. When we're in northern Italy, there's sure to be a private linguist who can assist."

"There won't be enough time to find one. You can be certain the Vatican has a PR army working overtime. The convention in Berlin starts tomorrow, and they're probably going to label all suicides the 'inexplicable work of God's will.'"

"That's what people will want to hear," he said.

"And the believers will believe it. In time, the Vatican will publish only those passages of the Q Document that reinforce their myth. And the whole thing will fade away. We'll be left shouting words like 'coverup,' and 'conspiracy.' Do you know what history does to people who shout those words?"

"Yeah-h-h, I know," he said on a long exhale. "You become a Wikipedia entry or a footnote in history."

"A minor footnote most likely," Wharron said. "And when you look up that footnote, it says something about 'the passionate intensity of paranoid morons.'"

Whoa.

Was she intentionally paraphrasing Yeats, whom he'd been thinking about earlier, or was it coincidental?

Well, in our own separate ways, we are both slouching toward Bethlehem.

Still considering their proximity to Greece, she said, "Professor Teagarden, what if I got sick and required an airlift?"

"I've got a better idea. It's probably a dead-end, but it's a Hail Mary and worth a try. C'mon."

"I prefer calling it a long shot instead of Hail Mary," she said. "Lead the way."

They hurried to his cabin where, instead of using the phone, he swiped his cardkey on the scanner to summon the Sicily Deck porter. Before Kanakaris arrived, Teagarden keyed-in 7777 on the safe, withdrew the envelope containing the Q Document, opened it, and laid out the pages on the coffee table. Sensing his intention, Wharron picked up the page Zurbarán labeled "Fragmento Diecisiete."

"This is the key," she said. "It's the one he called 'The Holy Shit Fragment.'"

He took it from her. It was the one he felt looked vaguely familiar. The lettering seemed more like modern Greek, though he had no way of knowing for certain, and because it was so short, he assumed it was much decayed. Other longer texts were cut off by deterioration of the ancient papyrus, or by what looked like water damage, or both.

Less than two minutes after summoning the porter, there was a knock at the door. Kanakaris entered and swiped his own cardkey on the scanner in the foyer of Teagarden's stateroom. Despite the hour, his appearance was impeccable. His white deck shoes appeared newly polished, his khaki slacks perfectly creased, and the turquoise pullover fit his tall, slender frame like a tailored glove.

The three of them exchanged pleasantries about Wharron's seasickness and her recovery aided by the ship's doctor. At first, Kanakaris was reluctant to sit. When he did, he perched formally on the edge of the couch, his long-fingered hands poised carefully atop his knees.

"Theo, this is a working cruise for us," Teagarden began, making it clear that Wharron was a colleague. He picked up a handful of the pages to gesture with them for emphasis. "We find that we're in need of assistance with translation of the Greek language. Ancient Koine Greek, in fact. And unfortunately, we have an extreme deadline. I'm hoping you can assist."

When Kanakaris heard that, his shoulders relaxed, and he smiled.

"I'm sorry, Mr. Sanchez and Ms. Wharron. I did not mean to be rude. It's just that, my movements are closely monitored. They know where I am at all times. If the software detects anything questionable, such as being inside a stateroom longer than it should take to assist with routine requests, I can be summoned to make explanations."

"Jayzuss," Wharron said. "As many times as I've taken this ship, I never knew it was a police state like every corporation the world over."

"Just between us," the porter said, "and in defense of my company, in my work as a ship's steward, I've received every thinkable request. And some that are unthinkable."

"I can imagine," said Teagarden. "We'll make this quick. Tell me, have you studied the ancient versions of your native language?"

"No, not much. But most speakers of modern Greek can grasp basics of the ancient tongue."

Teagarden handed him the nearest fragment at random, which happened to be one of the longer encrypted passages. "Take a look at this, please."

Kanakaris settled deeper into the couch as he inspected the document. He turned it sideways, and upside down. Then he spun it right side up again and held it close. After a few moments, his forehead wrinkled with exasperation and he handed the page back to Teagarden.

"Mr. Sanchez, as you say in America, it's total gobbledygook."

"Because it's ancient Koine?"

"Oh no, because it's not anything. It appears to be Greek. The lettering appears authentic to the ancient version of my language. The wording, however, is nonsense. It looks a little like some sort of puzzle. Like a parlor game with jumbled spelling."

Teagarden and Wharron exchanged glances. His choice of words reminded Teagarden of the first day of class in Advanced Probability when he drew the numbered stops of the Number One train on the board and asked students to discover a pattern. They balked when they heard the answer and called it a "parlor game."

"It actually is a puzzle. That much we know," Wharron said. "It's encrypted. Unfortunately, we don't know how complex the code is. It could be simple; it could be complicated. Because we don't speak the language, we have no way of deciphering it."

"Theo, if you are willing to work on the puzzle, please photograph each page with your cell phone. Then try basic translation of the letters from ancient Greek to modern Greek. Once that's done, maybe I can figure how to decrypt the 'parlor game' as you call it."

"Certainly, Mr. Sanchez. I can try."

He stood over the table and angled his cell as Teagarden and Wharron positioned the pages while he snapped close-ups. As he was leaving, Teagarden sealed the deal with two yellow chips, each stamped with a value of one thousand American dollars. Eyeing them in his palm, Kanakaris was astonished.

"Oh, sir, I—"

"Oxford is expensive," Teagarden said. "If you meet with any success on the word puzzle, I'll do better than that."

"Mr. Sanchez, I don't know how to thank—"

"No thanks necessary. Listen, Theo, there's one more thing. Keep this to yourself. No roommates, no fellow porters, no Benjamin Adoram. Is that agreed?"

"Perfectly," said Kanakaris. He swiped his cardkey and, staring at the twin doubloons, departed Teagarden's stateroom.

# CHAPTER THIRTY-TWO

The balance of the evening went from worrisome to strange, then from strange to freakish. By the time it was over, Teagarden's paranoia index surged into untested territory. Ironically, none of it related to the Q Document, Elad, religion, nonreligion, or any other aspect related to Operation Five O'clock. It had to do—exclusively—with Gretta Wharron's libido.

Perhaps it was fueled by marijuana and two martinis. He wondered if there was something in her e-cig besides pot, or whether her passion was kindled simply by her close proximity to resolving the Q Document mystery. For her, that would be spellbinding. Whatever the cause, after Kanakaris departed, she became intensely absorbed with her cell phone. When she finally put it down, her personality morphed from FFG warrior to a woman in the throes of raging lust.

"Now, Ms. Wharron, wait," Teagarden stammered as she began to disrobe. She ignored him. "Excuse me...hold on, now...what...um...are you—"

"What does it look like I'm doing?" she snapped. "My political motives are naked to the world. And now I am as well."

His eyes told her that—yes—he was drawn to the beauty of her well-proportioned body, and that he enjoyed what he saw.

"Listen, I'm happily married," he protested. "And what about Mara?"

"Mara is the love of my life. She's also an adult. She understands these things."

"My partner is an adult too, but Cynthia wouldn't much appreciate—"

"Hush." She plucked her e-cig from her purse. "I'm going to the balcony. Why don't you join me there for a little THC break? Afterward we can move on to the boudoir, or back here to the sitting room." A sly smile came over her. "Or we can simply fuck on the balcony. I love fucking in the moonlight. Don't you?"

Without waiting for a reply, she sauntered toward the balcony door. Though nude, she walked with the confidence of a runway model in spiked heels. As she passed him, Teagarden saw that the whites of her eyes were shot through with red, and her lids were droopy from tetrahydrocannabinol. So, his suspicions were correct. There was a lot more than marijuana in her e-cig. She pulled back the drapes and drew open the door, sending a gust of Mediterranean warmth into the room.

"Did you know that in Hebrew, the word for fuck is 'lech tiz-dayyén?'" she asked. "There is something so very unfortunate with that. It sounds wrong no matter what inflection you give it. In Spanish, the word is 'joder.' That's better. Still, I don't care for it. In French, it's 'foutre,' which isn't at all bad. But, oh, the grand Italian language!" She sawed the air with her open palm for emphasis. "In Italian, the word is 'scopare,' or 'fanculo.' They are magical words, don't you think?"

Teagarden said nothing. He watched her step into the darkness of the balcony. The FFG symbol tattooed on her lower back seemed to undulate as she moved. Once outside, she flared her e-cig and began loudly shouting straight to the sea and stars:

"Scopare! Fanculo! Oh, yes. Scopare! Fanculo! Yes, yes. Scopare! Fanculo! Yes, yes, yes."

Each time she inhaled on her device, the tip brightened, surrounding the back of her neck with a ghostly aura. Nearby, he noticed her opened purse on the floor. He withdrew her cell phone, opened it, and pushed the spongy button to revive the screen. It displayed the page she'd been obsessed with before entering full libido mode: the LOLA website. The subhead read "LOLA, your means to an adventurous Life of Love."

Her login was still active, so he scrolled down and saw that under "Social Developments," she'd keyed in two entries after Kanakaris departed:

> Consumed two Martinis...
> E-cig w/hyper-potent THC...two shallow pulls

Boy-oh-boy, what a lie! She's been puffing steadily now for nearly an hour.

Under "Mission Updates" she'd entered the following:

> Contact with Teagarden going well. With him now. Met native speaker of Greek. Possible full translation imminent. Next up: public release of Q Doc in Berlin and celebration at FFG convention later in Rome!

He scrolled farther and read random entries posted earlier:

> Teagarden arrived at Megiddo. I ordered Team Two in Mercedes to peel off due to GPS monitor. Team Three at prison has eyes on.
>
> Took close up risk at convenience store in Negev to plant new GPS tracer. FFG members managing mobile surveillance, take note: it went well.
>
> At coffee shop in Haifa. He's researching Italian Tricolore Line.
>
> He's on board Blue Voyager. I will also board, deliver Q Package, then make direct contact.

He clicked on "Urgent Advice" and noticed in the upper right corner that she'd muted LOLA's voice so that all instructions would be issued in text only. The latest exchange read:

Hi LOLA,
Please advise, am alone now with Teagarden.
—Gretta

Hi Gretta,
You are making great mission progress. Stay close.
Recommend compromising target by sharing hyper-
potent THC followed by heterocopulation. You've
got this, girl!
—LOLA

Whoa!

She really was relying on a computer app to tell her what to do and when to do it. There was even a heading called "Body Functions" which he did not click. He dropped the cell phone back into her purse and scooped up Wharron's clothing from the floor to drape over the couch back. On the balcony, he stood beside her.

"No thanks," he said, when she passed the e-cig. "I quit a long time ago. That cigar was my first in eons."

"Well, then—" she said.

She flexed one knee to lean closer and reached into his jacket with both hands where she felt the .22 and withdrew it before he could regain his senses and stop her.

"Ooo," she crooned, "who was it that said, 'Is that a gun in your pocket or are you happy to see me?'"

"I believe it was Mae West," he said. "And I'm saying 'no thanks' again. Not that you're not attractive. You are. But I'm happily married, and you are spoken for as well, to a woman in Israel." He easily snatched the .22 away from her. "It's time for you to go."

"Very well," she huffed, pulling away. "Your gun is made of plastic anyway."

Teagarden stayed on the balcony while she returned to the main sitting room to redress. Moments later, he heard the stateroom door close with a solid thump. In the night sky, the nearly full moon winked on and off behind fast-moving clouds.

# CHAPTER THIRTY-THREE

*Friday, March 21, 2025*

"So simple," the voice said directly into his ear. "So, so simple."

Teagarden had been sleeping fitfully. With open balcony doors, the sounds and smells of the Mediterranean had a tranquilizing quality, yet barely eased his frantic state of mind. When the state-room phone rang, and those two words were the first spoken, the only thing he could imagine was Elad.

Elad, the Impaler. Elad, the Vatican's master murderer, the modern-day samurai warrior. Elad, who once possessed a license to kill as the "tip of the spear" for the Mossad and who was now killing for a living as a globe-trotting freelance assassin.

So simple.

Simple was one of his favorite words. All mathematicians loved it. And Elad had spoken it several times while taunting him in the tunnels at Megiddo. He couldn't remember the exact phrase, but he'd never forget the context. Elad boasted that it would be easy to kill him.

Simple. Simple. Simple.

"Excuse me?" Teagarden said. "What are you talking about?"

"Mr. Sanchez, I'm speaking about the document. As Ms. Wharron said, it may be simple or deeply complicated. It's not complicated; it's simple. I know you only wanted me to translate the document, which I did. I was able to do much more than that. There was nothing to it."

Ah, God. This is not Elad. It's not even Gretta Wharron with her LOLA app manager. It's Theo.

"Would you care for me to email it to you?"

Teagarden rubbed his eyes and looked at the clock. It was five sixteen a.m., Friday. After the unusual evening with Gretta Wharron, he'd slept very little. Outside, the distant murmurs of loud conversation from another balcony and the vague *kah-chinking* sounds of the casino carried to him on the wind. He saw on the caller ID that Kanakaris was using his own cell instead of the ship-based phone line.

"Theo, I'm not doing email. Let's meet in person. Can you come to my stateroom right away?"

"Mr. Sanchez, please understand, I cannot make another prolonged visit at this hour. It's because of my cardkey. Last evening was risky. You know, my cardkey registers my movement about the ship, who I visit, how long, and so forth. Unusually long visits cause my name to blip up on the ship's software. After last night, if I spend more than a minute in your cabin, well—"

"Say no more. Where, then?"

"Perhaps you will enjoy watching the sunrise. You may want to request a special breakfast to be served at the Observation Garden which is on the Sun Deck at the ship's stern. It should be mostly empty at this hour. As your personal steward, I can arrange it."

"Done. I've seen the menu. The ship's regular breakfast is good. I'll meet you there in fifteen minutes."

Teagarden quickly showered and dressed, again wearing his new sports coat. He considered phoning Wharron, then decided against it after remembering the previous evening. True, they were still working together. Sort of. But there was no need to partner with FFG for this next chapter where he was finally making progress on the job. His mission, assigned by Klassen, was to learn what was causing mass suicide and do something to help end the madness, or to help the FBI and CIA to help end it. Besides, he'd contact Wharron soon enough, probably by midmorning.

On the way out, he scooped up his remaining yellow and black casino chips, his sunglasses, cell phone, and another cigar.

Outside, the corridors were quiet. The elevator smelled of residual vomit, bleach, and carpet cleanser. At the top of the ship, he saw that the Sun Deck's Observation Garden was perfect for early morning privacy. There were only a few scattered tables among a dozen olive trees thriving in large pots. And Kanakaris was both correct and incorrect about privacy. The deck wasn't mostly empty as he guessed. It was totally empty. There was not a soul present to enjoy the arrival of dawn on the Mediterranean.

Teagarden found a table at the railing where the ship's wake could be seen churning in the ambient light cast from lower decks. Overhead, the early morning sky was a patchwork of receding starry glitter.

"Simple," Kanakaris had said on the phone. Yeah, I doubt that. Nothing about this journey has been simple.

He started to nod off and thought of lighting the cigar to help him stay awake. Instead, he opted to let sleep overtake him in the moist air. The aurora of sunrise was breaking in the east when the same voice startled him awake a second time.

"Good morning, Mr. Sanchez." Kanakaris carried a large round tray overhead with one arm and shifted it to a folding table near Teagarden with the ease of a gymnast. "In Great Britain, this is called a full English breakfast. We call it the full Blue Voyager." He narrated each dish while shifting them to Teagarden's table. "Orange juice, fresh melon, two poached eggs, buttered toast with two kinds of jam on the side, three strips of bacon, sautéed cherry tomatoes with Spanish onion, and one full pot of freshly brewed coffee with a saucer of warm cream and your choice of sugars." He concluded by flipping the napkin with a flourish and placing it over Teagarden's lap. "Finally, a copy of our ship's newspaper, *The Daily Blue Voyager*."

Kanakaris stood butler-like beside the nearest olive tree planter as Teagarden opened the blue presentation folder and plucked the newspaper from the right inside pocket. There were three printed pages of standard paper with fancy scroll at the edges. The lead story was about ship's master, Captain Gaetan Bardolo, who formerly served as commander of a cruiser in the Italian Navy named *Cristoforo*, after Christopher Columbus. The balance was a calendar of onboard daily events: yoga classes, magic lessons for children and adults, karaoke night at the Blue Grotto bar, and the "Friday Night Special Show featuring the Neapolitan Beatles."

Thanks. I'll pass on catching that particular show.

Teagarden took a few disinterested bites of melon and toast. The second page of the newspaper reported the day's weather: "Sunrise at 6:15 a.m., partly cloudy with morning drizzle, followed by spotty sunshine, high of 21 Celsius/70 Fahrenheit."

Stuffed behind the weather page was the purpose of his sunrise subterfuge. There were several legal-pad pages filled with perfectly printed handwriting. To create room on the table, Teagarden transferred the bacon and toast to the plate with the poached eggs and tomatoes, then handed the empty dishes to Kanakaris. He placed the handwritten pages atop the blue folder and, because of the breeze, weighted them with the blue salt shaker. He sipped hot coffee while glancing over the first page where the lettering in English was so artfully constructed it could pass for that of a fastidious medieval scribe.

"Good job."

He flipped through to number seventeen, the one Wharron said was rumored to be called the "Holy Shit Fragment." With a mouthful of poached egg, he read:

> We have chosen this laborer from Nazareth whose homily the Caesars found troublesome. I shall contend his resurrected spirit came unto me. Hence, we are beholden to call him Messiah.

"Holy Mother of God."

Teagarden accidentally knocked his coffee cup to the

teakwood floor, where it shattered. He hastily tucked all pages back into the blue folder, handed Kanakaris a fistful of yellow chips, and hurried back to his stateroom feeling like a man with a nuclear bomb tucked under his arm.

# CHAPTER THIRTY-FOUR

He was obsessed with caution.

Teagarden locked his stateroom door. He checked and double checked that the balcony doors were secure. He patrolled all three rooms, carefully running his hands over walls, floor, and furniture. He moved a chair from place to place to use as a stepping stool for inspecting the crown molding. He knew it was meaningless.

Totally useless. I'm having a complete panic attack.

Still, he couldn't stop. He was in the grip of an obsession that could only be satisfied by the reassuring touch that nothing had been altered since his departure to meet Kanakaris. It may have qualified as full-blown clinical paranoia. Or it may have been little more than anxiety. Regardless, he was possessed of a need to verify that no cameras or recording equipment had been installed, and that no one was lurking inside or hiding behind peep holes cut into the bulkheads that separated cabins.

Back in the sitting room, he clicked on table and floor lamps, leaving off all ceiling illumination. Inexplicably, overhead fixtures challenged his comfort zone. He put the blue folder on the coffee table, sat on the couch, flipped it open, and began reading decoded translations of the Q Document provided by the remarkable Theo Kanakaris:

14th FRAGMENT:

...these avowals we shall make, and that I shall commit in letters to our gentile and Jewish believers, must be unvarying in assertion, else we shall encounter questions that we, indeed that history shall find unsteady in foundation. Our teachings must be as fixed in their order as the stars of the night. Likewise our public prayers and public and private conduct must reflect our chosen beliefs as though we are one with our...

15th FRAGMENT:

Do not allow converts to question our chosen Triad. Yes, it is borrowed from the Aventine Triad. This shall render our declarations familiar to the people and therefore allay natural reluctance. So, too, for the Caesars. Our chosen avowals of worship of three gods: father, son, and spirit constitute a just and civic linkage to their many and multiple gods, and therefore pose diminished threat to the pantheism of Apollo, Mercury, and Jupiter and to the faith of Moses and our own triad of founding fathers: Abraham, Jacob, and Isaac.

16th FRAGMENT:

...thus I say unto you in great confidence, these encoded communiqués are to be retained by you in utmost darkness and shall not be passed further in voice or set into script lest we be doomed to suffer detention and prosecution by the Caesars and found treacherous by the people. Though our hearts are loyal on their behalf, they would not understand. Therefore, our need for privacy in these matters is supreme.

Once fully well-ordered, our faith shall be like the sword and javelin of the warring Colosseum gladiators. The groundwork of our structure is to defeat them via their own artifice which they compose with army and false privilege. The one from Nazareth was chosen by me as both an invisible sword of fire and a harvest of survival for Jew and gentile. More than this, we also proclaim him resurrected so that our harvest may prevail and prosper beyond Rome, which shall fall of its own weight. Only the claim of Messiah, which shall be our privilege, can assist the task.

Be it known to all who read these words that the rabbi found troublesome by Caesar, and now known by the masses as "The Anointed One" was chosen by me, and therefore by you. There will be future Caesars. Thus, our descendants must know that by our proclaiming this faith, they are no less than us.

Be not dissuaded that he himself knew nothing of this. We shall amend that. That is the purpose of our written gospels. We shall tell the story we want them to hear. It is the reason we build this foundation, so that we may build our strength no less than the Romans built their own authority upon the shoulders of Apollo, the Greeks upon Zeus, and the Egyptians upon the Sun God Ra. As such, it shall become the only story ever told. And the greatest. It shall be the story of a man we resurrected so as to live forever, so that we may endure and defeat the Caesars of present and future.

In loyalty and faith to you all, I, Saul of Tarsus do hereby pledge...

17th FRAGMENT:

We have chosen this laborer from Nazareth whose homily the Caesars found troublesome. I shall contend his resurrected spirit came unto me. Hence, we are beholden to call him Messiah.

NOTES:
Mr. Sanchez:

I know you did not expect full decryption. Yet it was simple. I noticed the formula almost immediately. The lettering of each word was represented by the letter that follows it in the twenty-four characters of the Old Greek alphabet. For example, by applying the same code to English—"abc" becomes "bcd," and "xyz" becomes "yza." Simple. In English, this would mean spelling the word "ship" as "tijq," and the word "document" would be spelled "epdvnfou." Once I figured it out, it went quite fast.

Fragments 1-13 were not encoded and their translation was quite easy. Though in ancient Greek, they are straight passages from the earliest version of *Matthew* and *Luke* which date to 70 A.D., and which I know quite well.

Fragment Seventeen is odd. It is the final and shortest. Curiously, only the first two sentences are encoded. The last is composed entirely in ancient Greek. As noted, it means: "Hence, we are beholden to call him Messiah." The only thing I can figure as to why the final sentence is not encoded is that the scribe must have grown tired and simply spaced out.

Finally, I must say thank you for the opportunity to assist in your ancient Biblical research. I so thoroughly enjoyed the discovery of mysterious new voices you've uncovered that I stayed up all night.

Naturally, I am grateful for your generous gratuity.

Respectfully in Confidence,

T.K.

Teagarden had no idea how long it took Professor Pablo Zurbarán to figure out how to decode the cipher, but guessed it was considerably longer than it took this ship's porter. When the story is told, that will surely be one of the great ironies. Like it nor not, Mr. Theo Kanakaris may ultimately become a famous footnote to history.

Despite it being morning, Teagarden went to the liquor cabinet and poured two fingers of whiskey into a glass and plunked in two ice cubes. He opened the balcony doors and sat outside. The sun was fully risen in the east, yet there was a slight mist of rain from the west that joined the sea spray. He sipped the whiskey, which burned as it went down but almost immediately had a soothing effect.

They chose him.

The phrase stuck in Teagarden's mind like a broken record. *They...chose...him. They...chose...him. They...chose... him.*

Wherever you put the emphasis, it was scary. The Q Doc revealed that the founders of the most populous religion on Earth were championing a social movement as a means to combat oppression under the Caesars during the Roman Empire. It sounded like they chose him the same way any movement would choose a poster child to symbolize its struggle against abusive authority: Tank Man for the Tiananmen Square massacre, Napalm Girl to protest Vietnam, Rosa Parks to inspire the U.S. civil rights movement.

Teagarden saw that it was more than merely dangerous. It would electrify the ozone with offense and rage. The idea of playing a central role in releasing it to the world made him want to pack it in. Call it quits. Go home. He didn't want to possess this knowledge. It made him the man who knew too much. It was a burden just to have it reside inside his brain. Of course, it explained perfectly the freakish theatre of mass suicide. Some were so horrified they opted to kill themselves en masse; as Elad said in the tunnel, "they can't handle news that the Q Doc bears proof that you-know-who wasn't really the son of you-know-what." Militant atheists were equally willing to kill themselves, though only to ensure that the Q Doc was made public.

While looking at the boundless sea, he mumbled the same expression of disbelief he'd spoken before hurrying from the Observation Garden on the Sun Deck.

"Holy Mother of God."

# CHAPTER THIRTY-FIVE

He resisted the urge to take another shower to cleanse his mind of the problem. It would be just as useless as all that tapping on the ceiling and walls. He also resisted the renewed desire to phone his wife and Agent Klassen in New York.

Okay, so what should I do?

The answer came back in one desperate word: survive. It was Friday morning. He'd been safe on the Blue Voyager since departing Haifa and that reprieve would continue until docking later that day at Venice. The real problem was surviving after that.

Elad will probably be waiting in Venice.

He wasn't sure how Elad could possibly know he was on the ship, but it stood to reason that if FFG knew, Elad knew. When it came to the killer hired by the Vatican, the best strategy was to always assume the worst. Even if he safely debarked at Venice, he faced the wider challenge of surviving all the way to Berlin. He had Wharron and her FFG team to help with that. Finally, in Berlin, he'd hook up with FBI and CIA protection where he and Wharron would make presentations to the World Judeo-Christian Council, which should terminate Elad's contract.

Then reality set in.

Just because the Vatican would no longer want me dead doesn't mean Elad would stand down.

Just as with that psycho six years ago, Teagarden sensed this man was taking things personally because he was embarrassed for losing his prey, first in New York and second at Megiddo.

Professional assassins have a reputation to uphold. They tend not to like it when they're outsmarted.

He contemplated ways to disembark at Venice. He couldn't simply walk down the gangway like any other passenger headed for a gondola tour. The only alternative he could imagine was to slip out of the loading bay where forklifts deliver everything from stacks of toilet paper to Salisbury steak, while removing everything from booze bottles to garbage bags full of half-eaten Salisbury steak.

When the bell sounded, he peeked through the door's viewfinder.

"Theo, good." He swung open the door of his stateroom. "I apologize for my hasty departure this morning at breakfast, but…"

He stopped.

Kanakaris was stooped over in the doorway, his face bleached white, the flesh around his eyes tinged with an unnatural hue. Teagarden's gaze dropped lower, and another color caught his eye. With both hands, the porter was pressing his cell phone to a source of oozing red on his abdomen.

"Oh, Mr. Sanchez, I…I…" He staggered forward and fell into Teagarden's arms.

"Theo!" Teagarden supported Kanakaris by the waist during a stumbling lurch to the couch. "God almighty, Theo! What happened?"

"Oh, Mr. Sanchez, I…I…"

"Okay, don't talk. I'll call the ship's doctor. You just hold on." Kanakaris continued speaking while Teagarden ran to the telephone.

"Oh, sir…I emailed her…" When he shifted the cell phone, the hole in his gut squirted a burst of blood that landed on the decoded Q Doc pages where Teagarden had left them on the coffee table. "I sent her email…then she came to my cabin…"

"Hello, this is an emergency. Send the ship's doctor to the Taormina Stateroom on the Sicily Deck immediately."

"I…I emailed her…then she knocked on my own door…

and...and..."

"Yes, a man has been hurt. He's bleeding badly."

"She said...'I was smart'...then...then..."

"His name is Theo Kanakaris. Yes, yes, it's the ship's porter, Theo Kanakaris. He's hurt. Hurry, please!"

He slammed the phone and returned to where Kanakaris was doubled-over on the couch. He pried the cell phone from his hands and replaced it with a small throw pillow which he compressed with a knee.

"Listen to me, Mr. Sanchez...she said...'You're too smart'... that's what she said...'too smart'..."

"Yes, yes. You are very smart, Theo. Just like she is. You will be a great professor someday. Just stay with me. I promise, I'll pay your final year of tuition at Oxford. I can do it for you. But you must stay with me."

"No, no, not smart too...she said 'too smart'...'too smart'... then she...then she..."

"Shh," Teagarden interrupted, putting his finger to Kanakaris' lips. "You hush. Just try to keep it together."

"Please, listen...sir, I made a second discovery that you do not yet know of."

That caught his attention. Keeping his left knee jammed into the pillow, he leaned down to the wounded man's ear. "You mean on the Q Doc? You made a second discovery on the Q Doc?" Kanakaris nodded. "Okay, what else did you learn?" he whispered.

"I learned...I learned more...they date to the Middle Ages... perhaps around twelve hundred..."

"All right. Tell me, Theo, what dates to the Middle Ages?"

"It's phony."

"What's phony?"

"The Q Doc. It's a hoax. Oh, Mr. Sanchez...I told her...I told her it was a hoax...probably written in the Middle Ages...you do not receive email...so I emailed *her* with my discovery...then she...then she came..."

"She read your email and came to your cabin?"

"Yes...then she...she said, 'I was too smart for my own good'...then she...then she..."

"Then she stabbed you?"

"Yes."

Teagarden wiped Theo's bloody cell phone on the couch and tucked it into a side pocket of his sports coat.

"Listen, Theo, I'm confident this wound looks worse than it is. Just lay still. Don't talk anymore."

When the ship's doctor arrived with two assistants toting a stretcher, Teagarden stepped aside to gather all the Q Doc papers. He tucked them into the inside breast pocket of his jacket which made it bulge, like the outer pockets which held a pistol and wads of cash.

"Okay, Theo," Dr. Almonti said, "we're going to shift you to my downstairs clinic." His voice was confident and soothing. "We're going to get a blood line hooked up and stitch the wound. You're going to be fine."

While they transferred him to the stretcher, Teagarden departed.

# CHAPTER THIRTY-SIX

A hoax? Really?

That changed everything. Most obviously, it meant no more onboard reprieve. Elad would still be waiting in Venice, so surviving the next few hours on the ship was suddenly the challenge.

Why?

Don't be stupid. Because of her. That's why.

And why is that?

His brain was recognizing facts quicker than his mind could follow. He rushed to the nearest outdoor promenade.

All right, take it slow.

Did Kanakaris say the Q Document is a hoax?

Yes, that's what he said.

And did he say he was stabbed by Gretta Wharron after she learned of his discovery?

Yes, that is also what he said.

And that means—what—regarding the FFG lady with piercing brown eyes who uses an app for permission to eat, drink, and go to the bathroom?

Well, it means she's now looking to kill me just like she tried to kill Kanakaris. This is getting more complicated by the minute.

He ran down his new life-and-death facts. As a hitman for the Vatican, Elad wanted to kill him to prevent publication by him or FFG. As a member of FFG, Gretta Wharron wanted to protect him from Elad and help decode the document for full dissemination. Now their motives were reversed. She wanted to kill him to prevent public awareness of an ancient fraud. In time, when the Vatican learned the truth, Elad would be called off and, as he boasted in the Megiddo tunnel, he'd revert to protecting him—from FFG!

Yeah, I'll believe that when I see it. Besides, I can't wait for the news to filter down from the bosses at St. Peter's.

Meantime, Teagarden's job was still the same: verify Theo's work, publish the document, help stop mass suicides, and stay alive in the process.

"Lord help me," he whispered as he descended staircase after staircase, going from promenade to promenade, from stern to bow.

And all because of some disgruntled monk who was getting his shits and giggles by installing a phony religious script under the old Megiddo Church. I guess the Middle Ages had plenty of assholes just like us in the twenty-first century.

In shock, he wandered the perimeter of the busy Empire Deck where food was served in three restaurants: indoor cafeteria, outdoor twenty-four-seven burger grill at the stern, and sandwich buffet at the bow. He stayed well to the outside, blending with the crowd and keeping his face toward the sea to avoid security cameras, though he wasn't all that concerned about whatever passed for security on the Blue Voyager. Perhaps Ship's Master Gaetan Bardolo, who once captained a cruiser for the Italian Navy, would believe his story. And why not? It was a basic syllogism: A) anyone capable of running a cruise ship had a brain; B) anyone with a brain would see that he was telling the truth; therefore, C) Gaetan Bardolo would believe him and provide asylum in his own officer's cabin until Italian police and American officials boarded the ship in Venice.

Naw. Forget it. That syllogism is too tidy. It's so tidy it won't work. It would be like Edward Snowden expecting the NSA to believe he had the best interests of America at heart.

At the stern of the Empire Deck, he discarded his cardkey in a waste barrel near the hamburger grill. He needed it to open doors, but that key was the easiest way to track him around the ship, so he was safer without it. He wandered to the equally busy Ocean Wave Deck, which had an enclosed room for smokers that overlooked the hot tubs and two small swimming pools. Without his cardkey, he couldn't admit himself, so he waited until someone departed and courteously held the door open for him. At that hour it was mostly filled with women monitoring their children or grandchildren splashing in the nearby kiddie pool while they happily chatted and puffed. He didn't want to smoke but having a cigar in his pocket provided a good cover. He found a secluded chair, lit the cigar, and selected the two-day old *Jerusalem English Dispatch* from the reader's rack. The lead story was about another mass suicide, this time in South Africa. Forty-two members of a Pentecostal church near Cape Town had jammed into a fishing boat, motored into the deep waters of Table Bay, and intentionally sunk their own vessel, drowning everyone on board. Unlike past events, this time the minister left a note referencing a copy of the decoded source of Matthew and Luke, and that the knowledge found there was, "ukungenakubekezelelwa" Translated from Zulu to English, it meant "intolerable."

Good word. And I agree. This thing is ukungenakubekezelelwa.

His job now was to publish the fact that the Q Doc was a fake. That would end religious-motivated hara-kiri by groups that received copies of Zurbarán's decryption and believed them authentic. This minister in Cape Town who mentioned a motive in his suicide note helped because it provided a cognitive reference point for the public. As sad as it was, people would finally understand.

All right, it's time to break my silence. I need to contact Klassen. The FBI will get the hoax story to the media, and the CIA will tell the Vatican to call off their pit bull.

His phone, which had gone unused since landing in Jerusalem, was in one of his bulging pockets. Then he remembered he also had Kanakaris' mobile as well, a much safer option, in another pocket. He withdrew it and flicked away dried blood with both thumbnails. The screen was frozen with the image of Theo's last email communication. He pressed the off button. Nothing. He pressed the volume rocker panel. Nothing. He pried off the back, removed the battery, put it back in, and replaced the back cover. Still nothing. It was dead, killed by a cell phone's worst enemy—liquid. In this case, the liquid was human plasma.

He scraped and rubbed at the stains on the screen until he could read the last message frozen on the screen. It was to Gretta Wharron:

> **From:** tkanakaris@oxford.edu
> **To:** gwharron@ffg.org
>
> ...because modern Greek did not exist until about 1100...the old Roman cult of the gods was not called the Aventine Triad until much later...and construction on the colosseum began around year 72 so the timing is reasonable...BUT—it was called Flavian Amphitheatre until the year 1000! That means Fragments 14-17 were written AFTER the year 1000, which means they date sometime during the Middle Ages. And THAT means they are FAKE! Come knock at my cabin, we'll walk to Mr. Sanchez's stateroom together with this news.

Yeah, she knocked at your cabin all right, but you didn't do much walking together. She must have stabbed you in the gut the moment you opened the door.

He wondered why she didn't push into Theo's cabin, close the door behind her, and finish the job. He guessed a passenger or ship's employee must have stepped into the corridor, forcing her to back off. If Dr. Almonti got a blood line hooked up and clamped the bleeding, Kanakaris might survive until surgery. He figured the ship had already entered the Adriatic, which meant it was equidistant between Greece and Italy. A chopper could get him to the nearest ER quick and easy.

Teagarden placed the lighted cigar on a tray and let it burn out. Now that he'd calmed a bit, he realized it was a mistake to bolt from his stateroom and race through the corridors like the rats scurrying through the tunnels of Megiddo. Regardless of what Ship's Master Gaetan Bardolo believed or didn't believe, it was clear that his best option was to remain incommunicado in the ship's brig until docking at the city of canals. That was the best way to contact Special Agent Klassen—by being arrested!

That should be easy enough. Ship's bridge, here I come to get locked up.

He tossed the newspaper aside and stood to exit the smoker's room when he saw Gretta Wharron and Dr. Almonti outside. They were standing on an elevated causeway overlooking the swimming pools. Below them, at pool level, a pair of stud-type pretty boys moved among the sun-and-water-logged loungers, smiling and nodding as they scanned every face. They wore the Tricolore khaki slacks and turquoise pullover uniform with a couple of fashion accessories not normally seen in company attire. They each carried a Taser-baton tucked into side pouches on their trousers. And they each had a prominent bulge where bulges were not typically seen on tall, pretty-boy types—at the small of the back.

Teagarden's brain pulsed with red alert like the CIA's GPS ground alert system. His adrenaline-pumping brain rippled with clichéd warnings from epic movies like *Ben Hur* and *The Ten Commandments:* "Beware of Greeks bearing gifts," "Beware of the man with one sandal," "Beware the Ides of March." Then there was always, "Beware of If and If."

Oh, crap! I need to beware of everything.

It was suddenly clear: they were working together. Dr. Almonti was a member of FFG. That explained why she called him by his first name and why he responded to her seasickness so quickly the day before on the Sky Deck. It made sense because she frequently took the Tricolore line between Israel and Switzerland to avoid air travel. God knows if the two security guys were also members of their cuckoo club. No way could he go to the bridge now. Even if Ship's Master Bardolo wasn't an FFG member, someone would get to Teagarden and kill him inside the ship's brig.

Teagarden moved to the rear of the smoker's room to search for a hiding space but there was nothing. The only exit was the front door that faced the kiddie pool. It was just a matter of seconds before the two searchers wandered inside.

But how'd they know?

It couldn't be the security cameras. If that were the case, whoever was monitoring Big Brother central would send the security team straight to him in the smoker's room. It must have been some staffer who saw him and knew him to be Mr. Moneybags on this particular cruise. They saw him headed toward the Ocean Wave Deck and picked up an emergency phone to use as a tip line.

Wait, that's it. The emergency telephones. They're all over the ship.

He scanned the room. Halfway along the bulwark was a recess in the smoker's room wall covered by a plastic panel. Inside were two hardwired devices: a red emergency phone and a red fire alarm. He lifted the panel and pulled the receiver to his ear. The response was immediate.

"What is the nature of your emergency?"

"The suspect has entered the cafeteria on the Empire Deck," he whispered and hung up.

Only one of the cigarette people, a chain-smoking woman with orange-tinted lips, noticed what he'd done and stared with curiosity. Teagarden ignored her. He angled toward the window to see if the effort accomplished the desired results. It did. Within seconds, the two security men, Wharron, and Dr. Almonti withdrew their cell phones to study an incoming text. A moment later, they exchanged glances, turned, and hurried off to the nearest staircase.

Teagarden waited a ten count. With the curious lady still

watching, he opened the plastic panel a second time and pulled the fire alarm which set off a din of klaxon warnings. The sluggish smokers didn't move. Outside, the lifeguards blew their shrill whistles and shouted, "Everybody out of the pool." One lifeguard, a bronzed woman in a one-piece blue swimsuit toting a whistle in one hand and a bullhorn in the other, burst into the smoker's room.

"Everyone to your muster stations," she shouted. "Move out, now!" In the pandemonium, the gray-haired lady who witnessed Teagarden's trick approached him. He saw that the orange coloring around her mouth was not lipstick, but discoloration caused by tobacco.

"Where's the fire?" she asked in a gravelly voice.

"In the cafeteria. But they'll get it under control quickly."

"Oh, no," she said. "I left my husband and grandbabies there, so I could come for a smoke." Clutching her cigarettes and lighter, she pushed ahead of him to exit, leaving behind three possessions: a scarf, a book entitled *Shadows in the Fire*, and her cardkey.

Teagarden, meantime, had a brainstorm. He thought of one place that just might provide safe harbor from all FFG members for the few remaining hours until the ship docked at Venice. After the smoker's room emptied, he snatched the frightened woman's scarf and cardkey, and headed for the nearest staircase. His next stop would be the ship's chapel.

# CHAPTER THIRTY-SEVEN

It was mid-ship on a middle deck with no windows. The sign at the entrance read "All Purpose Faith Sanctuary, Entra tranquillamente, Entrer tranquillement, הזן בשקט," and the poetically mistranslated English, "Enter with Quiet."

The oversized door was made of heavy hickory or walnut. It was the only wooden door he'd seen on the ship and pushing it open required considerable effort. He recalled the deific weight of the doors at the Church of the Holy Sepulchre from which warriors of the Israeli Defense Forces burst through to surprise the FFG suicide cult. Perhaps there was something about places of worship that required heavy-duty entrances.

No one here. Good, they're all at their muster stations putting on lifejackets.

The large stained-glass panel on the far wall wasn't really stained glass but a plastic montage. It portrayed a golden ray of sunlight piercing white clouds to illuminate a green leafy tree. At the trunk's base, semi-concealed among the bushy grass, was a Crucifix, Star of David, Crescent and Star, Wheel of Dharma, and Om. A small side plaque named it *The Beauty of Faith*, dated 1997, and listed the artist as Maresciallo Melabianca, of Gorgonzola, Italy.

The klaxons finally ceased. They'd been so loud that their silencing seemed to quiet more than just the deafening alarm. It was as though an inner-ear tinnitus had also been muted.

"Thanks be to all gods for renewed silence," he whispered to the shrine of all faiths.

He worried again about the possibility that security cameras traced his movement to the chapel. In the year 2025, it was nearly impossible to go anywhere without video surveillance, even on a cruise ship. Yet they hadn't pinpointed his flight from the Sicily Deck to the smoking room on the Ocean Deck so, he rationalized, maybe the Tricolore Company hadn't bothered to update their Big Brother technology. His possession of the lady smoker's card-key helped to calm his fear. He was moving about the ship as Elana Bar-Levav.

*One thing is certain, her grandbabies in the cafeteria are fine.*

The plastic gun jammed his hip when he sat on the front pew. He removed it and placed it near his right buttock. He took off his jacket to use as a pillow and laid supine on the first pew directly under the cheesy plastic altar.

It made him think of a scene from the movie *Gone with the Wind*. Near the beginning, Ashley dumps Scarlett, then bolts from the library after telling her to forget their love affair. In her first display of arch-browed anger, and thinking she's alone, she heaves a tchotchke over the sofa back without knowing that Rhett Butler was lying there, eavesdropping all along.

*That's weird. Why am I thinking such nonsense?* First it was epic religion movies, now it's GWTW for the second time.

The ship's horn sounded two long blasts. He hoped it meant they were nearing Venice. If not, it likely meant the crew could stand down on the fire alarm because there was no fire. Either way, it meant Wharron and her allies were still searching for him.

*Of my three transgressions, I wonder which God considers the worst: using His house as a hideout, lying down in His house without praying, or carrying a gun into His house?*

Teagarden glanced again at the wall panel. The principal colors were green, gold, and white. Behind the white clouds, the sky was the same hue of blue as the ship's glassware and paper napkins. There wasn't a drop of red. That was fine with him. He'd seen enough red over the past few days to last a lifetime.

(Cynthia)
You know, it's probably all right if you pray.

(Sam)
Really? Do you think it will help?

(Cynthia)
Like the agnostics say, you never know.

(Sam)
Let's not get the agnostics involved. I've already got enough trouble with the believers and the nonbelievers. This is bad, Cyn, but I'm surviving.

(Cynthia)
That's important. Don't diminish the importance of that. Remember, Sam, your survival isn't just about you. It's about a lot of people who rely on you. Perhaps even great masses of people. Therefore, you must continue surviving to keep thinking and keep doing. And since you're thinking of saying a prayer, go ahead, say it. What's the harm?

(Sam)
Very well.

Since he couldn't get GWTW out of his head, he held to that theme while gathering his thoughts. Once the words came to him, and being alone in the chapel, he decided to speak them aloud.

"Dear God, whatever you are, and wherever you may be, since tomorrow really is another day, please allow me to survive long enough to see it arrive and reach Berlin so that I may contribute to ending this massive loss of life committed in Your name."

The slowing ship exchanged its rough pitch and yaw for gentle rocking. Just ahead of falling asleep, he felt the bump of tugboats as they tapped the bow and stern to ease it into port at Venice.

"Amen," he whispered aloud.

(Cynthia)
Very nice, Sam. I'm proud of you.

(Sam)
Thank you, Cyn. I...I...

(Cynthia)
Hush, Sam. It's okay.

# CHAPTER THIRTY-EIGHT

He awakened to a series of vague noises, sounds that went *chink*, and *plop*, and *tappy-tap*. They weren't alarming, but they were close. Very close. They were so close they seemed to be happening directly overhead. His eyes fluttered open. He saw nothing except the ceiling and the bland plastic coloring of *The Beauty of Faith*.

"Ah, you're waking up. Very good."

Teagarden bolted awake. The voice came from directly behind and overhead. Still recumbent, he tilted his head and saw all he needed. Dr. Niccolò Almonti was sitting beside him on the front pew. Perched between them was his leather medical bag.

"Nah-uh-uh," the doctor warned. "Don't sit up. You'll make me spill this. And believe me when I tell you, if I spilled this, we would both be very unhappy."

Teagarden settled back onto the pew. With head and eyes rolled back, he saw an upside-down Dr. Almonti holding a hypo-needle in one hand. In the other, he rapidly drew liquid into the needle's cylindrical reservoir from multiple vials. Once finished, he dropped the vial into his bag and picked up another. That was it. Those little vials were making the *chink* and *plop* noises. He again shifted to sit up.

"Professor Teagarden, do you see this vial?" The doctor held it over Teagarden's face. "It contains concentrated hydrochloric acid, the same substance that churns, albeit in diluted form, inside the human stomach. If I were to spill it onto your face, it would take less than one second for both of your eyeballs to become

225

boiling mush within their orbital sockets." Teagarden went immobile. "Very good," the doctor said. "Now put your hands at your sides." Teagarden did so. "Thank you."

Dr. Almonti finished drawing various liquids into the syringe. He tossed the last of the vials into the bag, crossed his legs, and leaned over Teagarden's face with the needle poised at Teagarden's jugular.

"You're going to inject me with acid?"

"Oh, not exactly. Yes, there's some hydrochloride in the mix to be sure. And other ingredients as well. It'll burn a bit. But don't worry about that because you'll be dead before you can scream." His lips broke into a droll smile. "There certainly will not be any dancing about or yelling, 'owie, owie, owie.'"

"And you're doing this to me because you're with FFG?"

"Oh, I most assuredly am with FFG. I am, in fact, one of the founding members, what we call the First Fifty. It was I who introduced Gretta to the group. I knew from the get-go that she would be a star for the group."

"Because of her emotional instability?"

"Now, now, Professor Teagarden, we tend to think of our rank and file as more stable than the flock belonging to any church, temple, or mosque."

Teagarden dared not move. His head, neck, and eyes were straining in a painfully awkward position. He could feel the doctor's hand resting on his collar bone where it held the needle a millimeter from his carotid artery. One slight push on the plunger, and the tip would sink. He played for time.

"Where's Wharron now?"

"Monitoring the exit ramp. We've arranged with Captain Bardolo to have only one exit for Venice."

"The captain is FFG too?"

"No, no, no. You're wanted in connection with an onboard stabbing. Considering the circumstances, the captain listens to any reasonable security advice, particularly when it comes from me."

"Naturally you saw to it that they blamed me for Theo.

How'd you find me?"

"Oh, tch-tch-tch, Professor Teagarden. You're not the only clever man on board. I too am a student of irony. Where else would a man hide from people opposed to the mass madness of magical thinking? And by the way, that was a tidy business with the fire alarm."

"Is Elad on board?"

"Ah, you're worried about the notorious one who, in this instance, is working for the Vatican and who murdered our dear Professor Zurbarán." He reflexively pumped his crossed leg as though keeping time to his words. "You see, the Vatican wants you dead because of your reputation, while we wanted a partnership with you precisely because of that same reputation—you know, Captain America, the New Prometheus, and all that."

"I figured out that part."

"Yes, of course you did. Now things have changed, so you needn't worry about Elad any longer. Besides, I'm about to do his job for him. Unlike him, I'm doing it totally pro bono."

"Because the Q Document is fake?"

"Oh, don't say that. I hate the sound of it." He sighed with impatience and stopped pumping his leg. "But, yes, that is the reason. No hard feelings, Professor Teagarden. Frankly, I wish it were the fool monk who perpetuated the hoax about to receive this needle instead of you. You see, my group has been searching for precisely this sort of evidence for decades. Once found, we naturally wanted it to be true."

Teagarden glanced at the plastic wall art. "Just as all religions want their version to be true."

Dr. Almonti smiled. He too gazed at the wall panel. His weight shifted slightly, suggesting their chitchat was nearly over, that it was time for him to jab the stick. Teagarden let his right-hand slide past his hip to the handle of the .22.

"Perfectly banal, isn't it?" Dr. Almonti said of the green and gold panel. "Like everything else in every house of worship the world over. Tch-tch-tch, what harm they've all done to our species."

Teagarden gripped the stock of gray plastic more firmly and played for time. To lift the gun, aim, and fire at such an angle, he needed to have the doctor look away.

"You're Italian?"

"Of course. From Milano."

"And you believe the master's *Pietà* is banal?"

"Tch-tch-tch." He looked away to roll his eyes with contempt. It was almost Teagarden's moment. "Do not confuse our great Renaissance with those who financed it. That would be like saying the slave masters of America deserve credit for the blues, jazz, and rock and roll."

A tactic for sparking distraction came to Teagarden. He played for more time before springing the idea of a verbal ploy.

"Is it epipoxilene?"

"No, for Christ sakes. The mother's milk of espionage makes death look like a heart attack. And its formula is a carefully guarded secret. My own concoction seeks no evasion on the cause of death. I call it 'Deadicillin.' It makes mortality overtake life with utter ruination of all blood, tissue, and organs from the inside out."

"Wow. Deadicillin sounds quicker than a knife to the jugular."

"Oh, it most certainly is. That's the big favor it offers the living—the speed at which it ends life."

Knowing his time for a needle stick was nigh, Teagarden advanced his only remaining idea while also maneuvering his right hand.

"Tell me, Dr. Almonti, did Theo Kanakaris get airlifted by helicopter to an Italian hospital?"

The doctor smirked and grunted. "Oh, come now, Professor. That too-smart-for-his-own-good Greek steward was dead before you departed your stateroom."

Teagarden's eyes bulged with astonishment. "But how? *How!?*" he cried. "Wharron's knife wound wasn't fatal!"

In that moment, Dr. Almonti's arrogance and pride got the best of him. He removed the needle from its position at Teagarden's neck to hold it three inches above his victim's face where he displayed it with cocky vanity. He meant to punctuate his hubris with the words, "What do you mean, *how*? With this—Deadicillin—of course!" But he never got there.

While the needle was temporarily removed, Teagarden seized the opportunity. He raised the plastic gun, held it upside down a few inches from his own chin, and fired.

Crack-k-k!

While rolling from bench to floor as fast as he could to get away from the needle, he guessed it was a misfire. That's not what a handgun sounds like. He guessed it was not even what a plastic handgun sounds like. He was preparing to shoot a second time when he saw that it was no misfire. Dr. Almonti was sitting perfectly upright, the unspent needle still poised in his right hand, his left hand pressed tightly to the left side of his face where blood spurted between his fingers. The doctor was stunned and still trying to understand what happened, which allowed Teagarden time to step away to a safer distance. He kept the .22 at the ready.

"Did I shoot you in the brain?"

"Apparently not."

"Where, then?"

Almonti gave his left ear a small tug as though plucking a flower from its stem. He extended his hand to display the pulpy mass of his own ear resting in his open, bloody palm.

"Wow," Teagarden said. "Your inner ear must be ringing."

"It is."

Teagarden was uncertain what to do next. Lines like "hands up," or "get on the floor," didn't seem appropriate. He steadied the weapon.

"All right," he said, "drop the needle. Stand up and turn around."

"Wouldn't you rather just shoot me?"

"No."

"No, you wouldn't, would you? What a shame."

Before Teagarden could respond, Dr. Almonti jabbed the needle into his own thigh. He grimaced with pain and flopped to the back of the pew where, for a moment, he appeared to gaze with curiosity at the trite universal celebration of faith. A dribble of bone-white saliva appeared on his lips a moment after the light went out of his eyes. Repelled at the sight but grateful to be alive, Teagarden caught his breath, tucked his weapon away, and rubbed his knees.

"I'm sorry, Dr. Almonti," he said, trying not to look too hard into the doctor's newly limp pupils. "Wherever you are right now, I hope it's not any worse for you."

Teagarden snatched his sports coat, swapped Elana Bar-Levav's cardkey with Dr. Almonti's, and hurried out the heavy door of the All Purpose Faith Sanctuary.

# CHAPTER THIRTY-NINE

Plunged back into run-for-your-life mode, Teagarden had no time to think. Autopilot kicked in as he descended flight after flight toward the bottom of the boat. He had no idea exactly where the cargo bays were located. He knew only that it was where forklifts rolled in with pallets of frozen orange juice, chocolate pudding mix, and giant bags of potatoes. Even if he didn't find the loading dock, at least he was moving away from Wharron's supervision of the disembarkation.

As for Elad, who knew? Teagarden assumed he was always around the next corner.

He struggled against the rush of exiting passengers. It was like trying to go up the down escalator at Grand Central Terminal during the morning surge of humanity. He turned sideways to let the flow of passengers reach elevators and staircases. Elderly for the most part, they were chubby and well-heeled Israelis and Americans with a smattering of Brits, Greeks, and Italians. All seemed excited to be going ashore to the magnificent Floating City, where they would walk along the canals and purchase forty-minute gondola rides that, afterward, some would say weren't as good as the gondola ride at The Venice Resort in Las Vegas. They'd return to the ship no later than five p.m. for a five-thirty departure. Come tomorrow morning, they'd all disembark again at Syracuse for a quick tour of Greek and Roman ruins on the Sicilian coast. All, that is, except Teagarden.

Eventually descending past the lowest level for general

231

passenger admission, he came to a faded directory on the firewall door:

Sicurezza
Infermeria,
Quarti di Equipaggio
Caffetteria Dell'equipaggio
Lavanderia.

It wasn't necessary to speak Italian to know the translation. The word meanings were easy enough. He didn't want to go to the security office, crew quarters, cafeteria, or laundry room. Since the ship's doctor was dead, it might be worth exploring his medical office. It would be easy since he now possessed his keycard. If he found nothing helpful, he'd resume his search for the cargo hold. Halfway down the narrow corridor, he found what he was looking for. The door was labeled "Infermeria, Infirmary, מרפאה."

He swiped Dr. Almonti's badge on the scanner and entered when the latch popped free. With no one home, the space was all his to explore. There was a tiny waiting room, a narrow hallway leading to two equally small examining rooms with portable gurneys, and a messy closet with shelves jammed full of medication boxes for treating sea sickness. The fourth door opened to a tiny office where a PC sat on a small desk cluttered with pamphlets about the norovirus. The final door was Dr. Almonti's private cabin. Barely large enough for a double bed and bedside table, it had a single porthole which he peered through.

The loading dock! It was farther aft and only one level below. He couldn't see it from that perspective, but he knew the loading bays were open because the forklifts were bustling in and out of view. They went in slowly, toting heavy pallets of beer barrels and five-gallon cans of olive oil, then emerged fast like go carts with the front prongs empty. Standing there, Teagarden worked details of a new strategy.

Yeah, it just might work, but even if it fails, it's still the best way forward. It's time to break radio silence because this has got to stop.

Dr. Almonti's Italian passport was on the bedside table, along with a small plastic baggie half-filled with white powder and a folded euro bill creased down the middle that still held white sprinkles.

So, Dr. Almonti was a junkie for the nose candy. What a surprise.

He snatched the passport. In the small office, he also took a white doctor's smock from the back of the desk chair and pulled it over his sportscoat. He clipped the cardkey with Almonti's photo to the front pocket, sat down at the desktop, and logged on to his email server as himself.

**From:** samteagarden@solarvector.com
**To:** cynthiablair@solarvector.com

first, know that am alive and well. i departed israel but won't say how, am now in europe but won't say where. yes, there is some danger. there is greater danger to those who seek to protect me or work with me as agent klassen can relate. Therefore i am working alone to prevent further bloodshed. i love you very much.
—sam

**From:** samteagarden@solarvector.com
**To:** bklassen@fbi.gov

it's only been a few days since we met, yet seems like a decade. first, allow me to express regrets for the horrible loss of life in Israel that i was lucky to survive. second, i am headed to the place you have no doubt figured. best not try to ride shotgun because the hitman stalking me is a killer so skilled that he rivals the grim reaper and I do not want you or others added to the growing kia list. just as bad, there is a global group called FFG also seeking to kill me for reasons i can't go into now (yes, i have made a significant q discovery). that doesn't mean i do not want to find deliverance from this hellish nightmare. please arrange for my salvation & rescue in the place referenced. third, and most important, continue with tight and ultra-secure protection of cynthia in the country house as FFG may seek to accomplish the unbearable. finally, be advised that if drakken had taken this assignment with greater respect for its significance and not redacted my briefing book, i am confident that lives could have been saved.

—teagarden

He logged off. He inspected the desk drawers, finding nothing of significance, though there was an old stethoscope which he attached to his neck before exiting the infirmary.

In the corridor, he found the internal staircase and descended to the cavernous storage hangars where the forklifts were busy delivering pallets of frozen fish, soda, and piña colada mixer. Head up, shoulders straight, stethoscope flopping atop the doctor's white smock with the nametag reading "Dr. N. Almonti," he strode into the dungeon like he owned it. Staying clear of machinery and hard hats, he marched out to the loading dock and across to a narrow dead-end canal where water taxis queued for fares. He was tempted to look back, to see if anyone found his presence unusual, or if he could spot Gretta Wharron at the forward bow. In the end, he didn't do it.

I'm a doctor on a mission. Just keep going.

Most passengers walked to the nearby Grand Canal. Once there, if they wanted transportation, they boarded a vaporetto waterbus at the ferry terminal. Regretting there were no Quickie cab boats, Teagarden approached a queue of water taxis, signaled the first in line, and boarded.

"Train station."

The driver shrugged unhappily and muttered under his breath as he cranked the engine: "Non hai bagagli ed è così vicino che potresti camminare in due minuti."

Teagarden didn't need to speak Italian to know the problem. He'd ridden in enough New York City taxicabs to know the universal irritation of drivers when the destination was so close you could practically sneeze on it. This man's resentment and curiosity were reaffirmed by his eyes peering at him in the rearview mirror. Teagarden ignored it.

It's understandable. How many doctors walk off a cruise ship through the cargo bay and hail a water taxi?

He removed the stethoscope and stuffed it into a side pocket of the white tunic. Only when the motorboat chugged from the dead-end canal and entered the wider Grand Canal did he venture a cautious look back at the dirty white Blue Voyager. No one appeared to be chasing him. Neither did he see Wharron near the starboard bow disembarkation point. As for Elad, it was best not to make assumptions. All Teagarden could be certain of was that the ex-Mossad killer was not sitting next to him in the water taxi.

Teagarden paused his anxiety long enough to enjoy the beauty of the Grand Canal. Being there was like stepping back into the eighteenth century. For a moment he considered tossing the Q Document into the water, followed by the .22, and the white tunic. He'd then redirect the cabbie to a hotel where he'd spend the next few days in world-weary recovery, admiring the preserved beauty and sipping Italian wine. With pockets full of euros, he could manage it. While hiding out in deluxe comfort, he'd call on Special Agent Klassen to "bring him in." And that would be that.

Yeah, right. That's not going to happen.

At the dock, he paid the water cabbie. Hoping to minimize his memory of the short trip, Teagarden left only an appropriate tip.

After a last glance at the elegance of the ancient city, he strode into the modern Santa Lucia Train Station. Once there, he saw both his next problem and what seemed to be the solution while standing in the ticket line. The first train bound for Berlin was nearly an hour away. The next train bound nonstop for Rome departed in seven minutes.

Rome, the Eternal City. Home to the Vatican—where the Pope lives.

It seemed like a good idea. He scanned the crowd. All faces seemed normal. They fell into two basic categories: numb with boredom or wired with excitement. The first group was mostly locals, people working the tourist industry and headed home after their shifts as waiters and hotel maids. The larger second group consisted of tourists, happy about their next stop in Il Bel Paese, the Beautiful Country. For most of them, it would be Florence, Rome, and Naples.

They all seemed harmless enough, but his safety in such a public place was a risk no matter how benign the crowd appeared. Lingering in the train station increased the likelihood that some FFG adherent would recognize him.

That would be bad.

Right or wrong, he did it. He bought a one-way biglietto to Rome, made a quick stop in the men's room to dump the lab coat and stethoscope, then hustled to platform sixteen. There, irony of ironies, the train was named La Volpe Romana, The Roman Fox.

I hope that's a favorable omen.

Maybe. Then again, maybe not.

# CHAPTER FORTY

It was one of the ultra-new, hyper-fast trains that allowed Italy to leap past China in the evolving technology. Elevated enough to allow wildlife to pass under, it was neither a monorail, nor a maglev. It operated on old-fashioned electricity, with over-and-under wheels like a roller coaster. The engine was the length of an eighteen-wheeler and shaped like a Maserati. It pulled eight elongated bullet-shaped cars down a swath of the ancient boot that was once the heart of the heart of the Roman Empire. This particular fast train traveled from Venice to Rome in the seemingly impossible time of one hour and five minutes. This meant moving so fast that the view out the window was dizzying. Consequently, each window was also a video screen that displayed a new snapshot of the passing terrain every five seconds.

Once in motion, the effect was tranquilizing. The nearly silent hum of the sleek engine, the gentle sense of movement, and the monotonous sequence of photo images combined to lull Teagarden into a shallow trance. He dreamed the images were a funeral mass of the recent dead, starting with Wechter. They kept coming, flashing like clickbait on MotherBoard, the death masks of Eveillard, Cole, Sanchez, Nasri, and now Kanakaris and Almonti. He jolted from the video requiem when the train suddenly lurched to an unscheduled stop, causing all video screens to revert to their function as regular windows. The name of the town was Arezzo. It didn't seem to matter because La Volpe Romana barely halted before it was again tearing south at a speed approaching three hundred miles per hour.

"Why don't we have this in the States?"

It took Teagarden a moment to realize the woman was speaking directly to him. In the seat facing his, she plopped her high-gloss magazine onto the narrow table separating them. It was *Cose di Casa*, in Italian, yet she spoke English like an American. He'd studied her before departure and everyone else for any sense of threat. None of them moved the needle. They all seemed to be what their appearance suggested: tourists, business people, grandparents visiting their grandbabies. His primary goal was to be certain Elad was not onboard. He wasn't. At least, not in his car.

"Pardon me?" he said to the woman, investigating her appearance a second time. Elegant and professional, with a model's good looks, she was black, about thirty-five, with intelligent eyes and short hair streaked with multiple shades of light brown.

"I said, 'why don't *we* have this?'" She was admiring the latest full-window snapshot: a pastoral olive field with sheep grazing in the foreground, rolling Tuscan hills in the background.

"Oh, right. Actually, the U.S. does have olive vineyards, you know—out west." He pursed his lips to indicate indifference.

"Oh, not the vineyards," she said. "I meant fast trains. They're such a wonder. It seems like every president since Ulysses Grant promised them. Yet here it is 2025 and Americans are still clunking along like hobos in boxcars. We get the hustle, while Europe gets the real deal."

He turned to their shared window displaying a new image of the passing Tuscan hills, now with a tidy stone farmhouse in the near distance. He didn't want to talk but feared unwanted attention by being dismissive.

"Oh, yes," he said. "If we had a service this fast, we could go from midtown Manhattan to downtown Washington in about forty-five minutes. Only teleportation would be faster."

"Now there's an idea. When that gets invented, I hope they prevent spiders and flies from getting stuck inside the teleport terminal. Did you ever see that old black-and-white movie about—"

Boing-buong!

She stopped to listen to the announcement made in Italian, letting him know she wasn't just looking at photos in the magazine. She spoke the language.

"La tua attenzione, per favore. Come controllo di sicurezza per la tua sicurezza, gli agenti della Polizia di Stato passeranno attraverso il treno per ispezionare i tuoi documenti di viaggio. Ti preghiamo di preparare i tuoi documenti identificativi."

A moment later, the same announcement was repeated in English: "Your attention, please. As a safety check for your security, officers with the State Police will be passing through the train to inspect travel documents. Please have your identity papers ready."

Uh-oh.

He tried to collect his thoughts. That explained the unscheduled stop. They must have boarded at Arezzo. Could Elad be behind it? The answer was—yes. Yes, he most certainly could be. Like Teagarden's rule for never underestimating the power of mathematics to explain the infinity of the universe, he was resolved to never underestimate that man. Yet, would he merely check passports? Then it dawned on him—Almonti. It wasn't Elad or FFG. It really was the Italian State Police, which meant they'd found the doctor's body and ordered a canvas of all trains, planes, and buses that recently departed Venice. They were likely searching for someone using a passport under the name Mateo Sakonnatayak Blackhorse Sanchez, which he no longer possessed, or Dr. Niccolò Almonti, which he did. There was one other possibility. They could be looking for someone using a passport with the name Sam Teagarden.

This is bad. Getting arrested and hiding in prison could be good. Unfortunately, nobody would believe this story, which would be bad. Still, avoiding Elad and FFG in a jail cell would be good. On the other hand, getting beat to death in prison by someone hired by Elad or FFG would be bad.

Everything is so complicated.

The announcement came again, this time in French, and again

the woman across from him listened intently: "Votre attention s'il vous plait. En tant que contrôle de sécurité pour votre sécurité, les agents de la police d'état traverseront le train pour inspecter vos documents de voyage. Merci d'avoir vos papiers d'identité prêts."

The woman put her shoulder bag on the narrow table, dug inside, and withdrew her passport as he retrieved Dr. Almonti's passport from his jacket pocket. Behind him, at the end of the long car, the doors swished open, sounding like the doors on the Starship Enterprise. Straining to look over his shoulder, he saw a man and a woman. The man was plain-clothed in a light full-length duster. The woman was uniformed in a light blue skirt and darker brass-buttoned blazer.

No question. Those two are definitely Italian State Police.

Before he could figure his next move, or even turn back around, the woman sitting opposite him snatched the passport from his waiting fingers.

"Don't stare at them," she said. "It will only arouse their suspicion." She opened the little booklet as she leaned forward and turned her head to speak in confidence so no other passengers would find the exchange unusual. "Funny, you don't much look much like Dr. Niccolò Almonti, born in Milano and died about ninety minutes ago onboard The Blue Voyager." Her voice was soft and friendly, almost sisterly.

His face said it all. He was astonished. "But, how—"

"A combination of sources. I've read the report on you." She picked up her cell phone and waved it casually. "I also viewed the emails you sent a short while ago to your wife and FBI Agent Klassen. That was a smart move. And I've read the police APB. You're wanted for murdering the Italian doctor and a Greek ship's porter."

"I did not—"

"Never mind," she interrupted, "It doesn't matter. We know there's a far-reaching contract on you." He was set to snatch the Almonti passport from her, which she saw coming. "Easy, now," she warned, almost chuckling. "In addition to not looking over your shoulder, let's also not make a scene. And do keep your voice down."

"I want to know—"

"Shh, we'll talk about all that later." She gave quick sidelong glance to the nearest passengers. "I was pleased when you purchased a first-class ticket for this train. There's not only more space, but more privacy as well." She tossed Almonti's passport into her bag, a trendy black leather satchel with shoulder straps, and again rummaged inside. This time she withdrew another passport and handed it to him. He knew from its coloring that it was American. "Take it," she said. "Think fast and try to keep it together. That's kind of important right now."

He accepted the document, opened it, and flipped to the main page. It was him. Everything about him was correct: DOB, signature, photo. Everything that is, except his name. It identified him as Lawrence Samuel Eagleton. Stunned, he looked at the woman sitting opposite him. Her face was neutral except for the eyes. Her eyes glistened with understanding.

"But how—"

"It was flown in this morning from Tel Aviv, compliments of my company and FBI Special Agent Klassen, who's still in charge of Operation Five O'clock. It's been ready for a couple of days. We expected you to turn up somewhere in Israel. Then you popped up on a cruise ship docking at Venice. Cute move. Unfortunately, we don't keep active agents in Venice. They had to fly it over on a U.S. Navy drone. Very tidy. One copy for each of us."

"You're with Langley?" She nodded in the affirmative with a slow up and down signal and a small eyeroll that, in a friendly manner, accused him of being slow on the uptake. "I don't believe you," he said. "If they don't keep agents in Venice, how come you were in the Venice train station?"

Her shoulders slumped as she spoke fast. "The captain of your ship issued a general alert about a stabbing and a fire alarm on board. We all took a fast train up from Rome immediately after that. Four of us. While waiting for you to show somewhere in Venice," she waved the cell phone again, "we learned you'd emailed Klassen and your wife. That confirmed your presence on board. I was already posted to the train station. Agents Bascom and Long were waiting for you at the airport. We double-teamed the airport because we figured that's where you'd go. Agent Platcher was sent to the Venice bus station." She smiled thinking about him. "Poor Robert Platcher. He always gets the crappiest surveillance gig. He gets sent to places like garbage dumps, home-less shelters, the chicken slaughterhouse. He once had to pose as an Italian meat inspector in a Croatian slaughterhouse for two weeks. Earned him his nickname—Platchy Cacciatore. He claims he hasn't eaten bird meat since."

Teagarden was pissed. He was relieved to finally be with an American ally, but her effort at disarming humor wasn't working for him. Since landing in Tel Aviv, he guessed he'd pumped more adrenalin and seen more death than most soldiers during a full tour in a warzone. He was ready to let her know his feelings when she leaned forward to intercept his momentum.

"Look, Mr. Eagleton, I'm intentionally talking shit to distract you. Got it? After all the scary crap you've been through, you need to listen to me. And you need to think fast. Prepare for what's coming down that aisle. Settle back in your seat and don't think about anything except being an American tourist headed for Rome. Your name is Larry Eagleton." She patted his hand. "I live in Rome. The Eternal City is wonderful this time of year. Just tell the nice police officers you're looking forward to visiting it. If they ask, tell them your hotel is near the Piazza Navona."

He did as she instructed. He leaned back, took a breath, and glanced at the latest photo frozen on the window screen. Ironi-cally, it was a ramshackle farm with a prominent chicken coop and scores of clucking birds.

"Platchy Cacciatore," he said, mostly to himself. "Funny."

"Yeah," she said, "that poor bastard never gets anything right."

"There's one in every office."

She nodded, her eyebrows raised in agreement.

"And by the way," she said, "is your cell phone off?" He nodded. "Good. Keep it that way. Stay calm now, Mr. Eagleton." The two officers progressed down the aisle while examining passports, Italian driver's licenses, and EU ID cards. They occasionally made small talk, issued false apologies and muttered casual comments of "thank you" and "grazie." At Teagarden's position they said nothing during the quick check of his document. It was a different story for the black woman sitting opposite him.

"Parli Italiano, Miss Karen Carrie Jantry?"

"It's—*Ms!* E sì, parlo italiano. Vivo e lavoro a Roma come ospite a Italia."

The man in the duster ignored the correction of her preferred form of address and switched to English. "Where were you born?" he asked, testing her while looking at her passport.

"Clarksdale, Mississippi."

"Are you traveling alone?"

"Yes."

"It's yes, *sir*," he corrected, imitating her own request. "Why do you go to Rome?"

"As I just said, I live there."

"And your business in Venice?"

"My business was in Milan. For my company, New Italia Cellular Technologies. I drove to Venice afterward for a visit. Now I am going home."

"Where do you live in Rome?"

"Trastavere."

"And you work for New Cellular?"

"No." She punched the word just enough to make it stand out as being unaccompanied by the word "sir." The plain-clothed officer closed the passport and held it while looking dead on into her eyes, waiting for additional information. The uniformed female officer stood beside him and slightly to his rear. The nametag clipped to the breast pocket of her blazer read "Poliziotto S. Russo." Teagarden studied her for any indication of discomfort

243

at her senior officer's line of questioning but saw none.

"I'm an investment banker with New York Trust and Finance," Jantry said. "New Cellular is going public on the Borsa. The IPO is currently valued at two and a half billion. In euros."

"Did you acquire that skill in Mississippi?"

"No. Harvard Kennedy School of Business in Boston and Goldman Sachs in New York." She flashed an acerbic smile. "Though I did acquire a few skills in Mississippi that have served me well."

A moment of visible enmity passed between them while the plain-clothed officer considered posing more questions. Instead, he returned the passport and moved on. After the Star Trek doors swished open to admit both officers into the next car, Teagarden asked, "Did he suspect you're with Langley?"

"No-o-o," she droned quietly so that only he could hear her. "He only suspected me of being a hooker or a hustler. All he knows is that I'm black, a woman, a non-Italian, and that I'm traveling alone with my disrespectful blackness. It's a cop thing. I'm used to it." They held each other's gaze. After a moment, she said, "But I know something important about that man you do not know."

"Okay?"

"He's looking for you. And if he knew who you were, emphasis on the word '*if*,' he would have dragged you off the train and beat you before turning you over. Afterward, he'd visit a confessional booth for absolution, then go home and sleep like a babe."

"But he's—"

"He's what? An officer of the law?" Teagarden nodded. "Mr. Eagleton, we're in Italy. This nation has played host to the Vicar of Christ since...well, since forever. Any challenge to that office presents unparalleled danger. Frankly, you were safer in Israel. And as you know, you were *not* safe in Israel."

He understood. The Vatican wanted him dead. Still, she wasn't fully up to speed. She had no idea that he'd learned the Q Doc was fake and that consequently FFG *also* wanted him dead.

Why would she? No one knew it except him and Gretta Wharron. He wanted to tell her, wanted the entire story to quickly gush out. If she could help him release the news, then the Vatican would flip Elad into being his protector instead of his assassin. He tried to speak. "Ms. Jantry, the Q Doc, it's…it's not what…"

"Hush."

"It's not…it's not the real…"

"Easy, Mr. Eagleton."

There was no point in trying. He was too upset. It was a bad time. Very inopportune. Unfortunately, he couldn't stop it, perhaps because of the relief he felt in understanding that she really was there to help him. Or perhaps simply because, enough was enough. Either way, everything culminated in that moment: drones, Wechter's death plunge, woman on fire, Megiddo, Gretta Wharron, and Dr. Almonti. When he broke down, he put one hand over his face and wept as quietly as he could. The CIA agent tucked a tissue into the palm of his free hand.

"Easy, Mr. Eagleton," she whispered. "I'm here to help."

# CHAPTER FORTY-ONE

The train maintained full speed until reaching a railyard that track workers called "La Signora con le Gambe Lunghe," a salacious nickname that meant, The Lady with Long Legs. It was a lengthy slowdown zone that consisted of a widely spaced pair of tracks that merged where they entered the tunnel. When it halted, it discharged all passengers inside Roma Termini at their own showcase platform dubbed "La Pista Veloce," a cantilevered track given the equally salacious sobriquet, L'Afterglow, by station workers.

Like every city boasting major metropolitan status, Rome's principal train station teemed with humanity. It wasn't peopled merely with passengers entering and leaving a travel hub, but also with office workers and various diverse urbanites—meeting, dining, and shopping; lovers sauntering; sullen teenagers desperate for distraction; pickpockets and panhandlers hoping for an easy touch.

Into this hubbub there entered two more: the fugitive, Professor Sam Teagarden and his new ally, CIA agent Karen Carrie Jantry, for whom he was suddenly filled with appreciation and awe. It was understandable. She not only saved his life but did so with great composure in the face of his own doubt and the malevolence of that Italian Ku Kluxer.

Watching her maneuver in the station crowd was like watching an off-duty dancer. She walked on her toes nearly like a cat, which he guessed couldn't be easy in high-stacked dark pumps that matched her gray-and-black high-waisted cigarette pants. If she was armed, the weapon must be inside the leather bag bouncing off her shoulder. It had to be, because there was nowhere else on her body to conceal a gun.

Departing the controlled chaos of the station, they emerged into the warm sun of the ancient city of Rome. Unlike Venice, it was modern and metropolitan yet somehow maintained the essence of antiquity. Teagarden imagined that the very cobblestones in the streets were once tread by Romans who ruled the known, not-so-wonderful world.

"Where are we going?" he asked a few minutes into the trek when they could barely stand abreast on the narrow sidewalk that lined a side street. When she didn't answer he said, "What about a taxi or an Uber?"

"Too dangerous. Unknown drivers are a big risk to covert operatives." She took his elbow as they walked the uneven stones. "Tell me something, Mr. Eagleton, why did you go south to Rome, instead of north to Berlin which, according to Agent Klassen, is where you were expected?"

Her comment about taxis worried him. He glanced nervously over his shoulder, then back and forth on a side street as they crossed an intersection. She turned and led him down another narrow sidewalk that seemed like it should be sparsely travelled, except that it wasn't. It was jammed with crowds of noisy American teenagers discharging from buses for the walk to the Roman Forum and nearby Colosseum. There were so many that Jantry and Teagarden couldn't avoid falling in with them.

"Did you intentionally embed with these rowdy tourists?" She gave a vague smile indicating that, yes, it was intentional. "Are you going to, as they say in spy movies, 'bring me in'?"

"Mr. Eagleton, you're neither a company employee nor a security risk to the U.S or its allies." She glanced at the noisy teenagers surrounding them and decided to choose her words carefully. "My assignment is to assist the Bureau with, shall we call it, another indelicate situation they've gotten themselves into. I am not going to, as they say in those movies, 'bring you in.' Although, yes, I am going to take you to my office for your own safety. If you wish to call that 'bringing you in,' be my guest."

He sighed. "What happens at your office?"

"We'll work that out soon enough. Answer my question. Why Rome?"

He looked away. For a moment the crowd of noisy teens thinned.

"The departure board in Venice," he responded. "The train to Rome was only a few minutes off. The first train bound for Berlin would have been an hour delay. I've got more people trying to find and kill me than you know about. I'll explain that when we get to your office. Plus," he hesitated, "I had an idea that I could speak to someone at the Vatican."

"About?"

"About canceling a...a..."

"Business contract?"

"Yes."

"You were just going to walk into St. Peter's and ask to speak to His Holiness?"

He exhaled another defensive sigh. "I wasn't thinking straight. You saw how upset I was on the train. This shit has got to stop."

"I get that part. You're stressed. Really stressed. You've got PTSD. I'll help you with that when we get to the office. But you're still smart enough to know that the top guy did not hire Elad. It's never the top guy. That sort of decision is always made by some mid-level capo. Even at my outfit."

"You know Elad?"

"Not personally. Everyone in my line of work knows *of* him. Word is, he did a job or two for us in the past. Plus, according to the report I read, he was behind the attack on you in New York."

"Yeah, that much I know."

"He's nicknamed The Israeli Shadow. Respected for his talent."

Teagarden stopped dead on the narrow sidewalk. Several squawking American teens caught up and bumped shoulders while passing. "Talented?" he asked. "Are you still talking shit to distract me?"

"Mr. Eagleton, I don't mean to say—"

"Talented. Really?"

"That was not meant as—"

"You actually said that. 'Talented!'"

She turned away and walked ahead. The raucous teens passed, then turned down one of the wider avenues, while Jantry and Teagarden stayed on narrow cobblestone side streets. The last time he was in Italy was with his first wife who was killed years ago in a horrible auto accident on the New York State Thruway. He still missed her, just as he missed his present wife, who helped him survive the ordeal wrought by another darkly talented man bent on killing him. That man's name was Harry McCanliss. Funny how his pathology seemed much like Elad's: macho, arrogant, thin-skinned, smart yet really dumb. Or, perhaps it was more accurate to say, dumb yet really smart. Either way, the result was the same.

The fact is, smart people are some of the dumbest people I know.

While walking, he noticed a difference in how they looked about with caution. He tended to rubberneck people for any sense of danger, particularly those coming up from behind. She, however, tended to inspect motorized traffic, paying particular attention to motorbikes and Vespa scooters that zipped everywhere in such a hurry they reminded him of the rats in the tunnel at Megiddo. She also carefully eyed small cars like Fiats and unmanned Quickie cabs. For the most part, she let her eyes do the work without moving her head much, which made him wonder if she knew something he didn't. Then he realized, well—yeah, of course she does. She's CIA. It was her job to know more.

Soon, the great preserved symbol of the Roman Empire came into view. It was also the principal reason that made Theo Kanakaris realize the Q Doc was fake, which in turn was the reason he was stabbed by Gretta Wharron and poisoned by Dr. Niccolò Almonti. Teagarden caught up with her on the pavement and stayed with the subject of Elad.

"Ms. Jantry, I've seen the results of that man's talent firsthand, so much so that I've come to think of him as supernatural. Tell me, did you know FBI Agent Aaron Wechter, CIA Agent Emmanuel Eveillard or Lieutenant Joseph James Cole? How about Sergeant Mateo Sakonnatayak Blackhorse Sanchez?"

At each name, she shook her head slightly. "I didn't know any of them, though I crossed paths with Eveillard a couple of times. Once at Langley and again in New York. He was much higher up the food chain than me. Had a full staff in Tel Aviv and, before that, in the Central American quadrant. I heard he once got a citation from the president for an operation that saved lives in Venezuela."

"Well, then you—"

"Never mind, Mr. Eagleton. I've said too much on the subject already. I just want you to know that I understand. I get it. Like it or not, it's the risk all Company operatives signed up for."

"What's the answer to my question? What happens at the office?"

She glanced at the looming façade of the Colosseum two blocks away.

"I'm still in phase one analysis," she said. "And you're still in security verification mode. Come on, let's go."

# CHAPTER FORTY-TWO

Jantry moved to the shortest queue labeled "Privato" to enter the Colosseum. When a bored security guard approached, she displayed her State Department diplomatic shield with such easygoing subtlety that Teagarden nearly missed it. Afterward, they breezed past the ocean of humanity to enter the arena's main floor. The same throng of noisy American teenagers that jostled them on the street was already there, crowded around their English-language tour guide, taking selfies, and looking at the maze of corridors.

"That's called the hypogeum," the guide said, gesturing to the exposed cellar. "How many of you have participated in a school play?"

"Me," called a dozen excited voices.

"Did you have curtains, and lights, and special effects?"

"Yes," the same dozen shouted, then some added: "fog machine," "we had strobe lights," and "a gun that fired blanks."

The tour guide enthusiastically approved. "All right," she said. "That's the sort of thing that happened down there. That was special effects central. It's where CGI happened before CGI. During the shows, workers down there tugged on a complex system of ropes and pullies that could hoist a gladiator or a lion straight to the arena floor, making it appear as though they magically popped up out of nowhere."

The delighted teenagers said "whoa," "wow," and "whoo."

Jantry tapped Teagarden's elbow, and they eased past the crowd to walk along the circular aisle where they took in the spectacle of preserved history. He'd visited the Colosseum during that Italy trip many years earlier with his first wife. It was wonderful then. Now, even under dangerous circumstances, it remained a stunning relic of history to witness. This was where all levels of Roman society came to witness men murdering men, animals killing and eating humans, and humans killing wild animals—all for the pleasure of the audience who enjoyed the spectacle of suffering. Patrician, plebeian, and prole—they were all admitted free of charge to the pageant of blood that he knew, thanks to Theo Kanakaris, first opened in the year 80 A.D. That made it 1,945 years old.

It was their…their…their what? Their NFL? Their religion? Their church? Their opium? God almighty, what kind of society found that pleasurable? And why?

Then he remembered Elad.

That former Mossad killer would have done well here. As a gladiator, he'd have put on a good show for the crowd and the emperor. Lots of blood. Lots of drama leading up to lots of blood.

Teagarden wondered again if Eveillard, Cole, and Sanchez managed to put up much of a fight against the latter-day gladiator from Israel's killer-elite. Probably not. He wondered if stealth played well in the crimson grandeur of the Roman games. Again, probably not. That crowd wanted losers to die well after a good fight, like the bull after a good bull fight in Madrid. Romans would no more love a stealthy gladiator with a black belt in karate than Spaniards would love a matador with a machine gun.

"Yes, women too," the tour guide said, responding to a question from one of the teenagers. "There were women gladiators. They too fought to the death, just like the men."

Again, the American teens cheered noisily with comeback comments about "Wonder Woman" and "Katniss Everdeen" from *The Hunger Games*.

"This way," Jantry said. "Let's go around. My favorite surveillance spot in all of Rome is on the other side."

They hustled past thick crowds until they circled one hundred eighty degrees to a series of concentric tunnels. To the left of the first tunnel was a scale model of the original Colosseum about the size of a small car. Jantry turned right to enter a cloistered space shadowed by the ancient arcade. From there, behind the safety railing overlooking the hypogeum, she could monitor the entire arena, including the main entrance, without being seen. In this spot, except for the tourists enchanted with the scale model, the only other group was directly below them in the hypogeum listening to an Italian-language guide.

"What are we—"

"Hush," Jantry interrupted. "I need to make certain we weren't followed. This tourist trap is great for that. It originally had eighty entrances. For today's visitors, there's only one entrance and one exit."

"That's what Elad said about the tunnel at Megiddo."

"Stop worrying about him. There's reliable intel that he's already bound for Berlin."

Well, that's some good news. Maybe coming to Rome was the right thing to do.

He stood behind her as she watched tourists enter the preserved arena of death. After a minute, she kicked off her pumps and let them flop beside her feet clothed in beige stockings. Somehow it made her seem relaxed, which made him feel a little less stressed.

"Did you really go to Harvard?"

"Yes."

"And do you really work as an investment banker?"

"For a few years. Not anymore. You know who I work for, Mr. Eagleton."

"That was a sweet narrative you laid on that jerk policeman on the train. Very smooth."

"Thank you, Mr. Eagleton. Give me a minute here, will you? I need to concentrate on faces in the crowd."

He wandered to the scale model. It had a cutaway section of the interior revealing details of seating, crowd control passageways, and underground corridors with trapdoors, cages, pullies, and levers. Nearby, he read educational placards posted on the wall. Exits were called "vomitoria" which meant "to spew forth." Seating sections were called "cavea" and were composed of sections named "podium, gradatio, and porticus." One label detailed construction materials: "Roman cement and travertine, a limestone still used today throughout Italy."

Minutes later, he was back at her side.

"Hey, did you know the exits here were called 'vomitoria'?" She still ignored him. "No? Well, do you know what a cavea is? How about travertine? No? Okay, I'll tell you. Travertine was an important building material vital to Roman engineers. If this is your favorite place to detect undercover bloodhounds, you really should know what it's constructed of."

"Do you find this amusing, Mr. Eagleton?" She held a steady gaze upon the main threshold where anyone following them would enter. "It's your safety that I have in mind."

"I appreciate that. Tell me, Ms. Jantry, how long since you graduated from the Farm?"

"How do you know about the Farm?"

"I worked at Langley a bunch of years ago."

For the first time, she broke her focus and looked at him. "That wasn't in the report."

"You must not be cleared for my full bio."

"It must have been a college internship."

"Close," he said. "As a numbers analyst I skipped the Farm and went straight to the office of encryption/decryption. It was boring. The worst job I ever had, which is why I quit in the first year."

After a pause, she said, "I graduated five years ago. After the Farm, I was dumped in record redacting." She turned back to her surveillance. "And that was the worst job *I* ever had."

Behind her back, the tie cord of her black leather shoulder bag was undone, causing it to flop open. Inside, he saw what he suspected. It was the rectangular handle of a Glock. He wondered if she knew he was packing a loaded .22.

"How long have you been in covert operations?"

"Never mind."

"That long? The suits must have liked having you in record redacting." The muscles around her mouth gave a small twitch, letting him know she didn't care for his snarky sarcasm.

"Mr. Eagleton, you had an understandable indulgence of emotion on the train. Now it seems that you're finding relief in being silly. Unless you're hitting on me. Be advised, I'll be tolerant of the former, not the latter."

That shut him up.

The noisy American group was on the move, their tour slowly advancing toward them. He glanced again into her shoulder bag that draped open at her back. Under the Glock was a pair of neon blue Adidas sneakers. Tucked inside one sneaker was the passport belonging to Dr. Almonti which she snatched from him on the train. Teagarden was about to warn her to cinch-up the gaping satchel when he noticed something else. Something familiar. It was a necklace.

Wait, what?

He reached into the opened flap and, with thumb and forefinger, withdrew the necklace from the other blue sneaker. The ornament dangling on the silver chain was the reason for his astonishment. It was the civil defense symbol for an atomic fallout shelter.

Un-fucking believable.

While ogling the pendant, he failed to see Jantry's eyes markedly flinch at something on the opposite side of the Flavian Amphitheatre.

# CHAPTER FORTY-THREE

Teagarden backed deeper into the overhanging travertine labeled "maenianum primum," the first balcony. He felt in his coat for the comforting handle of the .22 and found it. He said nothing, but it was as though a voice of clairvoyance had spoken, making her sense something was amiss. When she turned, she saw the dangling necklace in his left hand and understood everything in an instant. The fingers of his right hand tightened on the pistol grip inside his pocket.

"Mr. Eagleton—"

"I wanted to fill you in on new details. There's no need to explain that more people than Elad are now trying to kill me. You already know all about them, don't you?"

"Listen to me, Mr. Eagleton."

"And you're one of them. You're a member of FFG. Right, Ms. Jantry? Freedom from God. You're one of those militant anti-god people. They're so crazy that they want to kill me just as badly as Gladiator Elad."

"I'm not a member of—"

"Of course you are." He jangled the necklace.

"Mr. Eagleton, now is not the time—"

"You're smarter than Gretta Wharron, who, by the way, was not stupid. Crazy, but no dope. What's your role with FFG? Are you global chairwoman? Or just head of the local chapter?"

She breathed hard with suppressed exasperation.

"Goddamit Eagleton, that trinket doesn't prove—"

"It's all the proof I need. And keep your hands where I can see them."

She held steady and kept her voice low to avoid unwanted attention. "All right, Mr. Eagleton, I apologize for not listening to your story earlier. Go ahead, lay out your case. What happened on the ship?"

"My story is a little more complicated than just the ship. There are four parts. Part one: fearing I'd decode the Q Doc, the Vatican put Elad on me in New York because of my reputation. By the way, there was no chance I could do the job because I don't speak Greek. Nonetheless, the church didn't figure that out, so it wanted me dead like the Spanish professor who actually did decode it."

"Got it. I'm with you on that."

"Part two: the FBI wanted me to hook up with the CIA as window dressing to make it look like they were doing something meaningful about the suicide crazies, when in fact, they're not doing shit."

"I get that too. It's all show business. For them, you're as good as a series on Netflix. Plus, there's no love lost between my company and the Bureau."

"Part three: FFG suspected why Zurbarán was killed in Santiago de Compostela. When they heard I was on the job, they stepped in as an ally. All that changed on the ship once the Q Doc was verified as the handiwork of some asshole prankster from the Middle Ages. That's a fact Zurbarán missed when decoding the words without researching their meaning."

Mindful of her job, Jantry quickly scanned the arena floor, found what she was looking for, then turned back to him. "Listen, if there's a part four you better get to it quickly, because we don't have much time."

"Why?"

"Mr. Eagleton, do you recall on the train when I told you to 'think fast and keep it together'?" He said nothing. "I'm doing that again. Think fast and keep it together."

She let her leather bag flop from left shoulder blade to left breast. To him, it was a hostile move, like when a gunslinger tosses aside his coattail, making ready to draw down. In response, like a gangster in an old mob movie, he poked the barrel of his gun from inside his coat pocket, making it clear he was armed.

"I'm thinking fast and keeping it together just fine," he said with a nod to the protrusion.

She looked at the cylinder-shaped bulge in his side pocket. "I haven't seen a gesture like that since I stopped watching old gangster movies on TCM."

"I wouldn't know. I'm partial to ESPN. I like the Yankees."

"Tell me Mr. Yankee Fan, does the name Russo mean anything to you?"

"No."

"It should."

"Why?"

"It was the name of the police officer on the train. Not the skeevy detective who questioned me for living while being black. I'm referring to his backup, the one who wore a skirt. Officer S. Russo. I'll bet you a plate of fettuccini Alfredo the S stands for Sofia."

"So?"

"So she walked into the Colosseum just as you decided to poke your piece at me. And she'll be strolling past us both any second now. If she does the job she's here for, it's a win-win for her. She'll get a cop citation for popping the killer of Dr. Almonti and a Greek ship's porter. That's *you*. Later, FFG will throw her a congratulatory blowout poolside party, complete with raw bar and live music."

He leaned a little to the left, then right, to peer past the columns supporting the maenianum primum, but saw no one familiar.

"I don't believe you."

"I get how complicated this has become Mr. Eagleton." She sighed. "But you need to know, I am not FFG. I am CIA. And I have that necklace only because it was taken from a suicide crew in St. Peter's Square on Tuesday, the same day and same time as the bloody demo you witnessed in Jerusalem. I'm holding onto it in case it can be used as a cover."

"Nice effort, but it doesn't work for me. You need to understand that if you reach for the Glock in that shoulder bag, I will shoot you."

"Oh, Mr. Eagleton—now *I* don't believe *you.*"

"Ask Dr. Almonti if you should believe me."

"You mean you really did kill him?"

"No. Not exactly. But I did shoot his ear off."

She nodded as though she understood more than he could imagine.

"Look, Mr. Eagleton, we did not know about your discovery of an ancient fraud. That's very important. As for FFG, they've been on the radar a long time."

"Eveillard didn't say so."

"I'm saying so. As for Elad, I already told you he's headed for Berlin. It was mainly FFG I feared following us from Roma Termini. And clearly that fear was justified because she's headed toward us now."

"Officer Russo is FFG?"

"Why else would she show up here?"

"Why didn't we see her following us?"

"Because she wasn't following us. But someone was. More likely, it was more than one someone watching, following, and making calls. Plus, FFG's enrollment is big and getting bigger, thanks to Gen X, millennials, and Gen Z. It's not a crime being an atheist. The challenge is pinning down who's in FFG's militant branch, which is the same problem we've had for two generations with Islam."

"Is Russo still in uniform?"

"Yes. And by the way, I can now finish part four of your saga for you: FFG wants you snuffed to suppress discovery that the Q is fake, while the Vatican still wants Elad to do his job because they don't yet know it's a fake."

"As someone once said to me, 'now you're fully downloaded.'"

"Unfortunately, you're not," Jantry said. "Listen, this was supposed to be an easy day-shift gig for me. A basic grab-and-go. I hook up with you, confirm no bloodhounds, and escort you to the company office, which is a couple of blocks from here. Once there, you'll be debriefed, then turned over to the Bureau. They'll take you to Berlin or send you home, or whatever. For me, that's simple. You're lousing that up with that toy gun you found in the emergency case in the back of the company Ford." She paused. "It is the plastic .22, right?"

He nodded. "Yes," he said. "How'd you know where I got it?"

"Oh, brother. That stuff is standard issue for all company cars. And you need to stand down because this is going to put a fat fuck-up on my record. Officer Russo, however, will get a shiny medal pinned to her chest after she rounds that corner and drills four extra buttonholes into your two-button sports coat."

Before he could respond, Italian State Police Officer S. Russo edged into the columned arcade. Her eyes obsessively scanned tourist faces while the butt of her right palm rested atop the grip of her holstered Beretta 93 machine pistol. It was a fluke of luck that Russo turned first to examine the opposite side of the gallery where a crowd was drawn to the cutaway scale model of the Colosseum.

It was the quickest decision he'd ever made. The moment he saw Russo, he believed Jantry. Watching his eyes and hands closely, Jantry instantly recognized his change of mind. The grant of a micro-moment provided by Russo's turning away was a bonus neither of them intended to waste. They pivoted to the opposite direction and hurried in total silence down a flight of steps to the hypogeum.

Seconds later, Officer Russo couldn't miss the conspicuously out-of-place pair of lady's dark-colored pumps resting near the top of the steps. Leaning over the safety railing, she caught sight of her prey bolting through the ancient maze like panicked tigers on their way to centerstage.

"Fermate! Fermati o ti sparo."

# CHAPTER FORTY-FOUR

Teagarden's normally well-adjusted and analytical mind hadn't functioned properly since Theo Kanakaris fell bleeding into his stateroom while warning that the puzzle was a hoax. Now he was *inside* a puzzle. And this puzzle was no hoax. It was the original fun house. The primal maze where violence and death awaited presentation as entertainment.

The tunnel at Megiddo where he violated the house of rats was bad. This was worse.

Now I am a rat. What's more, I'm a rat in the original Roman rat maze of death.

He feared his thoughts were symptomatic of continuing mental impairment. Yet he couldn't stop obsessively thinking once again about his freshman psychology class at Chapel Hill.

Rats are not intelligent because they can navigate a maze to find the bread crumb. That's a false assumption. It only makes them appear intelligent. Fact is, that's precisely what rats have done for millions of years. Rats are natural maze runners. They've evolved the talent of navigating networks of holes, tunnels, pipes, paths, channels, burrows, nooks, dungeons, vaults, webs, and concealed chambers. It's what they must do to eat, survive, and live another day. When the first shrink, who dubbed himself a behavioral psychologist (and probably smoked a pipe) decided to run a rat through a maze and call it science, he was not only an academic fraud, he was also a total asshole.

Once in the hypogeum cellar, they did not stop as Officer

Russo commanded. Instead, they continued fleeing through the ancient maze: right, left; right, left.

Teagarden loved science and math but despised Psych 101, mostly because of that once-a-week lab session. He consumed the Morgan & King psychology textbook. Then came his turn on lab day to run the rat and push the red button.

And he did it. As an eighteen-year-old undergrad, he pushed that button. He actually gave that plump, white, pink-tailed laboratory martyr an electric shock and took notes as instructed: "mild shock—rat jumps in pain, keeps going; medium shock—rat jumps in pain, defecates, pauses, appears confused, finally keeps going; severe shock—rat jumps in pain, defecates, pauses much longer, appears paralyzed, refuses to move forward."

Once Officer Russo reached the bottom of the steps and entered the hypogeum, she called out her warning again, this time in both Italian and English: "Fermate! Fermati o sparerò! Stop or I will shoot!"

He even remembered the name of that poor rat: White Girl Number Two. And he tortured her with a push of the red button.

They did not stop. With Jantry in the lead, they ducked and hustled through the ancient narrow corridors where gladiators and tigers once trod before hastening to their stage entrance and ultimate death.

Later came a demo which the professor called "a measurement of self vs. selflessness." Two white lab rats. White Girl Number Two and her husband, Gray Leg, were put in the narrow network. Only the lead rat received shocks. When minimal, the male leader held position to protect his partner. When the shocks became severe, the leader pushed his partner to the front, then turn and ran. "Aha! Let that be a lesson to you all," the professor said, "it doesn't matter who's leading, whether male or female, the poetry of love is not written in stone. It is written in self-preservation! It is written in—**save my ass!**"

Officer Russo was good on her threat. She withdrew her weapon, aimed, and fired.

It wasn't a mere shot that went "bang" or "pop." It sounded like a high-pitched M-16 set to burst mode: *blaam-alam-lamm!* Then it came again: *blaam-alam-lamm!*

Teagarden snapped back to reality.

I'm being shot at. Not only that, but I'm being shot at with a machine gun inside the two-thousand-year-old Flavian Amphitheatre full of twenty-first century tourists. This is really—really—not good.

In that moment, his odd thoughts about lab rats stopped while his mind shifted to total panic. He halted, he spun about, gawked at the upstairs arena level where tourists were stampeding, fleeing for their lives, and running for cover behind ancient Colosseum stones. He too was ready to bolt and run without regard for anyone else. Jantry, however, kept her head. She grabbed him by the hand to lead the way, going straight for a short distance, then left, then left again. Reaching a dead-end, she pulled him into a tightly covered niche.

"Squeeze in here with me," she whispered.

He pulled in his legs and sat facing her, their legs interlocking like puppies in a shoebox. Her knees were flexed high and her stockinged feet were pulled in so tightly that she was nearly sitting on her toes.

Above them, the sounds of animal fear pierced the air as people ran in pure terror. They didn't know that Officer S. Russo wasn't after them. They knew only that it was happening—a gunman was roaming the corridors, killing anyone unlucky enough to be in the wrong place at the wrong time, turning the Colosseum into a real-life video game of death.

"Cops with machine guns. Really?" It was his voice, though it seemed someone else was speaking.

"Don't talk. It's a machine pistol," she whispered. "It fires three-shot bursts."

"Oh, only three. I feel so much better."

"Pull in your feet."

"You left your nice shoes back there."

"Never mind them. We have to wait here until she returns to the front of the hypogeum."

"How will we know?"

"*We* won't know. *I* hope to know by doing something called listening. For that, I need you to be quiet."

"Then what?"

"Then we'll have enough time to exit through the gladiators' back door."

"Is that where they carried out the dead? Hey, I thought there was only one entrance and—"

"I said *hush*. Whisper if you must talk." She cautiously poked her head out for a turtle-like look. "I told you already," she whispered when she pulled back in. "The company office is close by. We're forced to study this place inside-out. It's good for many uses: shaking a bloodhound, confidential talk, a dead drop, threat elimination. I know more about maneuvering in this old stadium than I do in my own apartment building."

"What is this nook we're stuffed into?"

"Base of an elevator shaft." She looked up at the fragile roof covering them. "That was once a trapdoor for sending big cats and gladiators into the fight."

"Great, we're hiding in a dumbwaiter. Are we going to rise and pop out on the arena floor?"

"Shh. Don't be more stressed than necessary. The traps haven't worked in over a thousand years."

"How many were there?"

"Dunno. Bunches."

"And how do you know Officer Russo will circle back to the front like you want her to?"

"I don't. We're safely concealed for now, as long you keep your voice down. We cut through the maze toward the front. After she fired a second burst, we cut back to this old elevator shaft at the rear. She has no idea where we are."

Listening to her made him wonder if she majored in psychology, then he hoped she did. That would mean she was experienced in running the rat maze. "Where's your Glock?"

"In my bag, where it belongs."

"But—"

"I have no intention of shooting an Italian State Police Officer," she whispered. "I'd surrender before doing that."

"But you're okay with her shooting me?"

She considered his question before answering. "Good point. It is a moral dilemma. I wonder if the company has an E and J form for that."

"E and J?"

"Explain and justify. There're E and J forms for nearly everything."

"Including sex on the job?" She ignored him. "Wow. That means if 007 had to fill out E and J's he must have done a lot of stupid deskwork we don't know about. In Italian, I believe that's called 'lavoro stupido.'"

"Here's some Italian for you: if you don't *silenzio* you're going to get us both *molto morto*."

Danger or not, scrunched up in a three-sided chamber that once hoisted lions to the arena floor was not to his liking. He withdrew the bulky .22.

"I'll tell you what," he said, displaying the weapon, "*this* is my E and J. And since you won't shoot her, I will."

"All right 007, put that thing away. The stress is affecting your head. You're displaying all kinds of clutter-brain phenom ranging from despondent to euphoric. I'll requisition a nice valium for you when we get to the office. Besides, that gimmicky spy toy you found in the company car wouldn't stand a chance against a machine pistol. It has no muzzle velocity and even less impact. Not to mention that she's wearing body armor. The only way to take her down with that toy is a direct shot in the eyeball. Even then it would have to be at close range."

After a pause, he said, "I apologize."

"Apology accepted. Not entirely your bad. It's foxhole mentality. What the shrinks called 'Band of Brothers,' and all that."

Wow, maybe she did major in psychology.

He sighed and let the revolver rest on his knee. A little piece of blue sky was visible past the decayed walls of the hypogeum maze. The sounds of panicked humanity had faded, which meant the crowds of tourists had safely escaped. He wanted to share something with her but feared she'd notch it somewhere on her chart of emotional despondency. He was about to tell her that he liked her, but that she was just the latest of several partners: Klassen, Eveillard, and Wharron. One was wounded, one was dead, and one had turned on him. Now, there was Jantry.

"Listen," he whispered, "I don't want..." He stopped and started again. "I don't want you to be the next—"

Before he could finish, he was interrupted by squawking police radios and the echoing stomp of hobnail boots. That was followed by the metallic clank of multiple automatic weapons being readied for discharge. All the sounds were coming from above them on the main floor at the Colosseum entrance.

"Russo?" a masculine voice loudly shouted, "c'è il sicario lì?"

"Shh-h-h," came the response.

"Oh, scusa."

"Grazie per aver annunciato la mia posizione. Stronzo!"

"That's our cue," Jantry whispered, pulling Teagarden by the wrist. "Russo is at the front of the hypogeum. Let's go before the backup storm troopers spread out and find us."

They hurried west, ducking low in the open-air channels of the hypogeum, then entered an enclosed maze of covered tunnels that twisted in multiple directions, including farther below ground. Jantry led the way, occasionally grabbing Teagarden's arm or shoulder to silently indicate which turn she'd take, and which darkened passageway he should follow. They came to the door just as sounds of pursuit could be heard in the halls behind them. It was a modern door, metal and painted battleship gray. Jantry pulled him close to whisper straight into his ear.

"This must go fast and smooth. On the other side of this door we go up the steps, to the sidewalk, then across the street. Don't stop for traffic. Make the traffic stop for you, and don't worry about getting run down. Italian drivers are okay with dodging brazen pedestrians. Then we descend into the Colosseo metro station. Once there, no turnstile jumping. I'll card you through. Got it?"

"Got it," Teagarden said.

Her plan went exactly as described: door, steps, sidewalk, street, traffic, metro entrance, turnstile, escalator, metro tunnels, platform, train arrival, board train, quickly deboard train before doors close, platform again, metro tunnels again.

Agent Jantry had successfully lost the trigger-happy police-woman secretly pulling double-duty for FFG. At the same time, they also evaded backup police responding to the "shots fired" call, only to foolishly reveal Officer Russo's position. Though he didn't speak much Italian, Teagarden lived in New York City long enough to know that the Italian word "stronzo" meant asshole.

Back on the surface, they walked toward the CIA's satellite office which she pointed out from the nearest intersection. It was typical twentieth century architecture for the city of Rome, a postwar six-story building made of thick stone, currently under-going renovation. The façade was brimming with flimsy-looking scaffolding, populated by hard hats using risky construction tech-niques common in Europe. At that moment, a heavy bucket was being raised from sidewalk to rooftop by a man hoisting a rope hand-over-hand. The hard hat sending the bucket aloft from the sidewalk had stepped aside to heave a hand trowel twenty feet into the air to another man standing in a third-floor window.

"Getting the place remodeled?" Teagarden asked.

"Has nothing to do with us. We've got the top floor and the roof. Let's skip the main public lobby and enter through the courtyard just beyond. That's our private entrance."

Behind them, the Colosseum's rounded battlement loomed overhead. No one was pursuing them on the one-way street so narrow it seemed barely wide enough for a single Fiat to pass.

Yet it didn't matter. Their problem wasn't to the rear. It was at the front.

Teagarden saw him first. He was standing on the opposite side of the street, across from the gated driveway he and Jantry were about to enter.

Elad!

# CHAPTER FORTY-FIVE

Teagarden's spinal fluid chilled to dry ice.

He was grateful that Jantry didn't notice the ex-Mossad agent on the street. Maybe she didn't because she'd never seen a true photo. Or maybe the Elad he knew looked significantly different from the Elad that CIA agents knew. Either way, it was a lucky break. He was more grateful that he didn't panic and blubber the name aloud. For a moment it felt as though he'd shouted, "ELAD!" Even a reflexive mumbling of the name would have triggered Jantry into full commando mode, and that would have been the end of them both.

He had to think fast. There were several obvious choices: turn and run, calmly explain the situation to Jantry and tell her to "keep it together" as she'd twice admonished him to do. Or he could withdraw the .22 and do a Marshal Matt Dillon right there on Rome's ancient cobblestones.

They all sucked.

Fortunately, there was one more option. Simply behave as though he'd failed to notice the world's most efficient killer as he casually loitered on the opposite curb. After spotting him, and before completing a single additional stride, he'd made up his mind.

Pretend!

It was the least risky choice. It was a gamble that he and Jantry would survive the next thirty seconds, about the amount of time they needed to walk to the gate, through the courtyard, and into the building. It all had to be done without being made *molto morto*. And preferably they needed to arrive more than merely alive, but without the need for tourniquets.

Just don't look at him!

So much for Jantry's report that he was headed for Berlin. Three more steps and they'd pass through the gate. Inside the courtyard stood a plain-clothed security guard trying not to appear like a guard.

Good luck to you, sir. I may be the principal target, but you'll be the first to die if you jump to my defense.

Once inside the courtyard, the larger main gate swung open so an Alfa Romeo sedan could exit the circular drive. Even with smoked windows, he could see a silhouette of one man in the back seat. Teagarden guessed the driver was a professional chauffeur.

If he's a CIA agent like Eveillard, then he too would get a star etched onto the Memorial Wall in the lobby at Langley.

The vehicle paused at the sidewalk. Teagarden stole a glance at the guard. He appeared unruffled. That was another moderately good sign. The engine of the Alfa Romeo revved as it turned onto the street that seemed too narrow to accommodate a car of its size.

We're at the building door, and still no fuss.

In the threshold, he decided to make a precautionary glance. He felt for the handle of his .22 and turned as casually as he could to gaze toward the rear in an untroubled manner.

And there he was.

Elad!

Elad, the quick and quiet.

Elad, the ex-Mossad hitman.

Elad, the killer elite, silent assassin, mass murderer.

The bastard was smoking a cigarette, coolly reclining against a shuttered tin shack that, when open, sold newspapers and tobacco. His chin was cocked skyward as he vented both lungs of whitish-gray smoke that fluttered skyward and dissipated. In that moment, nearly one hundred feet away, their eyes met. It was like radar. Like the fixed gaze of a gliding vulture when it locks onto the nest-sitting robin.

Do you see me? Do you see how easy it would be for me? You know I am unshakeable. I am unstoppable. I am Elad. I am the man who will...who will...who...

Teagarden unlatched from the eyes of the beast. Inside the doorway, he was relieved to see a heavy security contingent. Uniformed American Marines bearing M-4s monitored a tight screening process that included metal detection, full-body scan, and iris recognition. There were also non-uniformed men and women whom he took to also be Marines at the ready for any requirement. When he asked if they wished to see a passport, the response was a curt, "Sir—no thank you."

Jantry waited for him on the other side of security with all his effects confiscated by the guards and passed to her. She sealed them inside a clear plastic bag labeled:

U.S. Government
Proprietary and Confidential
Made from Recycled Products

When he approached, she was putting on her neon blue Adidas. He waited until she stood to make his outrage known to everyone within earshot.

"You are so lucky to be alive" he said, wiping his forehead suddenly bursting with perspiration. The entire security team heard.

"Easy, Mr. Eagleton," Jantry said. "We're an elevator ride away from home base. No need to have another breakdown now."

"The only breakdown to discuss is yours." He turned to the team of security Marines. "And theirs."

She didn't like it. Neither did a plain-clothed man with the security team who Teagarden took to be the ranking officer. Of intimidating height, he was a black man with a complexion darker than ebony, yet also with a case of vitiligo on his neck where a prominent blotch of skin was as pink as cotton candy.

He stepped closer to Teagarden and Jantry on the secure side of the metal detector.

"Is there a problem here?" he asked. His tone let it be known that any problem within his venue was his business.

"Yes sir," Teagarden blurted, "there certainly is."

"Never mind," commanded Jantry. "We'll discuss it upstairs. The elevator bank is around the corner."

"Sir, I'm listening," the Marine said.

"Unbelievable," Teagarden continued, refusing to be intimidated by either of them. "Why didn't you people see him?" He gestured to the gathered audience of security personnel. "Agents, officers, spies, soldiers, Marines. What does it take for you people to earn your salary? To pay attention? To actually see the trees that stand in the forest?"

"Hold it right there," Jantry demanded. "Who did I not see?"

The Marine nodded as if to say, *yeah, who?* Seeing that Teagarden periodically glanced at the entrance, they too gazed to the door flanked by armed, uniformed Marines. To them, nothing appeared out of order.

"All right, all right," Teagarden said. "I apologize. After having a breakdown on the train and getting chased through the Colosseum by cops with machine guns, I think I'm allowed to get worked up." He turned to Jantry. "There's no further value in discussing it here. Let's go upstairs, please."

"I appreciate that," the Marine said. "But hold on a moment. I want to know, who, or what, I missed?"

Teagarden exhaled a long sigh of exasperation. "Elad. That's who. Agent Jantry, you also missed Elad." He turned to the full team. "You all missed him. He was standing directly across the street, watching us as we entered. He was smoking a cigarette and standing there, just watching us like a gladiator waiting to make his entrance."

"Are you—"

"Yes, I'm sure," he interrupted, glaring at Jantry. "So much for your report that he's in Berlin. And moreover, he *wanted* me to see him. I'm telling you, he wanted me to know how easy it is for him. That means he wanted me to tell you what I am, in fact, telling you right now. You missed him. For all I know he's already upstairs waiting for us. Or maybe he'll be on elevator when the doors open."

The Marine stepped away to issue an order. Within seconds two men and one woman, all plain-clothed in khaki slacks and blue dress shirts, hurried from the building. Teagarden watched them depart, shaking his head.

"Easy," Jantry said. "If it's your own wellbeing you're worried about, I can assure you that you are now safe. I've taken good care of you since Venice, have I not? And I will continue doing so."

"You still don't get it," Teagarden said. She cocked her head with disapproval. "A minute ago, while we were on that sidewalk, it was *me* taking care of *you.*"

She tucked the padded bag under her arm. "Let's go upstairs," she said.

# CHAPTER FORTY-SIX

There was nothing unique about the sixth-floor office to reveal it as a nest of spies. It was like any other corporate space crammed with cubicles and surrounded by smaller private offices on the perimeter. It was the same floor plan at Langley when he worked in encryption/decryption over three decades earlier. The big difference now was the number of computers. Some desks had as many as six screens, each with its own specialized keyboard that ran programs of encrypted code via differing command-line interface languages. To him, it was a sad sight, and made him guess that working there was utterly without meaningful occupational reward.

There were, however, plenty of deep comfort amenities for workers and visitors that most offices do not have. After Jantry gave him the basic tour, Teagarden availed himself to some of the creature comforts. He passed the kitchen where stainless-steel counters held fresh sandwiches, snacks, fruit, and a salad bar. One corner of the kitchen held a butcher block counter with stacked racks of little liquor bottles like the kind they serve on airplanes. They were locked by a small sign reading, "Company Happy Hour 6-7 pm." Down the hall was a gym with all the usual workout machinery, plus a sauna and steam room. He passed on all of it, opting only for a shower with rich shaving soap and fresh razor blades. On the bench he also found a waiting change of clothing that included new boxers, slacks, and a casual pullover shirt. He left behind the socks and continued wearing the sports coat purchased by Blair specifically for the trip to Israel. Like his new passport photo and birthdate as Larry Eagleton, everything was a perfect fit.

Well, it is the CIA and they are spies. They're supposed to know everything about me, apparently, even my shirt size.

He wondered how the clothing package came to be waiting there, then remembered Jantry's colleagues named Bascom, Long, and Platcher. He guessed poor Platcher had the dubious honor of toting his new clothes from the Venice bus station to the CIA substation in Rome.

Poor Platcher. When he got a CIA job, he probably thought he was signing up for a life of espionage adventure.

Well, somebody has to tote the laundry.

After showering, he sat with Jantry in the kitchen where he selected a pod labeled "Dark Javanese" and made a mug of coffee.

"This is no ordinary office," he said. "Full workout gym, free deli sandwiches. Even booze."

"Yep," Jantry said, "there are times when we have to live here. Besides, we take all the risk, so we receive all the reward. That's the culture. The company joke is that working here will make you a hunk, a chunk, or a drunk."

"Great. My tax dollars at work. I'll be sure to include that in my book."

"You can't write about this. Well, okay, you can try. Many try. But it'll have to be run past the Company Publication Review Board and they'll tell you what I just said which is—'you can't write about this.'"

Teagarden didn't care because he had no plans to write a book. The only thing he wanted was for the pain to stop. Overhead, a large television monitor mounted on the wall was tuned to an American all-news station. The volume was muted. The bottom headline read:

Little Girl Blue Put in Drug Induced Coma, Fate Unclear

"Stop looking," Jantry said. "The twenty-four-hour news cycle only feeds anxiety. Speaking of which, here, take these."

From a small white envelope, she dropped two bright red tablets into his palm. He looked at them, then back at Jantry.

"Really?" he asked.

"Do you trust me now that you're safe?"

"Yes, I do, but—"

"Good. Take them. They'll help with your anxiety and prevent another—well, never mind that. But you'll feel better in about a half-hour." She'd obviously caught herself ahead of using the word "breakdown" or "crackup," which made Teagarden's shoulders slump. "Look," she said, "I apologize for the way I spoke to you in the lobby. And don't get me wrong. There's nothing wrong with weeping. I do it all the time. But there's a time and place. Know what I mean?"

There was no value in arguing. The truth was, he agreed with her. Besides, after all he'd been through, he didn't mind if he got a little stoned on a couple of pills.

"All right," he said. "I'll take them, but only to demonstrate that I do trust you after suspecting you were playing for the other team. And I'm sorry you lost your nice shoes."

"I appreciate that."

He washed down the pills with dark Javanese. The clear plastic bag labeled "U.S. Government" sat on the adjacent table. He could see that it held the .22, sunglasses, his cell phone, wallet, and passport.

"You're confiscating my wallet?"

"No. Only the silly .22 and the God Glasses." She reached to pat the bag. "And by the way, those glasses are proprietary. We invented them. The public doesn't know about them. So you must keep that to yourself."

"What are you talking about?"

"You didn't know? The sunglasses you took from the Ford. They're metal detectors and night vision lenses with auditory enhancement. Real Superman stuff. You didn't use them?"

Stunned, he remembered what Wharron said about a new development in eyeglasses, and Klassen's use of a monocle back in New York.

"No, I didn't. You mean I missed the chance to have X-ray vision?"

"Looks that way. If you'd used them, you may have gotten the upper hand against FFG on the ship." She smiled with a sense of irony.

"How long have they been around?"

"God Glasses are super new. Technically, they're still in development. They're manufactured one at a time in Winchester, Virginia at a CIA front called X-Futura Corps, which is more than you need to know." She patted the bag again. "Now, let's get back to business. Your wallet and passport as Lawrence Eagleton will be returned to you as soon as you're cleared in debriefing, which will be soon. Everything else, we keep."

"There's a load of money in my wallet."

"I saw. That too belongs to the U.S. government. I'll leave enough for you to purchase personals. That'll be easy to fudge on my E and J."

"This is getting annoying. What am I going to be cleared of? Do you doubt I am who I say I am?"

"No. Don't worry about the formalities." She looked at the clock. "Unfortunately, clearance requires a meeting with the bosses that begins in a few minutes. Don't stress. If it gets unpleasant, I'll speak for you. Between my help and the pills, you'll do fine."

On the opposite wall, a faded poster outlined federal regulations including OSHA safety standards and workers' rights to be free from all forms of bias and harassment regarding gender, race, sexuality and sexual orientation. She took a long chug from her one-pint water bottle.

"Are you feeling better after a shower?" she asked.

He wanted her and everyone in the office to be focusing on Elad instead of him, instead of little red pills, instead of debriefing, instead of adhering to formalities about "clearance."

"Yeah, yeah," he said, letting her see his irritation. "I feel great. There's nothing like a good ole shit, shower, and shave."

"Nice! You're starting to talk like a veteran company man on a long-term stakeout. Listen, I know you're stressed. You'll feel better soon. If you need a nap, which you likely will, there are private rooms in the back." She again glanced at the clock. "Just FYI, I did communicate with the company nurse while you were showering. She'll swing by soon. You know, take your pulse, BP, listen to your pump."

"Listen, I appreciate all this, but it's really more important that—"

"I know, I know," she interrupted. "Elad. Stop worrying about him. If that really was him out there, the recon Marines will get him."

"Please believe me. That really, really was—"

"Stop worrying. You're in protective custody now. You're going to be fine. By the way, in addition to the nurse, I had a chat with Klassen in New York. He's arranging to put you in a drone to Berlin courtesy of the U.S. Air Force. It's one of those X-num-bered-thingies. A little flying saucer that'll land on the hotel roof. No airport. No economy seating. No baggage claim. It's the wave of the future."

"And he'll meet me there?"

"Us."

"Excuse me?"

"He'll meet *us* there. I'll be going with you. Remember, the CIA handles American international interests. Not the FBI. And right now, you are what's called an 'international interest.'"

"Okay. And Klassen will meet *us* there?"

"Eventually. They're making him travel commercial, so we'll get to Berlin ahead of him."

Teagarden didn't like the sound of it. Klassen was already way overdue to make an entrance.

"Listen," he said, "I'd like to say, thank you. It's clear that without you I'd have been nabbed by those two Italian cops on the train for having Almonti's passport. Same thing for your smart work in the Colosseum. Thank you."

"It's my job, but I do appreciate being thanked. I don't hear it often."

"How often to do you get shot at during one of your grab-and-go operations?"

"That was my first. Do me a favor, don't tell anyone."

"How many grab-and-go's have you done since leaving 'record redacting'?"

"Tons. It's what I do. I escort people in and out of Rome and Vatican City or I watch others escort people in and out. Once in a while I get to do in-person contacts, dead drops, pass and receive messages. It's called being a spy."

"Sounds more like 'Spy 101.' What's the next step up in the food chain?"

"Now that is a secret."

"I bet it's working angles on the world's hot spots. Running informants. Arranging delivery of firearms across borders. Maybe even hooking up with the right people, get 'em drunk, slip a little something into their vodka or Maalox, depending on their age."

She gave a wry smile. "Could be," she said.

"All that stuff can be done from Langley. But trust me when I tell you that you're better off here," Teagarden said. "The food in Rome is superior to the strip mall chains in Northern Virginia."

Jantry assented with a head bob and took another swig of her water bottle as she glanced at the clock a third time. Overhead, the all-news station was airing a report on FBI efforts to prove or disprove that the February terror attack in New York was part of a wider network. The lower graphic read:

Still No Confirmation of Pro-Gun Terror Group

Jantry was ready. "Okay, time for our meeting, Mr. Eagleton. Just a wee bit of business before your zonk kicks in."

"You can stop calling me Eagleton now. And I thought I was

only going to chill and have a wee nap on those pills. Now I'm going to have a 'zonk.' That's not such a good idea with Elad on the prowl."

"Let's stick with your cover name while your cover is still active, Mr. Eagleton. And don't worry. We've got plenty of Marines on security duty, and I'll be right with you the entire time you're—uh, napping."

He thought of making a snarky remark but changed his mind. She tucked the clear plastic bag under her arm and escorted him down a dimly lighted hallway to a heavy glass door sealed with thick gaskets that required her identity card for entry. Inside was a windowless, soundproof room where six others stood near an oblong conference table. Jantry introduced him to two of the six: Station Chief Manfred Orden and Station Underchief Beatrice Jolly.

Orden, the boss, was a textbook case of the all-American office backstop. His countenance possessed a visible blessing of the gods of government: upper-middle-aged WASP, green eyes, alabaster skin with cheeks and nose marked by clusters of burst red capillaries, and a beer-belly manifest of near-term congestive heart failure. His number two, Underchief Jolly, was another stock character from the classic government office. She was a middle-aged white woman with searing blue eyes, a pug nose, and a facial expression fixed with righteous anger that only a fool would miss as a warning to keep a safe distance.

Of the others present, he recognized only the senior Marine officer with the blotch of vitiligo on his neck. Once small talk ended, Station Chief Orden got down to business.

"All right everyone, please be seated." He gestured to the conference table. "This is a routine oral debriefing ahead of the formal 10-77 Report for Record. It is being tape-recorded and should not take long."

Jantry spoke first. Teagarden knew most of what she recounted because he was there for it. When invited to speak, he quickly stated his own story from the moment he landed in Jerusalem and was met by Eveillard, to the moment he and Jantry walked past Elad before entering the CIA substation. He also took the liberty to issue a warning, trying to convince them of the danger they all faced because of the deadly shadow lurking nearby. He suggested halting all building repairs until Elad was dead or captured.

Judging from the silence after he concluded, his presumptuous safety lecture did not go well, though no one voiced objection at his temerity. He wondered if the resentment was because his wasn't a formal CIA case, or because they saw him as FBI chump of the week. It made him worry that they were considering turning him over to the Italian police for the murder of Dr. Niccolò Almonti. Whatever else they had in mind, it was clear that they didn't want to take any action until they were confident it wouldn't backfire against their own reputation and retirement pension.

The debriefing was interrupted when a young lady knocked and walked in. She had red hair and freckles and looked barely old enough to vote, yet there she was, standing at the head of a CIA conference table in Rome, holding a steno pad.

"Urgent notice, sir," she said. "Just fielded."

"What subject?" Orden asked.

"Operation Five O'clock."

"Oh, okay," Station Chief Orden said. "Since we're now debriefing Operation Five O'clock and that certainly pertains to Mr. Tea—uh, Mr. Eagleton, you may read it aloud to all gathered."

"Very well, sir." The redhead held the pad filled with squiggly lines and began reading: "Classified communiqué for substation Colosseum. Status: Urgent. Subject: Operation Five O'clock. Category: Eyes and Ears Only. From contact codename Cassius, street-based liaison with Italian State Police...three Marines... two males and one female dispatched at 3:30 pm GMT, i.e., thirty minutes ago, from satellite-station 'Colosseum' to search immediate area around satellite station...have been found...two dead... one is alive and talking, but seriously injured...all were concealed inside a padlocked sidewalk retail shack two blocks from office...

no reported noise, no gunshots, no disturbance, and no one nearby saw anything...conclusion of eyes and ears only con-com."

Teagarden glared at Chief Orden with the most accusatory *I-told-you-so* scowl he could muster.

# CHAPTER FORTY-SEVEN

Only the ranking Marine reacted. His eyes bulged with shock and the baby pinkness of his neck pulsed red with anger as he brusquely departed the conference room. Everyone else held in slack-jawed silence. The only reaction at the table was made by Jantry who bowed her head. When the collective shock of the news passed, they reflexively reached for their cell phones with such timing that it appeared choreographed. They grabbed, cradled, tapped, and swiped as they read confidential data on the three casualties being transmitted in real time.

Orden was the first to speak: "Agent Jantry, did you check with the Bureau in Washington before this debrief?"

"Yes sir, I did, though not Washington. I communicated with FBI Special Agent Bernard Klassen, stationed in New York. I let him know that my grab-and-go was successful, and that Professor Teagarden, thanks to Station Jerusalem, is now ID'd as Larry Eagleton, and that he is presently secure here at Colosseum substation."

Teagarden decided the chief probably had a wife and grown children in Northern Virginia or suburban Maryland. Rome was probably his final posting and he wasn't going to let any FBI patsy ruin his good will with Langley, which two dead and one seriously injured agent could easily do.

Still speaking to Jantry, Orden said: "And did Klassen express any preference as to what should be done with Mr., err, Eagleton now that we have him?"

"Yes sir, he did. Several things. It was Klassen who made arrangements with the U.S. Air Force for transfer via drone to Berlin." She looked at the clock. "Rooftop departure is planned for twenty minutes from now." She swallowed before continuing, a clear signal that she knew her boss would not like the next piece of info. "Additionally, sir, Klassen advised that the FBI's Operation Five O'clock does remain active, and the Euro desk at Langley has reasserted a status of 'continued total cooperation.' And, yes sir, I did confirm that on the encrypted communication channel from Langley." She looked at her notes and continued, "For verification, it posted at 15:15:42 Greenwich Mean Time."

Orden's veiled contempt for Teagarden grew less veiled.

"And did Klassen indicate with any specificity what our 'continued total cooperation' might, dare I ask, consist of?"

"He did, sir. Operation Five O'clock is to be delivered to the Charlottenburg Grüner Park Hotel in Berlin where Klassen and the Bureau will take responsibility. He also explained that lawyers from Homeland Security have approved domain linkage in this instance."

Station Underchief Beatrice Jolly could restrain her anger no longer.

"Oh, he explained it did he? Well, screw that!" she interjected, leaning into the table to emphasize her indignation. "We're not in Buttfuck, Botswana. This is Rome, fricking Italy. Doesn't the FBI have contacts with Rome PD?"

Jantry glanced toward Orden for indication as to how to respond. It was apparent to Teagarden and everyone else present that Chief Orden preferred not to address Underchief Jolly's complaint. He simply did not want to tangle with her. It's the same in every office. There's always some animosity among ranking bureaucrats that prevents the wheels from turning as smoothly as they should. Having seen it play out in hundreds of academic meetings, Teagarden knew that Jantry hoped to curry some small amount of favor with the station chief by stepping in to respond to the underchief's wrath.

"Ma'am," Jantry began, "I believe it's fair to say that it's the politics of designated boundaries. As a U.S. domestic agency, the FBI would be toast if the press learned of agents engaging in foreign intelligence activities, including linkage with foreign police departments."

"This is not legit foreign intelligence activity," Jolly said. "It's only show business so POTUS will look like he's doing something about all the kamikaze cult assholes."

"Yes, ma'am," Jantry said. "Of course, it's not actual foreign intelligence activity." She paused to take a breath. "However, as FBI Agent Klassen pointed out to me, American ambassador to Italy, Mr. Desmond Largoman, still supports the order that the Italy CIA shop must continue providing all possible co-op. And, by the way, his office is on the con-com list for Operation Five O'clock updates."

That set Jolly's rancor a notch higher.

"Why the hell is Ambassador Largoman receiving confidential communications on an FBI operation that's nothing but White House window dressing and which the CIA is ordered to handle?" She paused for a breath. "If all the assholes of the world want to stick swords in their necks because they believe in God, or because they don't believe in God—well, goddamn leave 'em alone and let 'em do it!"

Again, no indication from Orden on how to respond. Jantry cleared her throat.

"Ahem. Ma'am, I believe it's safe to say it's the FBI's C.Y.A. S.O.P. for any particular SNAFU. Not to mention that the ambassador is the FBI's fallback rabbi on this matter."

"That response," Jolly caught herself from cursing further, "doesn't answer my question, Agent Jantry. Why is Ambassador Largoman receiving confidential reports on Operation Five O'clock?"

"Right," Jantry began, "probably because as American ambassador to Italy, he's the ranking American in this nation, and is, therefore, entitled to receive those reports. Additionally, as a former U.S. senator from New Jersey, perhaps we can speculate that Ambassador Largoman has designs upon the White House and wants political credit for helping to end the suicides."

"Great. Just fucking great. Two dead American Marines and one wounded here in Rome may present a little problem for his presidential ambitions. Especially after the press finds out how connected he is to a Charlie Foxtrot of foreign intrigue with zero national interest. He'll have to own it. Not us." She looked at Chief Orden. "And he *does* own it."

Underchief Jolly gave a grunt, letting the room know that she was finished for the moment. Jantry again glanced at Chief Orden, hoping to see a small nod of the head that said, *well done*, or maybe a vague smile to indicate thanks. Even a glint in the eye would do it. There was nothing. He let her go it alone, let her take Jolly's ferocity utterly without appreciation. Teagarden saw it and knew what it meant. If there was heat to be had from higher-ups pertaining to Operation Five O'clock, Orden would let Jantry burn.

During the pause that followed, Teagarden thought again of warning about Elad, but there was no time. The PA system intervened, and all cell phones in the room simultaneously squawked with the same announcement.

"Attention...security breach...sixth floor...security breach... lockdown all systems...lockdown all access points...lockdown all egress points...ready all firearms...attention...security breach..."

All reaction appeared pre-programmed. The lights in the sound-proof conference room obediently clicked from ordinary fluorescent to a deep blue. In the semi-darkness, Teagarden saw the three unidentified men rush for the heavy door. When it opened, rapid reports of *pop, pop, pop* became audible. They were distant and muffled as though underwater, yet easily recognizable as the salvo of handheld weaponry.

The three men were quickly followed in order by Agent Jantry, Chief Orden, and Underchief Jolly. Teagarden went last. On his way out he grabbed the plastic bag that Agent Jantry left behind.

In the main office, company employees had already drawn their weapons and spread out in the blue twilight. He slid onto the nearest desktop where he became a spectator. The medication was kicking in, making him feel peculiar, not quite himself. Watching the event unfold, he had a sense of casually viewing a violent sport from the safety of the first balcony at the Colosseum, what the Romans called the maenianum primum.

If only they'd listened to me, this wouldn't be happening, and they wouldn't have to die when the tiger magically pops up from the trapdoor in the floor—which the tiger named Elad will certainly do.

Unworried about the consequence of breaking silence, he called out, "Hey, Jantry, what exactly was in those two tablets?" There was no answer. In the blue semi-darkness he could barely make out the silhouettes of dozens of people sprawled about on the floor, ducked under tables, stationed in doorways, each with a weapon-filled hand at the ready. The distant gunfire grew closer, as though it were descending an internal staircase from the rooftop.

"My bad," Teagarden announced, trying to make out who was who, and where they were crouched and crawling. "Sorry. I realize now that I should have eased you all into the facts about Elad so as to not damage your fragile little egos. I should have let *you* think of the idea of sending all hard hats home for the day. That might have saved you from this special-effects shit show."

More gunfire sounded, closer than before.

"Do you hear me, Mr. Orden and Ms. Jolly? Wherever you are in this disco dance, I should have let *you* sound the alarm, so it would be your idea. Now you're all in this silly mess."

"Teagarden, down!" That was Jantry's voice.

"Where're the Marines?" And that was Orden's voice.

"I can hear you-u-u," Teagarden sang. "If I can hear you, Elad can hear you too-o-o."

"Sir, backup Marines are in the elevator, on the way up from the lobby." Jantry again. "Teagarden, get down!" Still Jantry.

"Great, just great. We've got bogies coming down the staircase while the United States Marine Corps is taking the up elevator. That's a new one for the record books." And *that* was Jolly's voice.

"Not bogies, Ms. Jolly," Teagarden corrected. "Just bogie. One. One bogie. His name is Elad. He's lurking in the hypogeum, getting ready to pop up to the arena floor any second now."

It was the poor optics that inspired his next idea. He ripped open the white padded bag, dug out his wallet, passport, and .22, all of which he tucked into his various pockets. Then, for the first time, he put on the sunglasses taken from the big Ford at Shimon's Eleven in the Negev Desert.

He could suddenly see everything in the blue darkness. Moreover, every handgun stood out, found by roving crosshairs that re-coordinated with every shift of his head. Even the slightest movement of his eyes caused the lines to focus anew on nearby weapons as well as color-coding environmental danger like the GPS screen in the dashboard of the Ford.

"Oh, wow!" he crooned. "Gretta Wharron was right to call these things 'God Glasses.' They are truly amazing."

His announcement caused another flurry of unintelligible muttering around the office hiding places, though he could only make out a patchwork of words: "...Jantry what th'hell..." "...how many tablets..." "...get those goddamn God Glasses before..." "...great, just fucking great..."

Ignoring them, Teagarden's personality transformed into that of a sports announcer, something the Flavian Amphitheatre likely never had.

"Ladies and gentlemen," he began, imitating a broadcaster's rich voice in total disregard of the danger, "we've now arrived at the climax of our evening here at the Colosseum games. The valor of our gladiatorial men and women is on full display in the blue illuminated forum of death. These highly trained agents of the CIA squat courageously behind baffles and inside the knee wells of their desks, each wondering where he'll appear. Will Elad the Mossad Shadow Killer drop from the sky? Will he rise up from a trapdoor? Or, will he simply materialize out of thin air and cut all their throats one by one with the ease of a grandmaster assassin?"

"Teagarden, get down you fool." It was Jantry whispering to him from the floor near the kitchen doorway. More gunfire erupted in the stairwell.

Teagarden continued his narration.

"Ladies and gentlemen, as you can plainly hear, Elad is coming. He's closing in. We can expect his arrival at any moment. Whether you're a senator seated in the prestigious podium section, or a plebian in nose-bleed standing-room only—grab your spouse, your neighbor, your sex slave, and hang on for dear life."

He slid off the desktop and wandered deeper into the office, mesmerized that everyone was so efficiently coordinated. They were hiding, yet not hiding. The ones tucked into the knee wells were so odd looking it was amusing, as though they were kitty-cats hiding in a shoebox, waiting to jump and pounce. Standing directly over the shadowy outline of one crouching CIA agent, Teagarden began singing:

> All around the cobbler's bench,
> The monkey chased the weasel,
> The monkey thought t'was all in fun,
> Pop! goes the weasel.

"And now we've got a doped-up FBI patsy dancing through a CIA Def-Con Five while acting like a goddamn cartoon character. Jantry—do something!" (Jolly again.)

"Yes ma'am! Teagarden or Eagleton, whichever one is listening to me—listen to me! Get down! On the floor. Now!" (Jantry again.)

Teagarden ignored her. With the aid of the God Glasses, he half-danced farther into the maze of cubicles, each walled-in by baffles:

A penny for a spool of thread,
A penny for a needle,
That's the way the money goes,
Pop! goes the weasel.

"Jantry, just how much goddamn sodium pentothal did you administer?" (Jolly.)

"I spoke to the nurse via con-com. After hearing details of his condition, she ordered a double dose of Big Reds: sodium pentothal, propofol, and Valium. Her intent was to make him talk freely during debriefing, then sleep all the way to Berlin." (Jantry.)

Teagarden heard but did not assimilate the meaning. Time and space were playing tricks on him. So were dimension, circumference, diameter, and apex working on his head. They were all ganging up on him. Also math, algebra, trig, and calculus.

From the private elevator bank, two sets of twin doors swooped open and a score of Marines swarmed out, helmets and automatic weapons shining laser beams everywhere like mini-searchlights. The lead warrior was, once again, the Marine with vitiligo who recognized Teagarden standing in the main doorway looking like a one-man welcoming committee. Spotting the God Glasses, he removed them from Teagarden's face and slid them onto his own where they were framed by his arching Kevlar helmet.

"Have there been gunshots?" he asked, the twin laser beams of his helmet shining brightly in Teagarden's eyes.

"Oh, yes sir."

"Many?"

"You bet."

"Automatic?"

"Nope."

"Where?"

"Roof and stairwell."

"How many?"

"One. Uno. Un. Ein."

"How do you know only one?"

"Because, I know-w-w."

"Elad?"

"Oh yes. It is the second coming of...no wait a moment, it is the fourth coming of Elad."

"Okay."

The Marine glided into the office and toward the stairwell as though on Rollerblades. The others hurried behind him and fanned out among the cubicles. To Teagarden, it looked like the old Pac-Man video game. In the elevator bank, the bright overhead lights blinked in the blue darkness. The nearest elevator car made a *ding* tone. Seeing that, he stepped into the open elevator and pressed the button for the first floor. At the main lobby, he walked out into the courtyard and beyond to the narrow street where the rounded battlement of the ancient Colosseum rose in the near distance.

# Chapter Forty-Eight

*Saturday, March 22, 2025*

His neck and back ached with the morning-after pain of a gladiatorial survivor. It felt as though his uppermost thoracic vertebra, the T1, had been slammed with Thor's hammer. His mouth was more than dry. It was so grit filled that he used his left index finger to scrape his tongue because he hadn't enough saliva to spit or swallow. His right arm vibrated with ten thousand volts of electricity radiating from armpit to fingertips.

"Uh-h," he groaned when trying to shift.

People were moving around. Lots of people. They ignored him. There was nothing unusual about that because there was nothing unusual about someone sleeping in the airport. Any airport. Nodding off on a chair with head drooping to the chest, slouched over onto three chairs with backpack as a pillow, sprawled on the floor, out of the way of human flow, with a coat as a blanket. The presumption of every passing airline employee, airport worker, police officer, and passenger is always the same. That sleeper is no hobo. Neither is he a drunkard or panhandler. He's just a passenger. One of many thousands. Poor guy. Flight delayed. Held over. Canceled. There but for the grace of the gods of airline travel, go I. Just leave the unfortunate schlep alone. Let the sleeping flight victim lie.

When Sam Teagarden blinked awake on the industrial carpet, he knew it was morning because the sun was blasting through a floor-to-ceiling window. It gave him a headache. That was all he knew: morning, sunlight, window, headache. He had only vague memories of the recent past. There was the Colosseum shoot-'em-up and the sighting of Elad in front of the CIA satellite station. That much was vivid. Then came the shower inside the CIA office. After that, things went fuzzy. He knew there had been another shoot-'em-up yet he couldn't summon the facts. The memory of it was like an old movie you saw long ago, whose title you couldn't remember, but the key scenes were still memorable. Then came cars and planes, walking and waiting, pacing and sitting, more walking and waiting, and more pacing and sitting. There'd been a lot of excited talk with odd people and odd talk with excited people. Finally, there was exhaustion, nodding off, and sleep.

He rubbed his neck and rolled over on the floor. Underneath his head, he found his folded sports coat serving as a pillow. His lower neck had been pressing on the protruding .22 still inside his coat pocket. That explained the neck and back pain. As for his right arm, it was little more than a useless flapper, asleep to the point of being a phantom limb. He rubbed it with his left hand and looked out the window.

Aircraft! Lots of them. They were landing and taking off in the far distance, rolling back and forth in the near distance, and parked stationary at jetways visible from his carpeted berth.

Okay, I'm at an airport. Which one? And, how did I get here?

He waited for the pain and pulsing numbness of his electro-limb to ease before trying to sit up. When his arm finally returned to sentient flesh, so did the headache recede. His ears picked up the murmur of the flowing crowd. He studied the signage.

Tor/Gate B014. That still doesn't explain which airport.

He stood, rubbed his creaky knees, unruffled his clothes, and moved to a vacant seat where he rifled through everything: pants pockets—coins and euros, but no ticket; wallet—stuffed with euros and dollars, but no ticket; sports coat pockets—gray-plastic .22 revolver with four plastic bullets, and an American passport identifying him as Lawrence Eagleton, but still no ticket; shirt pocket—crumpled paper receipt.

Receipt for what? It's a certainty I haven't been to a grocery store.

He unfolded the wad, pressed the wrinkles out with the heel of his palm and held it to a position where his eyes could adjust and read the smeared black print:

Boarding Pass: Roma Airways
Flight #RA325 Rome to Berlin
Leonardo da Vinci Fiumicino (FCO) to Brandenburg (BER)
Seat 32B Economy

I'm there. I mean, I'm here. Here! I made it to Berlin on my own.

He should have understood sooner. It explained why B014 was listed as both "Tor" and "Gate." He rose and joined the human flow. On the way out, he made a stop at a restroom, bought coffee and a muffin, easily passed through immigration as Larry Eagleton, and climbed into a taxi at the transportation curb.

"Wohin möchtest du gehen, mein Herr?"

"Do you speak English?"

"A little."

"The Charlottenburg Grüner Park Hotel, please."

"Ja."

# CHAPTER FORTY-NINE

Berlin was a throbbing network of urban functionality. Since the fall of the wall and the divided halves reunited, it had reassumed its position among the great municipalities of the world. Unlike many important cities, the interconnecting parts of Berlin work with unique efficiency.

The effects of the drug Jantry gave him in Rome had completely passed. Thanks to the near catatonic sleep it induced, he felt better than he had in days, and that was despite having spent an unknown number of hours in transit and on an airport floor. The temperate weather of Berlin induced a welcome sense of composure. Anything would be an improvement over the stifling sun of Megiddo, the emotional bewilderment he felt in Rome, and the constant rocking of the Blue Voyager racing across the Mediterranean.

Near the hotel, he asked the cabbie to cruise the neighborhood instead of pulling into the circular drive of the main entrance. Unlike much of the German capital, the Charlottenburg district was quiet, upscale, and residential. It reminded Teagarden of Washington's Georgetown neighborhood. While the cabbie circled, he spotted what he wanted on the main commercial avenue, three blocks from the hotel. He paid the cabbie and did the rest on foot.

First stop was a men's clothing store, pricier than he wanted, but it would have to do. Not that he needed to be concerned about money, but he guessed that a shop catering to the affluent would mean having to wait for alterations.

After several selections, only the cuffs of new slacks needed adjusting. During the downtime he bought toiletries at Schneller Weg Apotheke, a brown leather backpack from a boutique luggage store, and sat for the local barber where he got a haircut far shorter than usual. When trimmed back, his thick streak of gray showed more prominently where it grew from the front of his head like an off-center stripe. To highlight his effort to change appearance, he combed his hair differently, straight back, instead of parted at the left. Ninety minutes after he stepped from the cab, he walked from Spandau Herrenbekleidung wearing a new suit, dress shirt, tie, and—though he hated them—socks. As for shoes, he opted for a new trend that, according to the salesman, started in Hamburg and was rapidly spreading across Europe. It was a type of shoe/boot, a throwback to Beatle boots of 1964, except that in this case, the heels were unusually high, which was the whole point. The advertisement called them "Pumpen für den Mann," which translated as "Pumps for the Man," though they weren't really pumps at all, not high heels, and certainly not stilettoes. They did, however, have heels that made him two inches taller than he really was.

The irony was, he didn't expect any of these feints to fool Elad. Nothing would fool that man.

Still, if he could delay Elad's reflexes for even one second, it would help. At least he'd be presentable at the convention of religious historians in the affluent neighborhood where much of the monied class of Berlin lived.

Okay, well, I've made it this far, so let's get on with it.

He packed his old clothes, sneakers, and revolver in his new backpack for the quick walk to Charlottenburg Grüner Park Hotel. At the front door, he paused to read the bronze plaque where the words were in German and English:

Constructed in 1593, once known as Köhler Beerhall, this classic German post-and-beam structure was damaged during Allied bombing in 1945.

It was rebuilt in 1960 by the firm of Fuchs & Wolfe.

"Great." Teagarden didn't speak German but knew the word "fuchs" meant "fox." It had been a persistent theme, so it may as well continue. "And I've encountered more than one wolf this time around."

Just past the main entrance, he paused again at directional signage posted in multiple languages:

Nippon Auto Group, Registration 2nd Flr.
World Judeo-Christian History Council,
Annex Bldg., (exit lobby at rear, through garden
courtyard)

The man at the front desk wore a plaid sports coat with a mismatching striped shirt and French cuffs. His right ear sported a dangling gold earring.

"Wie kann ich dir helfen?"

"Can you ring Bernard Klassen's room, please?"

"Yes, of course." He tapped at his keyboard. "Mr. Klassen has not checked in just yet. Would you care to leave a message, sir?"

"Yes, please leave the message that Larry Eagleton asked for him and say that I'll check back this afternoon."

"Yes, Mr. Eagleton. And, what room are you in?"

"I don't have one," Teagarden said. "I'm a late attendee to the convention. Is it possible that something has opened?"

"No, I'm afraid not. With two international conventions this weekend, we are fully booked." A few earnest clicks on the keyboard followed. "Oh, wait. Mr. Eagleton, you do actually have a room with us. It's on Die Terasse Level, on the tenth floor. It is, as they say in Vegas, the penthouse. Small, but cozy. There are three modest rooms on the top floor, all opening onto a common terrace that has the best view of Berlin in the entire hotel."

Teagarden was stunned. Then he thought, well of course, sometimes the bureaucrats think ahead and get it right, especially when it comes to their own creature comforts.

"Oh, my goodness. Thank you very much."

"Yes. In fact, it was Mr. Klassen's office in New York that made the booking and left a message to explain that he'll be directly next door to you. Also, your colleague, Professor Teagarden, who I see will be a presenter tomorrow afternoon at the seminar on the subject of archives authentication, will be in the third room."

He couldn't resist. "Oh, yes, Professor Teagarden. He's a damn good man. Tell me, do you have a copy of the full convention schedule?"

"Yes, certainly, Mr. Eagleton. I have an entire convention packet for you that includes helpful materials about the hotel and the Charlottenburg neighborhood as well."

The desk clerk busied himself registering Larry Eagleton. Teagarden turned to inspect the lobby. It was an eclectic mix of Middle Age feudalism with ultra-contemporary décor. The walls held ancient wood carvings from a nearby castle and many family crests. The door to the Kapitäns Bierhalle und Grill was flanked by a pair of life-sized armored knights. Yet the surrounding furniture was weird. The chairs and sofas were mod, boxy structures upholstered in starkly white leather, making them appear like geometric shapes in Styrofoam. The rug was white polyester filled with a white-on-white pattern of squares, triangles, and circles. The visual effect was dizzying.

He scanned the faces of people sitting on the white boxes but recognized no one. More importantly, no one seemed to recognize him as the American Prometheus. He also looked for evidence of anyone with affected disinterest, too obvious about *not* looking his way. Still no one. It all added up to only one thing.

I'm the first one here! I not only survived being squeezed on both ends by ecclesiastics and atheists, not to mention CIA incompetence, but I beat them all here. Klassen is still en route. And

Elad, the big bad wolf, is still...Uh-oh!

That thought triggered a new memory. Details of the second of two shoot-'em-ups in Rome bubbled to the surface in whatever part of the brain houses memory. It happened inside the CIA's Colosseum Satellite Station.

I remember now.

Elad was coming down the staircase from the roof. After the commanding Marine confiscated the God Glasses, they all headed up the staircase toward the roof. That's when Teagarden took a powder. Nobody noticed his casual strut to the elevator bank. Influenced by Agent Jantry's drugs, he calmly waltzed out of the blue-lighted mêlée. At that moment, Teagarden indulged in the fantasy that Elad was killed in the exchange with American Marines.

Yeah, right. Keep dreaming.

His wishful thinking segued to a fallback hope that at least Agent Jantry and all the others at the Colosseum substation survived Elad's latest invasion.

Let's hope. And the same goes for all the Marines.

"All set, Mr. Eagleton," the desk clerk said. "Here's your cardkey for room 10C, convention packet including ID badge to all venues, map of the Charlottenburg, and complimentary beers at Kapitäns Bierhalle which is straight between the knights in shining armor. Your convention is in the annex building. To get there, you exit this lobby at the rear doors which are just over there and walk through our greenhouse courtyard. My name is Gunther. If I may be of further assistance, please let me know."

"Danke," Teagarden said.

"Bitte," said Gunther.

Things were looking up. During the elevator ride to the tenth floor, Teagarden realized that for the first time since arriving in Jerusalem, he'd just had an encounter with a stranger who didn't leave him feeling paranoid.

The entry to his room had narrow double doors made of ancient wood and inlaid with many panels. Inside, it truly was an attic room, like an old-world French garret in the Montmartre quarter of Paris; snug but comfy, with two sleepy-eyed dormers for windows. And Gunther was right about the view. The small terrace shared with two other attic rooms looked east toward the city center where he could make out the Brandenburg Gate. Farther on was the giant Fernsehturm, the television tower in Alexanderplatz that once dominated the sky of Soviet East Berlin. To the north was the River Spree where, though narrow, many children drowned after escaping to the west with their parents. Ten floors directly below was the hotel's semi-circular cobblestone entrance. He wondered if those same stones once served horse-drawn carriages for the landed gentry to enter and drink beer amid raucous gatherings during the enlightened age of Frederick the Great.

At that moment, a group of black cars jockeyed for position to discharge passengers at the door: an Audi, a Mercedes-Benz, two BMWs, and a Toyota van. He waited to see if Klassen emerged from any of them. A family of four bounced from the Audi.

American tourists.

An Asian man slowly eased from the rear of the Mercedes, his pitch-black hair flopped forward in a thick clump.

Japanese corporate exec headed for the auto conference.

The driver jumped from the first BMW, ran to the rear door, and opened it for a lady with a small dog cradled in her right arm. Despite the unseasonably warm weather, she wore a full-length white fox fur.

And that's got to be the wife of some corporate auto tycoon.

The second BMW pulled into position. Instead of discharging, it picked up a waiting passenger.

That's certainly not Klassen.

Finally, the Toyota van found enough room at the curb to discharge. Twelve young men barely out of their teen years simultaneously emerged from multiple doors like the Ringling Brothers clown car. They were all trim and well-groomed which made Teagarden guess they were part of a religious entourage attending the Judeo-Christian gathering. Oddly, they were not behaving like typical young travelers. They did not talk, jostle, laugh with excitement, or even look about like tourists. Instead, they waited politely until a woman stepped from the front passenger seat. Once on the sidewalk, they fell in behind her to be led into the lobby. It took a fraction of a moment for the shock of recognition to hit home. Teagarden knew that woman.

Gretta Wharron!

Freedom from God had arrived in Berlin. And it was being led by none other than Getta-War-On.

"Oh, please Klassen," he whispered to the clouds, "will you please show up soon. I need help, there is no CIA backup, and I am desperately tired of this shit."

# CHAPTER FIFTY

Wondering if he was living up to Jantry's fear that he bordered on a thoroughly profound crack-up, he rushed to the viewfinder of 10C. No one was in the corridor—yet.

He guessed it would be only a matter of minutes. It was Wharron's mission to prevent him from presenting the Q Doc as a Middle Age forgery. For her, that meant killing him. He guessed the easiest way to get to him would be to start a mass suicide with her cult-eyed zealots, then demand his presence as a bargain for it to stop.

Once again, being a logic-minded math professor, he ran down his options: hide and wait for the Klassen cavalry, which meant letting young men die—or risk his life to try saving their lives. He already knew the answer. It was practically preordained. He would do whatever he could to prevent another matinee performance of suicide theatre. That much was written upon his...his what? DNA? Fate? Upbringing? Personality? Code of honor?

Whatever it was, it presented a problem. How do you save extremist groupies who belong to an anti-religion religion and are prepared to publicly cut their own throats just to prove their commitment? He'd witnessed how paralyzed the Israeli military was. If they were helpless, what could he possibly do?

*I'd have to be a comic book hero to stop them.*

He hurried back to the terrace on the off chance that Klassen had checked into the neighboring room since he arrived. He peered through the sliding glass doors of adjacent rooms 10A and 10B.

Nothing. He again leaned over the rampart to view the circular drive where there was no longer a queue of vehicles and the two valets stood idle with world-weary boredom.

In his room, he fully opened the sliding door, so Klassen could enter by way of the terrace. He withdrew the .22 from the sports coat. Jantry was right. Its ungainly design was perfectly foolish. Unless you fired it directly into someone's face, it hadn't the power to accomplish much of anything. Its principal value was that it would pass undetected though airport security. Understanding its inefficiency as a weapon made him all the more appreciative that he had survived his encounter with Dr. Almonti. Still, it was the only firearm he possessed, and he intended to keep it. He opened the cylinder. The four plastic missiles were still nestled in their silos. He returned it to his pocket.

(Cynthia)
Sam, you've got this. It's a tough situation. But you can do it. You've already thought it out. Now, you can do it. You can. You really can, I know it.

(Sam)
Cynthia, I can't say it with any more honesty. I'm scared.

(Cynthia)
I know. I'm scared for you. Sam, remember, many more lives need to be saved. The madness must stop.

(Sam)
I know. (Pause) Thank you. I'm glad you're there for me.

(Cynthia)
As always.

He again checked the hallway viewfinder. Still nothing. He opened the door and leaned out to peer into the corridor. Empty. The fire-exit stairwell was on the opposite wall. He stepped out, quietly pulled the door shut, scooted across the hallway, opened the metal fire door, entered the stairwell, and began his descent into the unknown.

If I really were a comic book hero, I wouldn't be one of those deformed musclebound types, or anyone wearing a cape. I'd be something new. I'd be an everyman superhero.

With his Pumpen für den Mann, his steps echoed loudly in the stairwell. Going on tiptoe helped quiet his footfall.

I'd be a superhero who performs remarkable deeds with intelligence and guided only by scruples. Although those God Glasses would really come in handy right now.

Farther below him someone entered the stairwell with a noisy clunk, then exited again. He redoubled his effort to step softly.

I'd be someone like...like...like...oh hell, who am I kidding? There are no everyman heroes. There is no Super Math Professor. That's a dumb idea. Which is why comic book writers endow them with capes, muscles, and magical powers.

Three floors lower, he came across a rollaway cart stashed on the landing. The tablecloth was haphazardly pulled to partially drape a tray of half-eaten food: chicken that oozed with congealed fat under a thickly translucent gelatin glaze, roasted potatoes with curdled cheese, and a hard roll that looked like an overtoasted tennis ball. In that partially consumed state, it reminded him of roadkill.

I hope I don't look like that when Operation Five O'clock is finished.

He figured the food cart was the clunky noise he'd heard a moment earlier. The porter was probably concealing it in the stairwell until he could get it to the service elevator. Eyeing the unappetizing mess, he made a mental note not to order the hotel chicken and continued his descent. Only a few more flights remained.

Superheroes? Really? Why was I even thinking such foolish

things? Stupid. I'm starting to worry about myself. I need to stay focused.

At the ground floor fire doors, he eased down on the push bar with his hip. It opened onto the courtyard conservatory that separated the main lobby from the Annex Building. It was a lush arboretum, sweltering hot and crammed with a thousand green shades of exotic flora lurching toward a high glass ceiling. Sitting obediently in the middle of the jungle, on a row of benches under a narrow double row of palm trees, was a twin line of twelve dutiful-looking young men. He could barely see their faces because the happy trees sprouted thick leaves along their trunks. Yet there was no doubt of their identity. It was the same twelve who arrived in tow behind Wharron. Standing behind a thick palm, he scanned the courtyard but didn't see her. Despite the foliage, there was no way he'd miss her height. She'd probably parked the FFG flock in the courtyard, then peeled off to inquire about him. Teagarden read the small label posted on the tree concealing him:

Zombia antillarum
Bekannt als die Zombie-Palme

A Zombie palm tree, how appropriate. And those one dozen automatonic young men really are a form of the walking dead.

Feeling the butt of the .22 in his pocket, he turned right, keeping in the shade of arching greenery and staying clear of open spaces. Beyond the courtyard, the Annex Building was a short walk through a connecting portico where more signage and calendars were posted. Unable to read the words from the arboretum, he exited, walked through the portico, and stood at the entrance to the Annex. The first floor had chambers for corporate assembly with names like Die Exekutive Suite, Die Brandenburgische Suite, and the smaller Sächsische Suiten Eins, Zwei und Drei. The second floor was one large conference space called Friedrich Halle that could accommodate up to four hundred. A timetable posted in English for that larger space mentioned Teagarden by name:

Sunday, March 23, Friedrich Halle, 4pm
Sam Teagarden, Ph.D., heroic American Prometheus who altered U.S. history, presents momentous research on historic documents uncovered at Megiddo, Israel.

Great. Nothing like advertising to Gretta Wharron and Elad precisely where I'll be tomorrow at four p.m.

He was the star attendee and the Germans were practically pimping him as a latter-day Martin Luther. Because he never formally agreed to be a presenter, he guessed his appearance was arranged by Assistant FBI Director William Drakken. It was exactly one week earlier that Klassen mentioned the conference while from his hospital bed. And it was Drakken who said he expected the whole mess to wrap up in Berlin: suicides, Teagarden's participation, religious document controversy, the whole thing. He wanted it all boxed up with a nice bow and stored away in America's memory attic.

"Yeah, and if I got killed," Teagarden said aloud to himself, "he'd be okay with boxing me up too."

"Who besides me wants to kill you?"

Teagarden turned to see Gretta Wharron's brown irises and overly large black pupils boring straight into his own eyes. Even with the two inches of additional height provided by his new shoes, she was still taller than him. She lightly gripped his right forearm. When he looked down, he saw the needle poised over the crook of his elbow. As with Dr. Almonti, it wasn't a horse-sized hypodermic, but a smallish plastic tube with a shallow thumb-driven plunger.

"Don't move, Professor Teagarden. I will jab you if I must."

His heart sank. It had been a great mistake to expose himself, especially since he knew she was on the premises. He should have waited in his room for the cavalry to arrive from America.

"I'm guessing your right hand is gripping that silly pop-pistol. Slowly remove your hand from your pocket."

He did what he was told. She interlocked the fingers of her left hand with his right. Her opposite hand remained poised at his right forearm, ready for a quick push on the plunger.

"I repeat, who besides me wants you dead?"

He had no intention of admitting that Assistant FBI Director William Drakken wouldn't mind if he ceased to exist. "Elad," Teagarden said. "He's at the top of the list."

"Ah, yes. You can stop fearing the Vatican's go-to cleaner who killed Professor Zurbarán."

"Too bad he's not on your side."

"I agree," said Wharron. "So tell me, where do I fall on the list?"

"Number two. Followed by," he hesitated, "all the others."

"You mean *all* FFG?"

"Yes. Doesn't FFG want me dead?"

"Don't be so presumptuous, Professor Teagarden. We're not that bad. Only those of us who know what you've learned about the Q Doc want you dead. That used to be a short list, only Dr. Almonti and me. Since you took care of him, I've made certain a few lieutenants in Rome and New York were bought up to speed."

"How thoughtful of you."

"Try to be more considerate. Mainstream FFG members are perfectly honorable. They seek only to unshackle the human race from toxic belief in everything from Zeus to Hay-Zeus. Once accomplished, the species will be free of killing in God's name."

"And you're willing to kill yourselves to get the job done?"

"Oh, so presumptuous. It's only a small inner group prepared to make the ultimate sacrifice. They are all volunteers. We call them Finis Orbis. It means 'the end of the circle.'"

"Take it from me, circles never end."

"Nonetheless, we must try."

"You mean your PIM LOLA tells you to try."

She didn't care for his sarcasm.

"That's enough." She turned him around. "Thanks to True Song Company, LOLA is available to all, including me, you, everyone in FFG, and everyone who isn't. It is an unbiased guide to achieving a meaningful life without the folly of Apollo." They slowly walked back into the tropical arboretum from the connecting portico. "This way, Professor Teagarden. No more cracks about LOLA, and *no* sudden moves."

He decided to try making her angry. If he could, it might give him a finely sliced window of opportunity to punch her and run.

"Tell me Gretta, would one of those FFG members you brought up to speed happen to be a policewoman in Rome named Sofia Russo?"

"Yes. As you've already learned, FFG members are everywhere and fill all occupations. And by the way, her first name is Stellina, not Sofia."

"Ah, yes, she was attractive. Even when she was trying to kill me in the Colosseum, I found her to be quite a looker. Just as I found you when LOLA instructed you to strip and convert to heterosexuality."

"Shut up."

"But tell me, does LOLA allow you to have as *deep* a relationship with Officer Russo as you do with Mara Baker-Mann who's now rotting in a Jerusalem prison?"

"Goddamn..." She caught herself mid-anger. Her grip tightened on his arm. "Don't test me, Teagarden. Mara is the love of my life. You make another homophobic, sexist crack like that and I will drop you right here."

He exhaled and said, "Okay, I believe you."

"Keep walking. We're going to walk through this jungle, enter the main lobby, and casually stroll, hand-in-hand, to the elevators. I've got a little job for you back in your room. Do not doubt me, Professor Teagarden, I will stick you anywhere along the way. So, do not tempt me."

"Don't worry."

"And you're going to smile."

He cooperated as best he could with a tight parting of his lips. Having seen how quickly Dr. Almonti died, he had no doubt about the potency of the concoction. If he attempted anything, she could easily thrust the needle through his coat sleeve and into the flesh of his forearm, instantly turning him into a cadaver. Afterward, she'd call for help and claim her husband had a seizure. During the excitement that followed, she'd slip past the EMTs, along with her entire moon-eyed gang of FFG zealots. That reminded him of something.

"Why did you bring along a suicide team?"

"You already know."

"Insurance?"

"Brilliant."

Just as he figured. If she couldn't find him, she'd order a death circle to do its thing. They'd demand that he be brought before them just as Mara demanded in Jerusalem, albeit for a different reason. Well, being nabbed by her at least meant those twelve boys would survive.

The main lobby was busy with people absorbed in their various reasons for being there. Some sat on the white-on-white sculpted furniture, leaning into their cell phones and tablets. Others gathered in spontaneous chat groups.

It was easy enough to know the Hasidic rabbis, priests, and Japanese men as being attendees to one of the two assemblies. Others were less obvious. He guessed them to be clerics of various cloth: ministers, parishioners, and biblical scholars. There must also be historians, researchers, and reporters keen on finding anything newsworthy, particularly at a scholastic-based, interdenominational conference that was normally boring as dirt. This year, however, was different. Global suicides and their rumored relation to the Q Doc had made this year's confab a must-attend event.

Teagarden sensed the crowded lobby presented another escape opportunity he mustn't pass up. He tried the only strategy he could think of—child psychology.

"You know," he began, "I'm no longer the only one who knows the Q Doc is a fraud. I told others. They're coming to the conference. You'll have to kill them too."

"Doubt it. Even if you did, it doesn't matter."

"The CIA and FBI will go public." His volume grew louder than his normal speaking voice. "They have proof that it's a practical joke straight from the Middle Ages. You...can't...kill...everybody."

Moderate success. A clutch of people, having overheard, turned to glance his way. He was prepared to continue when she tightened her grip and paused near the suits of armor flanking the entrance to Kapitäns Bierhalle.

"Look at these knights in shining armor," she said. "I read on the hotel's website that they're authentic to the fifteenth century. Now that's the *real* Middle Ages. I doubt whoever had to wear all that metal considered it to be a practical joke." She cocked her head and let her brown eyes give a phony sparkle. "Don't try that again," she whispered, squeezing his arm. "I told you to smile. If you don't smile, I'll jab you right now."

He smiled again, better than before.

"Good. Now kiss me. Nothing major. Just a peck on the lips."

He kissed her.

"Very good." With a slight increase in volume for the benefit of lobby eavesdroppers, she said, "*You're* my knight in shining armor."

Appeased, the curious onlookers turned back into their group chats as Teagarden and Wharron moved past the twin knights to the elevator bank.

Damn, this woman is not only smart, she's quick too.

He glanced at Gunther in mismatching plaids behind the main counter, absorbed with a queue of guests. Elsewhere, no one found them curious as they walked through the lobby, holding hands and chatting.

"Keep smiling," Wharron warned.

Both elevators were on upper floors, requiring them to wait. He hoped Klassen would step out when the elevator doors opened. Klassen too was smart. He'd understand the situation and save the day like a real knight in shining armor.

Ugh. More silly fantasy. C'mon, snap out of it. Think!

Teagarden's intellect overrode his indulgences in magical thinking. He needed to take real action regardless of the risk.

"At least grant my last request."

No one was standing nearby, so she raised her voice slightly. "This isn't a ridiculous American TV show, Professor Teagarden."

"Will just hearing it do any harm?"

"What is it?"

"Just tell me, why doesn't it matter that the FBI and CIA know of my discovery that the Q is phony?"

"Because there's only one American Prometheus." She smirked hard. "That's you. You convinced the world that two Kennedys and Dr. King were murdered by a team of halfwits managed by a black-ops FBI program. Funny, of all the JFK conspiracy theories, no one ever really thought of the one crazy plot that turned out to be true. Consequently, you're trusted. If you said Santa Claus sells crack in Miami during the off season, people would believe it. Can you say the same for the FBI? The CIA? Thanks to you, nobody believes anything they say."

"Therefore, I must die to preserve FFG's claim that religion is phony, not the document?"

"Uh-h-h—*yeah-h-h!*" Her eyes bulged like a comic hitting a punchline. "But don't fear death. As someone once said, we must all step over into the great nothingness sooner or later. And in the case of Deadicillin, I have reliable information that it's quick and painless."

"There will be others to decode the document and find it to be an ancient hoax."

"Not necessarily. The Vatican won't be releasing it. And anyone else will be crucified on social media as a crackpot."

"Oh, brother. What a twisted world we live in."

She shrugged with agreement. He watched her pupils as they locked onto his. Her mouth twisted to the side as she spoke with comedic irony.

"But it's not so bad in the end. Look at it like the mathematics teacher you are. When you multiply a negative number by another negative number, you get a positive number. Let's try that with religion. All religion is a lie...you have proof that the lie is itself a lie...therefore we end with a positive conclusion that there is no God."

Holy Mother! What mutation of human genetics made the mind of this woman? And just a moment ago I was thinking she's smart. Well, that's just more proof that smart people can also be some of the dumbest and most dangerous people walking the planet.

The elevator doors swooshed open and they entered.

"What's this final job you have for me?"

"Nothing difficult. It's generally referred to as a suicide note. What floor is your room?"

"Ten."

She pushed the ten button and the doors swooshed shut.

# CHAPTER FIFTY-ONE

Getting into room 10C required her to release his arm and hold the needle to the back of his neck so he could retrieve the cardkey from his wallet. She continued holding it at the base of his skull as they walked through the ancient double doors. Inside, she sat him at the room's desk, so small it was more of an antiquated, feminine-style vanity.

"Cramped but possessing old-school charm," she said. "Oh, and a lovely terrace as well."

She reached into the right pocket of his sports coat and withdrew the .22 while keeping the other hand with the needle fixed on the back of his neck.

"Is this my punishment for not copulating?"

"Shut up."

"Let me know if you're still interested in fanculo."

"You missed your chance. Put both hands on the table. Now, take a sheet of hotel stationery, and the pen, and get ready to write."

When she began reciting, he sighed heavily and scribbled the words in old-fashioned longhand.

> I, Sam Teagarden, do hereby assert that remnants recently found under the ancient church at Megiddo are indeed from the Q Document, a long-missing source for Matthew and Luke. Analysis of these fragments finds verification that the Christian

faith was founded upon complete mythology crafted during the late first century by men whose motives were likely pure of heart and designed primarily to improve the plight of Jews suffering mightily under the Caesars.

"New paragraph."

Being aware that this finding will create unbearable spiritual and intellectual burdens for so many, I have decided that the only viable option for me is to take my life as have so many others. For that, I am sorry.

"Now sign it."
He wrote:

Samuel Teagarden,
AKA, American Prometheus

When he finished, she read it over his shoulder and said, "Good. Now fold it neatly and insert it into one of those envelopes and hand it over."

She tucked it into a pocket. With the needle at the back of his neck the entire time, he did everything as instructed, although he knew no one would believe he wrote it voluntarily. First, he only went by the name Sam, never Samuel, which he privately abhorred. Second, he certainly wouldn't describe himself as the American Prometheus, a moniker the media gave him back in 2019. He especially wouldn't use that sobriquet in his own suicide note. His wife would know. And she'd make certain everyone else knew as well.

"Stand up," she said.
He did.
"Now I want you to understand your position. I have a

plunger filled with Dr. Almonti's Deadicillin poised at your neck. I also have your firearm in my other hand aimed squarely at the small of your back. If I shot you, it would probably only bust a vertebra or two, which would be very painful for you. Now get up slowly and walk to the terrace."

"Oh, good. I'm going to feel the sun upon my face one last time."

"Fair enough. How do you feel about your face slamming into concrete ten floors below?"

"Nuh-uh. That's not going to happen."

"Come along, now. Ah yes, you were right, there is plenty of sunshine. And the height of the terrace railing is just right. You'll sit on the edge and scoot over. It'll be easy for you."

Teagarden mind-flipped to another channel. Typical of his ruminative digressions of the past days, a series of childlike sleuth games flashed through his head. Quite annoying at such a moment, he tried to resist the mental intrusion, to no avail.

Question: In a totally empty room, there's a pool of water under the body of a man who hung himself. Why?

Answer: He stood on a block of ice to reach the noose.

Question: A man walks up many flights of stairs and turns on the lights. When he looks out the window, he sees many dead bodies. Why?

Answer: He's a lighthouse keeper and there's been a shipwreck.

Question: A woman with a poison needle and a relatively useless handgun prefers that her victim leap to his death. Why?

Answer: Because, you moron, there's no poison in
the poison needle!

Halfway across the terrace, he made his move. It was a back-
ward roundhouse with his left hand, though it was also a blind
shot. All he could do was hope it would land somewhere on her
face and buy him enough time to dodge the bullet if she managed
to pull the trigger. It wasn't much of a plan, but it was all he had.
With her standing directly behind him, because of her height, he
had to swing wide and high.

There. Done.

Then came yet another of his flaky stress reactions. This time,
during the slow-motion pirouette that followed, he visualized the
episode in compartments, like the outline of a poorly plotted high
school term paper:

I. Violent Scene of Self Defense.
   A) Backhanded fist connected with her chin.
      1) Audible solid crack.
         a) That's good.
      2) Her brown/black eyes rolled every which way like
         tumbling dice on a craps table.
   B) He wasn't dead which meant he wasn't jabbed with
      Deadicillin.
      1) Where is the needle?
         a) Gotta neutralize the needle.
         b) There it is! Still in her right hand.
         c) Gotta get it.
         d) But wait, what about the gun?
   C) Oh, look, the plastic .22 went skidding across the terrace
      floor.
      1) Excellentemente. (Why am I inventing Spanish
         words?)
   D) Back to the needle.
      1) There it is.

2) She's falling.
3) Was that a tooth that just popped from her mouth?
4) "Ploomph!" She's down. Dropped hard like a sack.
5) Grab her right hand.
6) Good. Jab needle into her neck.
7) Done. Right into her jugular.
   a) She deserves it.
      aa) Fuck her.
      bb) Not literally.
8) Roll away in opposite direction.
   a) But wait, there's more. She lives still.
   b) I was right. There was no Deadicillin.
   c) That's good and bad.
      aa) That's good because I'm not dead.
      bb) That's bad because she's not dead either.
E) Uh oh, she's scrambling for the .22.
1) She's much closer to it than me.

II. New Arrival Upon Scene of Violent Self Defense.
   A) Huh?
      1) Is it FBI Agent Klassen?
      2) Hell, no. That would be logical.
         a) Unlike Roy Rogers, the FBI never arrives just in time.
   B) Karen Carrie Jantry?
   C) The CIA?! Really?
   D) Well, I'll be damned. Yay!
   E) Standing in the entrance of adjacent Room 10B, Jantry draws down on Wharron.
      1) "Blam!" (one shot only).
         a) Shot missed!
            aa) Oh, shit!
      2) Wharron sees Jantry.
         a) Wharron's up.
         b) Wharron's scrambling toward the terrace railing.

c) Wharron's on the railing and...
    aa) Wharron's shouting "Freedom from God!"
    bb) Wharron jumps.
    cc) Holy crap.

She shouted again on her way down: "Free-e-e...dom-m-m...
from...God-d-d-duh!"

From where Jantry and Teagarden stood on the terrace, her
impact didn't sound like much of anything. There was no big
noise. Instead, they heard a nondescript *thump*, like when a dog
shifts position in the quiet of the night and re-plunks directly
beside the bed with an exhaling sigh.

At the railing, Jantry and Teagarden looked to confirm her
demise. There was no question. Gretta Wharron was dead. She
lay on her left side. Eyes and mouth open. Skull cracked. Blood
flowing from head and mouth to the curb.

"I wonder if LOLA told her to jump."

"Who's Lola?" Jantry asked.

"Never mind. I was wondering why she jumped after your
shot missed."

"I didn't miss. That was a warning shot. She knew it and took
the only other option."

"Thank you," said Teagarden.

"Don't thank me. I owe you."

"Why?"

"Because I screwed up in Rome. You were right. That really
was Elad and I didn't believe you. Plus, I overmedicated you. It
was the company's prescribed dosage for a man of your size
having a serious panic attack, but your anxiety was justified, and
you probably hadn't eaten in days. I should have known better
than to listen to the company nurse."

"Yeah. I don't remember much about how I got to Berlin. I
think I slept most of the way."

"I apologize."

"Apology accepted. Don't be too hard on yourself. You did

really good on the train and again at the Colosseum."

"Thanks. And the woman cop who tried to kill you at the Colosseum has been confirmed as FFG. She'll be fired and face attempted murder."

"Good. How many did Elad kill in the satellite office?"

"Three. All Marines, including the supervisor Master Gunnery Sergeant Nicholson. When they found his body, his neck was broken. Can you imagine? A big man like him?"

"I'm afraid I can."

Teagarden pictured the tall African American with vitiligo, the only one in the entire office who attempted to own the emergency. That's typical, he thought. The one possessed of the courage to do something is usually the one that others allow to take the fall.

"Orden and Jolly survived?" Teagarden asked. Jantry nodded. "And how is Elad's attack on your office being explained publicly?"

Reluctant to answer at first, Jantry said, "Well, it's confidential, but I'll tell you. Langley will announce that a plane on a humanitarian mission to aid Libyan refugees crashed in Sicily, killing five Marines and wounding one. That covers the two Elad murdered on the street, and the three he killed in the stairwell."

"What a surprise. And for my final question: what about Elad?"

"Total eighty-six. Over the rooftops. That guy is spooky. We found a trail of his clothes. He had at least three outfits under his work overalls. Plus an Uzi with big stick mags. Flash-bang grenades. The whole thing."

"He's here now."

"You've seen him?"

"No. He's here, though. You can bet on it. And where's Klassen? We need him."

"Told you before, he works for a different outfit. That means he's at the mercy of the airlines. He's already had a layover and a weather delay at Shannon."

"Great. More Drakken-arranged bureaucratic bungling. That

means it's you and me against Elad."

Below them on the driveway, gawkers stared at Wharron's body, including two boys from Wharron's FFG suicide team. True to their emotional detachment, they were unruffled by the sight of her body. They exchanged a few words, turned, and calmly walked back into the lobby.

# CHAPTER FIFTY-TWO

It wasn't possible for them to intercept the shit show that followed.

Within seconds, the confused din of screams and shrieks floated up to the terrace. Guests hurried from the lobby in a panic. Some ran with arms flailing, others stumbled to the circular drive where they stooped to wretch. Teagarden and Jantry knew what was happening. They'd both seen it the previous Tuesday—him in Jerusalem at the Church of the Holy Sepulchre, her in Rome at St. Peter's Square.

"How many were there?" she asked.

"Twelve. All boys, with nothing better to do than publicly open their own carotid arteries. C'mon," he said, "we've got to get down there and—"

"No, no, no. We're not going down there. It would risk your life. I'm not doing that again. Each of them wants you dead. I was assigned the job of protecting you, and this time I'm going to do it."

"That's going to look bad on your E and J."

She didn't respond. From the terrace, Teagarden pictured the scene playing out in the lobby. All twelve would be squatted in a circle around the ridiculously white furniture in a room where ancient plankboard walls were decorated with sixteenth-century family crests. Each would be holding a cutter to their own throat while chanting in Latin and English for him to be brought before them like a virgin to be sacrificed. Perhaps one of the twelve stood in the center, leading them on and warning all would-be heroes not to interfere.

"Here they come," Jantry said as sirens wailed in multiple directions. "Normally, they'd want to come up here to question us about the rooftop jumper, but they'll have their hands full with a suicide party in the lobby."

"There's nothing the police can do down there except make it worse."

"I know."

Teagarden figured Gunther had made the call. The front desk probably had an emergency button somewhere behind the counter. Or maybe it was a direct audio connection linked with a dispatcher. Two patrol cars hustled into the circular drive and skidded to a halt. Then came a dozen more. Then a score. When the ambulances arrived, they were blocked from close access by patrol cars which forced EMTs to sprint on foot with oxygen tanks, stretchers, and heavy kits filled with medical gear.

"Is this what it's like for God?" Jantry asked. "He just sits in the sky and watches people do stupid stuff?"

"Maybe."

They stood at the railing, sickened by the sights and sounds that permeated everything. The very air seemed to pulse with dreadful howls of fear and pain as the ritual of death took place in the lobby below where otherwise civilized people were horrified and simultaneously captivated.

"The ones who watch are just as sick," Teagarden said.

Jantry nodded agreement. "Maybe the German polizei can save some lives. Meantime, we need to plan for dealing with Elad."

"Forget it. The best way to deal with him is to get a message to the Vatican. Whoever's managing him needs to be told that the Q Doc has been confirmed to be a fraud, a practical joke from the year 1100. That'll get them to issue a stand down."

"Calling the Pope is above my paygrade. I'm guessing the same is true for Klassen when he gets here. Correction, make that *if* he gets here."

They entered room 10A on the other side of the terrace where the view was largely blocked by local high-rises.

"How'd you get in here anyway?" he asked. "My room is registered to Eagleton, and these other two rooms are registered to Klassen and some schmuck named Teagarden."

"I'm a spy. Remember?" She verified that the main exit to the corridor was secure. "This setup is good. When Klassen checks in, we'll be able to hear him from this room."

"Unless it's really Elad. Like you, he too knows how to get into a room without a cardkey."

"Tell me something, Professor Teagarden, Elad knows what you look like. Right?"

Teagarden made a snort. "Does he ever."

"Right. Now tell me something else. Does FFG know what you look like?"

"Sure. Wharron and Dr. Almonti certainly did. I'm all over the internet. Anyone can research me."

"How old are the FFG members presently killing themselves in the lobby?"

"Twenty at the most."

"And Elad obviously knows what I look like?"

He hesitated. "Well, he saw you approaching the CIA satellite office in Rome with me. Did he see you again inside, during the blue light attack?"

"No. He never actually got inside the office."

"Okay. What are you thinking?"

Jantry paced the room. She looked out at the terrace and twice went to the viewfinder to check the corridor. Soon afterward she resolved whatever was preying upon her mind. From her shoulder bag she withdrew the Freedom from God necklace and draped it around her neck. Then she withdrew her Glock and tucked it into her belt at the small of her back.

"One more question. How many FFG fanatics do you think are already dead by now?"

"Two. Maybe three."

"That means nine or ten are waiting their turn." She bolted

for the door.

"Wait!" he shouted. "What the hell? What are you...uh...oh, wait...I get it. No! No, do not even think of it. No, no, no."

"Professor Teagarden. You stay here. If anyone knocks at the door, do not answer. Though I doubt anyone will be checking in during the colosseum-style death game playing out in the lobby. And if you hear any movement next door in 10B, wait until you see the occupant walking out to the terrace before engaging."

"I forbid this. Only a miracle could intercept this disaster. No offense, but you're no miracle worker. You'll be killed. I won't have another Eveillard on my conscience. Another Cole. Another Sanchez. Another Wechter. It's too much!"

She grabbed him by the shoulders. "Professor Teagarden, you have to understand something. I signed up for risk. Taking the company's oath was the most courageous thing I ever did. All the rest is just another day at the office."

She marched from room 10A with the FFG's atomic civil defense necklace bouncing upon her chest.

# CHAPTER FIFTY-THREE

She took the staircase and emerged in the arboretum, teeming with botanical life. There were no humans to be seen.

Jantry eased toward the glass partition separating the green-house from the main lobby where she saw only the backsides of excited spectators blocking the action in the center of the lobby. When she pushed open a heavily sealed door, the chants and ululations became intelligible, except that they were in Latin.

"Libertatem a Deo, pro libertate nos mori, afferte nobis Vulpes... Libertatem a Deo, pro libertate nos mori, afferte nobis Vulpes..."

The police were inside the lobby, concentrated near the entrance-way, awaiting orders. It was the same hesitancy she'd observed in St. Peter's Square and which Teagarden spoke of seeing in Jerusalem. Once the suicide game gets underway, aggressive cops only complicate the problem. When they weighed in at St. Peter's, it quickly triggered mass hara-kiri. Yet if they don't weigh-in at all, everyone ends up watching it happen one at a time.

"Libertatem a Deo, pro libertate nos mori, afferte nobis Vulpes..."

Jantry pushed through the crowd until she glimpsed the center of the action. Teagarden had estimated correctly, ten young men were still alive, each holding a knife of various type and dimension. Nine sat cross-legged in a tight circle while one stood in the middle. Two already lay dead where they dropped, their hands still gripping their own blades plunged into their necks. Onlookers stood back, watching. Some were silent. Some screamed with objections while others screamed with sick encouragement, goading each participant forward as though they were spectators at the Roman games.

"These people do not qualify to call themselves people," Jantry muttered in disgust. "They'd love to see lions popping up from the cellar."

"Libertatem a Deo, pro libertate nos mori, afferte nobis Vulpes…"

Jantry spoke French and was fluent in Italian, which made it easy to know the basic Latin meaning of their chants. "Libertatem a Deo" meant "Freedom from God." Volpe was Italian for fox, so "Vulpes" was Latin was fox, which meant Teagarden. They wanted the clever American Fox brought to them, so they could kill him. If he wasn't produced, they'd continue to kill themselves one by one in a public display of bloodletting.

"Libertatem a Deo, pro libertate nos mori, afferte nobis Vulpes…"

They were all white boys with short cropped hair and engorged pupils that betrayed a drug-induced zealotry.

"Libertatem a Deo, pro libertate nos mori, afferte nobis Vulpes…"

She squeezed through the crowd, trying to be less obvious about her presence while looking for the man she needed to find. Knowing his reputation, her life depended on seeing him before he saw her.

"Libertatem a Deo, pro libertate nos mori, afferte nobis Vulpes…"

Then it occurred to her.

Of course, the police!

He was known to be a chameleon. In Rome, he arrived at the satellite office dressed as a hard hat. According to intelligence reports, he dressed as an archbishop in Santiago de Compostela, and as a UPS delivery man in New York. It was logical that he'd show up at the hotel impersonating a uniformed cop. She stayed well hidden in the crowd to maneuver closer and quickly scan each police officer's face. Nothing, nothing, nothing, nothing, and nothing. She shifted to survey the opposite side of the crowd of waiting cops. Nothing, nothing, nothing, nothing, and—

What?

They made eye contact from a distance.

"Libertatem a Deo, pro libertate nos mori, afferte nobis Vulpes…"

No!

But it was. He was standing in the middle of the crowd beyond the twin statues of armored knights, in the direction of the elevator bank.

It was not Elad—*but Teagarden.*

The man Elad chased from New York, to Israel, to Rome, and now Berlin. The man the Vatican wanted assassinated to save the faith from scandal. The same man these FFG cult members would instantly assassinate to prevent the world from learning that an ancient document questioning God was only a prank from the Middle Ages.

She bug-eyed at him with furious anger for leaving the safety of room 10C. He bug-eyed back, then darted his gaze and nodded his head to another spot in the crowd. Another spot directly in front of the glass-doored entrance to the arboretum. She looked to the place Teagarden's eyes were gesturing.

Elad!

No question.

She recognized him from old file photos. Squat and muscular, with deep-set eyes that radiated with cold, reptilian intelligence. And her theory was wrong. He wasn't masquerading as a cop. He was dressed as a hotel porter in a waiter's vest and short apron, so he must have entered through the Annex Building and passed through the greenhouse just moments after she did. He also wore a long, colorful, gem-encrusted crucifix, an accessory not normally seen draping from a hotel porter's neck.

"Libertatem a Deo, pro libertate nos mori, afferte nobis Vulpes…"

In that moment, time stopped. Elad found her at nearly the same moment she found him. Worse, he seemed to sense that she hadn't merely found him in the crowd but was directed by some other presence. His eyes shifted in search of that other presence. It was her fault—again.

Shit!

After his scan shifted from her, his resourceful eyes roamed the room to spot Teagarden. That gave her only microseconds to act. With no time to waste, she pushed through to the formerly white rug soaked with red, and into the circle where she held the Freedom from God neckless high for all FFG members to see.

"Libertatem a Deo," she shouted, "la Vulpes è qui."

# CHAPTER FIFTY-FOUR

It was linguistic corruption. She accidentally combined Latin with Italian. Still, it got the message across to every suicidal FFG cult-member. Just to make certain, she said the same in German as best she could manage: "Der Fuchs ist hier."

The suicide crew quieted. They looked on with curiosity and, she felt certain, veiled appreciation. To reinforce their confidence, she held the necklace like a badge as she made the rounds and spoke distinctly to each of the ten: "Der Fuchs ist hier"…"La Vulpes è qui"…"Der Fuchs ist hier"…"La Vulpes è qui"…

Thus far, her idea was working. They knew Gretta Wharron was dead. They'd never seen Jantry before, yet they all stood at the edge of total acceptance that she was Wharron's replacement. During a quick gaze of the wider crowd, she eyed cops, Teagarden, and Elad. The cops were itchy to move in, Teagarden held still, while Elad's crocodile eyes were going full-tilt with surging analysis. He was a razor's slice of time from morphing into full-blown violence.

Inside the circle, she edged closer, holding her focus on FFG members. She gestured for all sitting FFG members to stand. They did. "The Fox is here with us—*now*," she said in English, using the rhythms of a Southern Baptist revivalist preacher. "Be it known to all that upon this day, the Fox has come nigh. This is a momentous day in our struggle to be free from their God, from all gods, from false gods because all gods are false gods." For dramatic effect, she slowly raised both arms like a bible-thumper in Clarksdale, Mississippi. "He is present here and now." She stood before Elad. "He...is...there! There! There!" She pointed with both hands at the ex-Mossad agent, the world's most renowned and feared international killer for hire. "That man is your Fox. That man is Sam Teagarden!"

The result was unimaginable bedlam.

All ten FFG members charged Elad, their daggers rotating like windmill veg-o-matics bent on slicing and dicing a single man. They jabbed, stabbed, pricked, pierced, punctured, and gouged. The remaining spectators panicked. They bolted in every direction without regard for who got trampled. Without a go-code, the cops were the last to move. Finally, after seeing the FFG cultists charge Elad, they charged in as well.

Jantry caught sight of Elad reaching for his Glock and a moment later saw it go missing as the blades worked like a ravenous school of piranha. The last thing she saw before getting knocked down, lifted, and knocked down again as though riding waves in a tumultuous surf, was Elad attempting to use a shank pulled from the long crucifix. It did not stop his attackers.

When it was over, twenty-seven spectators were injured, three seriously from knife wounds. The remaining ten FFG cultists survived and were promptly arrested. The only shots fired were discharged by cops toward the floor like deputies in a western movie during a barroom brawl. The lobby was wasted. Every piece of furniture, ornament, and wall decoration was destroyed or splattered with blood. The two knights in shining armor lay smashed and heavily dented, fallen guardians of a once-valorous age.

As for Elad, his dead body had hundreds of piercings. Seven knives of various shape lay around him on the floor while three remained lodged in his flesh. A long and slender stiletto protruded from his abdomen. A Bowie knife with an inlaid wooden handle was jammed so deeply into his throat that its point protruded from the other side. And a vegetable peeling knife, curved like a mini-scimitar, resided in his left eye socket up to the hilt. The God

Glasses, taken from Master Gunnery Sergeant Nicholson at the Colosseum substation after he took them from Teagarden, lay near his body, smashed in the stampede. In the weird respite that followed, everyone stood about in various stages of trauma, relieved to be survivors. The police officers, too, stared in shock and disbelief.

"May the Lord have mercy on us all," Jantry said, as she walked through the fogged-up glass doors sealed with heavy gaskets. When Teagarden followed, he meandered the aisles of lush green life to find her semi-concealed under the enveloping screen of a drooping palm.

"I agree," he sighed after sitting next to her.

Not understanding, she gazed at him. Their eyes connected through the verdant patchwork. "You agree with what?" she asked.

"May the Lord have mercy on us all," he said.

"Oh, right. That's what my mom down South used to say when there was simply nothing else to say."

Teagarden nodded. They sat quietly in the hot shade of botanical life until the police ordered full evacuation.

# RECOVERING THEIR SENSES, ONE BY ONE
## CHAPTER FIFTY-FIVE

*Sunday, March 23, 2025*

"You're supposed to say, 'Welcome to the party, pal.'"

It was Supervisory Agent Bernard Klassen's effort at friendly sarcasm when he finally arrived an hour later. Still healing from injuries sustained on the roof of Teagarden's apartment building, his face showed latent bruising around the eyes. He found Teagarden and Jantry on the terrace. Jaded and still trying to recover from the horror show, Teagarden was not keen to participate in the banter. Jantry, however, was still on the job.

"Professor Teagarden, you once asked for a miracle. Well, I give you...the FBI," she said, complying with Klassen's suggestion that he should be greeted with sarcasm.

"Hey, nice of you to join us," Teagarden said.

Klassen sighed and tendered apologies for his tardiness. Though unable to assist in the climatic violence, he managed to quickly step in as diplomatic liaison with the Berlin PD who wanted to close the hotel. That would mean canceling all remaining programs associated with the World Judeo-Christian History Council. And that, he feared, would not only revive cult-driven passions, but also ignite worldwide suspicions of a conspiracy working to cover the truth. Klassen wanted the full story to reach the public to prevent continued flash-mob suicide and, he hoped, fully end the crisis. Because of his influence in Washington, phone calls were made that resulted in a convention restart for Sunday morning at nine o'clock in the Annex Building.

When word leaked that the resumption was the result of backroom arm twisting, the curiosity of the global media caught fire. Quickie flights from around Europe rapidly booked up. There were so many online reservations at GIN.vid for the video-conferencing hookup that the company had to rent two Chinese deep-dish uplink antennas to handle the overload. That was followed by an invasion of television satellite trucks to the upscale Berlin neighborhood which, in turn, wrought a second massive police presence.

At the appointed hour, with more than five hundred people squeezed into Friedrich Hall on the second floor of the Annex Building and no less than forty-eight television cameras in the back of the room, Abraham J. Isaac and William Franklin Jr., the dual council chairmen, made a joint-introduction for the next guest speaker. They referred to him as the "American Prometheus," "The Fox," and "the world's most important whistle blower." When they suggested he may also be a "new Martin Luther for a dangerously corrupted age," the already quiet room grew even more silent.

Once at the podium, Teagarden spoke for only six minutes. He briefly recounted details of his journey from New York City, to Israel, Venice, Rome, and finally Berlin. On the subject of recent sectarian violence, he made no distinction between those motivated by religious faith or the aggressive absence of faith. And without naming Drakken, he shamed American hesitation to assume a greater leadership role:

> No nation was better poised to intervene with
> both research and quick action to understand
> what was happening around our planet and move

to save lives. Because the U.S. failed, its star is diminished, the world is physically damaged, and its people are spiritually lessened as a result.

He listed the names of the dead as further proof of FBI and CIA bungling.

When he turned to the subject of the Q Document, he explained that it consisted of seventeen scraps. The final four were encoded, and when decoded, yes, those final four:

> ...did indeed cast evidence that the Christian faith, including its baseline claim to messianic divinity, was wholly designed by first-century Jews presumably to reunite through revival of faith all of those aggrieved by the wider diaspora, to force cessation of assimilation into pagan Roman polytheism, and to otherwise lessen suffering under the cruelty of the Caesars that governed every aspect of their lives.

Having already gone from quiet to silent, the room became a void of deep space filled with soundless nothingness. Snapshots of the individual Q fragments flashed on a screen behind him. The image of Fragment Seventeen, though illegible to all, appeared on the overhead screen longer than the others. Teagarden continued:

> Since first viewing these fragments, I have learned one vital and indisputable fact. The final four, and indeed all the wider Q Document extracted from the cave at Megiddo, is unmistakably a fraud committed with great perseverance of effort by person or persons unknown. Further, it is a certainty that the perpetrator possessed absolute knowledge of the deceit. Indeed he, and I believe it is safe to call the forger a "he," is probably the

originator not only of the document, but also of the lie contained therein. I believe this is, as the lawyers like to say, prima facie verification that the document is nothing more than a joke. A practical joke, if you prefer. But a joke nonetheless. It was executed in all likelihood by a monk living in the ancient church at Megiddo some time in the late eleventh century. If I am correct, it's fair to assume he was bored out of his mind, angry at the abbot for some perceived insult, utterly exhausted with lousy food, and in desperate need of anything to break the relentless tedium of his own monastic routine.

He paused for a modest ripple of audience laughter, part chuckle and part nervous giggle, which had a venting impact upon the atmospheric pressure in the hall. Jantry and Klassen exchanged knowing looks of satisfaction. For them, Teagarden's words about the document being a fraud meant displays of mass suicide would cease. And that, in turn, meant mission accomplished. It was a mission unduly prolonged and filled with bloodshed, but in the end, Washington officials, including POTUS, applauded the FBI and CIA for a job well done.

# CHAPTER FIFTY-SIX

That night, they dined in Kapitäns Bierhalle after passing between the twin knights who'd been re-erected to their post. The armor had newly added dents and dimples suffered in the lobby riot. Gunther, the plaid-clad desk manager, put a sign on one knight reading:

SIE SOLLTEN DIE ANDEREN RITTER SEHEN

"Nicht sprechen," said Klassen.

"It means," responded Jantry, who didn't speak German but nonetheless understood the expression, "'you should see the other knights.'"

"Ha, he who laughs—lives," said Klassen.

They ordered locally brewed craft beers that arrived in huge liter-sized steins. While drinking, the three of them made several toasts. Klassen toasted Jantry's "spectacularly quick thinking" that resulted in Elad's demise at the hands of the FFG. Jantry toasted Teagarden for "enduring and ultimately prevailing in his mission." Teagarden, having forgiven all oversights, toasted and thanked his two companions for helping him survive. And from Washington came Assistant FBI Director William Drakken's confidentially texted congratulations:

> Praise to you all: to CIA Case Officer Jantry for extraordinary action on Operation Five O'clock.

A special clap-clap to Professor Samuel Teagarden for being a discreet and loyal team player for his country. And to Agent Klassen, not only praise, but a forthcoming promotion awaits.

Klassen's reaction to the communiqué was surprising.

"Screw that," he said, "I'm done with that prick."

"You're mean you're quitting?" Teagarden asked.

"No, I'm transferring to the psych analysis department. Gets me away from Drakkenstein's field operations. Plus, it allows me to use my training as a psychologist. Saying that he will promote me is his SOP CYA and HR knows it. He totally screwed up on this one. If I know how the bureaucracy works, he'll soon learn the consequences of his toxic macho personality, but by then, I'll be in another department."

Jantry and Teagarden exchanged looks of mutual satisfaction.

Still addled from the many days of violence, Teagarden wasn't hungry. He managed only to nibble at a Caesar salad while both Klassen and Jantry heartily consumed the house specialty, Brandenburg chicken schnitzel with scalloped red potatoes.

# CHAPTER FIFTY-SEVEN

Teagarden departed before dawn the following morning. This time, the FBI booked him first-class. To make his spouse happy, he put on the beige socks purchased at the clothing shop in Berlin, though he hated wearing them. Made in Germany, they were nearly knee high and covered with little red teddy bears.

Ugh. It's only because I love and miss you, sweetheart.

While queuing for security, he wondered why he felt it important to keep the plastic .22. Neither Jantry nor Klassen asked for it to be returned, probably because they forgot. He figured, at a minimum, it was a fair memento of his involuntary plummet into international espionage. Perhaps it was also a final trick of prideful indulgence because, while unsnapped and concealed inside his carry-on bag, he could sneak it past all checkpoints. And that made him feel clever.

In the duty-free shop, he purchased a new Flexi-Flat computer with the cash left over from his roulette winnings. For his wife, he purchased a designer bag, which he filled with smaller luxury goods.

Before being called for boarding, he turned on and charged his cell phone for the first time since turning it off in Jerusalem. He also booted up his new computer to update Blair that he'd arrive at JFK in about ten hours. Her response made him smile with true happiness:

**From:** cynthiablair@solarvector.com
**To:** samteagarden@solarvector.com
**Subject:** Home Again

All my excellence, my beauty and figure, were ruined by the immortals at that time when the Greeks took ship for Troy and with them went my husband, Odysseus. If he were to come back to me and take care of my life, then my reputation would be more great and splendid. (*The Odyssey*, Book Eighteen, 251-255)

Am thinking of what to do for celebration of your wonderful accomplishments.

Love you,
Cynthia

With spring break concluded, he arranged for his prize student, Aken Okeke, to take charge of the one class in Advanced Probability he would miss. Unlike with his wife, Okeke's response did not bring happiness:

**To:** Professor Teagarden
**From:** Aken Okeke
**Subject:** Captain America 101

It shall be an honor. I will direct the class to seek the quantum formula demonstrating probability that a humble math professor can be twice stricken by a lightning bolt tossed by none other than Zeus himself. Congratulations! I understand both the Pope and the President plan to personally thank you.

Regards,
Aken
(see attachment)

He clicked on the attachment to find a front page story from
*The New York Times* website:

Heroic Math Professor Serves Again
Works with FBI & CIA to End Suicide Madness

NEW YORK – Sam Teagarden, the man known
as the American Prometheus, has again played a
key role in resolving a matter of major international importance. This time, instead of running
for his life from black-ops FBI hitmen, he worked
in tandem with the Bureau and other agencies to
help end the mysterious and bloody phenomenon
known as "flash-mob suicide." The violence recently afflicted both religious and organized atheist
groups following word that a biblical document,
long thought lost, had been discovered beneath an
ancient church in Megiddo, Israel...

"Oh crap!"
He feared this would happen. Just like last time, there would
be more media gangbangs jamming his apartment building and
probably his campus office too. He could imagine reporter questions he'd soon be facing: "How'd you get hired?"..."Did you
witness flash-mob suicide?"..."Did the CIA give you a gun?"...
"Training?"..."Do you feel like a secret agent?"..."How does it
feel to save so many lives?"..."Will you accept an invitation to
the White House?"..."To the Vatican?"..."Did anyone try to kill
you?"..."Did *you* have to kill anyone?"..."Do you feel you qualify
for a Nobel Peace Prize?"
He ran down his choices. He could be a team player as

Drakken called him and tactfully answer all questions.

No, thanks.

He could stonewall and speak with no one.

That's not very civic minded and would only make me look bad.

Searching for a middle ground, he remembered the business card belonging to Mateo Sakonnatayak Blackhorse Sanchez that he'd taken from the glove box of the Ford spymobile. He withdrew it from his wallet:

Moira Gray
Network News Producer
Mideast/Europe
mgray@solarvector.com

Hmmm.

That may be his best option. He could sit for a long interview with a broadcast news pro who would know how to tell the full story with video. It would make a good one-hour story for *60 Minutes*. That way, all the answers would be out there for better or worse. He tucked the card back into his wallet.

Scrolling news websites, he learned that the FBI was claiming that because there had been no further terror attacks in other large and liberal cities, the Manhattan bomber had truly acted alone.

That's their evidence? Great, the Federal Bureau of Incompetence at work.

He also learned some good news. Little Girl Blue had emerged from her drug-induced coma and was going to make a complete recovery. Teagarden read the latest *New York Times* story in its entirety on his laptop. Doctors used the phrase "the luckiest unlucky girl in the world." More than once, they employed the word "miracle."

Good, good, good. This world needs a miracle. Whoever you are, Little Girl Blue, I hope you grow to make it a better place for all.

When first-class boarding was called, he found his seat and obediently converted his cell phone to airplane mode. A parade of routine aviation tedium followed. Once in the air, he took a nap, awakened, ate a meal, flipped through the airline magazine, then watched the beginning of the fourteenth Jason Bourne movie. Bored, he turned it off and turned to his Flexi-Flat for the debriefing forms emailed by Klassen and Jantry. In the mode of speaking truth to power, he also wrote assessment reports of the whole misadventure to higher-ups in the FBI and CIA. This time, he blamed Drakken for "unnecessary loss of life in double digits," which he hoped would only add to HR's decision to punish him with a demotion or a transfer to some cheesy post in document redacting. To help him recall specific details, especially about the tunnel in Megiddo, he consulted the photo file on his phone. It should have been a simple task. It wasn't. He paused at the image snapped by Emmanuel Eveillard of him and Deacon Nasri in the tunnel. Neither of them was smiling. They only stared into the camera like men doomed to an unpleasant fate. Overhead, the glare of the flash just barely caught the engraved wording in the If and If Arch.

Scrolling back, he studied multiple photos of the wall of bones. That's when he saw something that he'd only sensed while looking on in the blue-lighted darkness.

"Oh wow-w-w," he sang under the roar of four jet engines. "How did I miss that?"

Unlike when he was staring at the tunnel of bones in person, he saw immediately that within the patterns of femurs and fibulas, there were skulls, ulnas, and many smaller bones arranged in the vague order of the syllogism:

$$\alpha \!\!-\!\!-\!\!-\!\! \beta \quad \beta \!\!-\!\!-\!\!-\!\! \gamma$$
$$\alpha \!\!-\!\!-\!\!-\!\! \gamma$$

When in the tunnel, it appeared to be artfully arranged graphics. Yet there it was. Aged, chipped, and deteriorated, but still discernable. In its simplest form, it was a visible iteration of the age-old syllogism formula:

if $a = b$ and $b = c$ then $a = c$

He scrolled forward to his photo of the carving in the stone arch over the niche that concealed the Q Document:

προειδοποίηση
αν και αν

According to Deacon Nasri, it translated as:

beware of
if and if

That clinched it. The overhead arch was not a warning about the phony document, but a supplement to the graphically inlaid math formula written in the wall of bones. The first line was a warning about the most basic syllogism known to all human logic.

beware of

The second line was the basis of the formula itself:

a=b...if and only if...b=a

Together, the combined message said:

beware of the formula that says a=b, if and only if, b=a

The probable logical consequence jolted him:

Fragments 1-13 are true, if and only if, encoded fragments 14-17 are true

Then there was the opposite formulaic assertion:

Fragments 14-17 are false, if and only if, fragments 1-13 are false

"Holy shit," he said, though no one heard above the drone of four jet engines. "I'm keeping this to myself. Let the next guy conclude that instead of a practical joke from the Middle Ages, it's actually a cryptic formula spelling out something incomprehensible about faith versus absence of faith."

He finished the debriefing forms, turned off his cell phone, and resumed watching the Jason Bourne movie.

# CHAPTER FIFTY-EIGHT

Upon arrival at New York City, he was again targeted by GPS-based advertising. While chugging forward on a long autowalk at JFK Airport, a huge electronic billboard on the opposite wall promoting nonstop flights to Honolulu wiped to a blank neon blue. A moment later it blossomed back to life with personalized messages directed to him, with lurid lettering one foot high:

> Welcome home, Professor Sam Teagarden...
> (wipe)
> As the heroic broker of peace among persons of faith...
> (wipe)
> The President has invited you to the White House!

In the background was the same selfie of him and Cynthia Blair happily trudging through the deep snow of Central Park. Embarrassed and hoping no one would recognize him, he looked away. When the billboard wiped again, it blossomed with one final message:

> To honor your great accomplishment,
> (wipe)
> we proudly offer you a free Quickie!

"Lord have mercy on us all," he muttered.

# ACKNOWLEDGMENTS

Many thanks to my amazing readers for their valuable input.

To Chris Rhatigan for your copyediting skills.

To Frank Zafiro, a former law enforcement officer, for your advice and guidance, particularly on firearms.

To Barbara Shapiro for your tough kindness that pushed me to strengthen many aspects of the story.

To my wife, Lisa Weiss, who patiently read many versions of the manuscript, providing helpful advice with each review.

To Eric Campbell and Lance Wright of Down & Out Books, thank you for your dedication to finding and publishing new writers in the crime fiction genre. As editors and publishers, you are doing important work.

Finally, as the Coen Brothers did not phone after reading *Flight of the Fox*, the prequel featuring math professor Sam Teagarden, I can only assume you are waiting for this sequel. Therefore, when your forthcoming call is received, all will be forgiven.

**GRAY BASNIGHT** worked for almost three decades in New York City as a radio and television news producer, writer, editor, reporter, and newscaster. He lives in New York with his wife and a golden retriever, where he is now dedicated to writing fiction.

GrayBasnight.com

BOOKS

On the following pages are a few
more great titles from the
Down & Out Books publishing family.

For a complete list of books and to
sign up for our newsletter,
go to DownAndOutBooks.com.

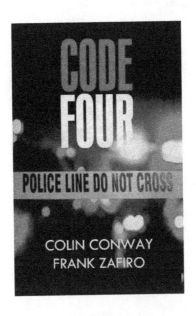

**Code Four**
A Charlie-316 Crime Novel
Colin Conway and Frank Zafiro

Down & Out Books
November 2020
978-1-64396-157-6

The last two years have been tumultuous ones for the Spokane Police Department. The agency has suffered from scandal and police officer deaths and underneath, a secret and deadly game of cat and mouse has been playing out.

Now the Department of Justice has arrived to determine if federal intervention is needed. This disrupts everyone's agenda and threatens to expose dark secrets, and end careers.

*Noiryorican*
Short Fiction
Richie Narvaez

Down & Out Books
November 2020
978-1-64396-120-0

A reluctant assassin is born. A con man tries to sell the Grand Central clock. A superhero is dying to lose her powers.

In thirteen fast-moving stories, the author of *Hipster Death Rattle* explores the tragic world of noir fiction with a wide range of Latinx characters.

These stories define noir as tales of people who fall not from great heights but from the stoop and the sidewalk.

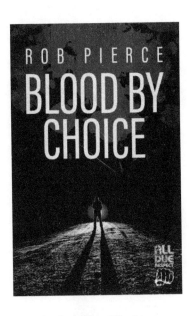

***Blood by Choice***
Rob Pierce

All Due Respect, an imprint of
Down & Out Books
September 2020
978-1-64396-116-3

Two women and a child are murdered. Dust, who unknowingly set them up, returns to Berkeley to find the killer. With his old buddy Karma in tow, Dust discovers that one of the culprits was Vollmer, a ruthless hired gun working for Dust's former boss, Rico. When Vollmer finds out Dust is in town the hunt becomes mutual.

In this, the third book of the Uncle Dust series, old debts are paid and new ones incurred. Brutish, dangerous men lurk in every corner and slaughter runs rampant.

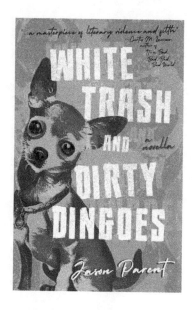

*White Trash and Dirty Dingoes*

Jason Parent

Shotgun Honey, an imprint of
Down & Out Books
July 2020
978-1-64396-101-9

Gordon thought he'd found the girl of his dreams. But women like Sarah are tough to hang on to.

When she causes the disappearance of a mob boss's priceless Chihuahua, she disappears herself, and the odds Gordon will see his lover again shrivel like nuts in a polar plunge.

With both money and love lost, he's going to have to kill some SOBs to get them back.